Books by W. Warren Wagar

H. G. Wells and the World State

The City of Man: Prophecies of a World Civilization in 20th-Century Thought

H. G. Wells: Journalism and Prophecy, 1893–1946 (editor)

European Intellectual History since Darwin and Marx (editor)

Science, Faith, and Man: European Thought since 1914 (editor)

The Idea of Progress since the Renaissance (editor)

Building the City of Man: Outlines of a World Civilization

History and the Idea of Mankind (editor)

Good Tidings: The Belief in Progress from Darwin to Marcuse

Books in World History: A Guide for Teachers and Students

World Views: A Study in Comparative History

World Views: A Study in Comparative History

World Views: A Study in Comparative History

W. Warren Wagar
State University of New York
at Binghamton

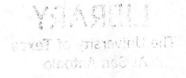

The Dryden Press
Hinsdale, Illinois

Copyright © 1977 by the Dryden Press
A division of Holt, Rinehart and Winston, Publishers
All rights reserved
Library of Congress Catalog Card Number: 76-55505
ISBN: 0-03-088043-2
Printed in the United States of America
789 059 987654321

Preface

World Views is an example of something seldom attempted in the field of modern intellectual history: a comparative study. I have sought to chart and explain the principal differences between several great national traditions, the British, the French, the German, the Russian, and the American. *World Views* also serves as an interpretive synthesis of the thought of the modern era. It argues that Western culture since the seventeenth century has been ordered by four master-conceptions of reality and truth, the four "world views" of rationalism, romanticism, positivism, and irrationalism. In the Epilogue, I venture—not without a few honest palpitations!—to predict the world view of the next century.

I wish to thank four eminent scholars who have helped, knowingly or otherwise, to make this book possible. The first is my mentor at Yale, Franklin Le Van Baumer, who continues after two full decades to guide my steps in the endlessly fascinating realm of intellectual history. The second is Leonard W. Levy of Claremont, who challenged me long ago to cast *World Views* in the form of a comparative study. The third is Norman F. Cantor of Chicago Circle, whose stimulus and encouragement have been decisive in recent years. The fourth is James W. Alexander of the University of Georgia, who read the manuscript with rare diligence and persuaded me to purge it of some of its excesses. None of these scholars is in any way responsible for the excesses or errors that surely remain.

November, 1976
Binghamton, New York

Contents

World Views:
A Study in
Comparative
History

Chapter One

World Views and National Souls

Intellectual History

Historical studies are now undergoing a fundamental change, a long delayed change foreseen many years ago by scholars on both sides of the Atlantic but only now affecting the profession as a whole. Until recently, most academic historians restricted their attention to politics and studied in public and private archives with something like a monomaniacal concentration of effort. They construed "politics" broadly enough to include diplomacy, warfare, church affairs, and constitutional and legal history. The rest of life rarely attracted their interest, or did so only when it directly influenced politics.

Today, history embraces economic and social life, psychobiography, demography, and the culture of masses and elites. The new historians draw freely on the methods of the behavioral sciences and the humanities; they find no part of human life outside the historian's province. All this should (and could) have happened in some earlier generation. Every movement in the contemporary revolution in historical studies goes back to the innovations of scholars long in their graves. It is a clear but painful case of better late than never.

Inevitably the new movements do not all sing together in perfect concord. Since they take inspiration from radically different external sources (Freudian analysis, sociological behaviorism, Marxism, and existential philosophy, to name a few), they sometimes quarrel with one another more fiercely than with the old political historiography. We are a good distance from anything like cognitive synthesis in historical studies. In broadest terms the new movements divide into two schools: the quantifiers and the explorers of consciousness. The quantifiers are the heirs of Descartes and Newton; the explorers of consciousness descend from Kant and Hegel. The new historical sociology and demography belong to the first school; the new psychohistory and intellectual history belong to the second. One views humankind as a measurable social animal, the other as spirit or mind. It is the old clash in Western culture between naturalism and idealism reenacted in new costumes with new possibilities of fruitful interaction or mutual invalidation.

This book is a comparative study in intellectual history, a discipline that explores consciousness. At least in American academic circles, intellectual history is one of the oldest "new" fields. It has been a field of historical study on American university campuses since the 1940s. It is still little recognized elsewhere, except in the German-speaking world, which knows it as *Geistesgeschichte* (or *Ideengeschichte*). The German fields, for that matter, developed earlier. But only in the United States has intellectual history achieved the status of an autonomous branch of historical study.

Perhaps "autonomous" is misleading. Intellectual history has no generally accepted definition, methodology, or professional societies. Some universities, such as Johns Hopkins and Brandeis, have given it special attention. There are several textbooks, many courses, and since 1940, *The Journal of the History of Ideas*.[1] But most intellectual historians are academic lone wolves. They do not divide into competing camps, found institutes, or swarm together at annual meetings of the American Historical Association. All they share is a sense of engagement in a common enterprise, for which "intellectual history" is the most familiar label.

What is intellectual history, in and of itself? Let us say first that intellectual history is a field of historical studies, and not of philosophy, sociology, or any other related discipline. It investigates humankind in its existential mode of being, as real men and women acting in the real world. It seeks to describe and explain events. Its goal is not to produce an abstract model of human behavior, or human nature, or society; it does not proclaim laws with predictive power; it has no license to identify the good, the true, or the beautiful. Even though much of its subject matter is the work of social scientists and philosophers, its methods and purposes are those of history. It seeks to know humankind existentially.

The only fundamental difference between intellectual history and the rest of history is the kind of events that it sets out to describe and explain. At its furthest imaginable reach, the jurisdiction of intellectual history extends to all the events that happen in human minds: acts of will, desire, memory, imagination, cognition, reasoning, intuition. In such a schema the rest of history would study only "action" in its narrowest sense: the physical behavior of rulers and warriors, workers and consumers, migrants and felons. But since all such behavior is to some degree mind-initiated and mind-controlled, even the most orthodox varieties of political history become inescapably involved in the reconstruction of mental activity. In practice the intellectual historian tends to limit himself to a particular kind of mental activity. He traces the development of the general ideas, beliefs, and values that underlie action in given times and places.

He is interested in these general ideas, beliefs, and values whether or not they exert any immediate or demonstrable effect on "action." Unlike *The English Historical Review*, which declared in its first issue (1886) that history "occupies herself with theology or metaphysics or natural science not as independent branches of inquiry, but only in their bearing on the acts of men,"[2] the intellectual historian argues that a dogma, a cosmology, or a biological theory is itself an act of man, an event in history. To hold otherwise is to capitulate, once again, to the claims of political history to historiographical sovereignty. Theology, for example, does not become unhistorical as soon as we leave the Reformation; the natural sciences were not less historical in the fifteenth century than they are in the twentieth.

All the same, some events in intellectual history obviously cut a wider path through the ages than others. Some have a more powerful impact on thought itself, or on other modes of human activity, or both, and will command a disproportionate share of the historian's attention. There are also serious questions as to what constitutes the "events" of intellectual history. Few scholars who have committed themselves in print to a definition of the field share the definitions of their colleagues.[3]

For some, intellectual history is the study of the "climate of opinion" prevailing in given areas and cultures. It describes the temper of thought, the spirit of the age, the presuppositions from which formal movements of ideas take rise. But the objective existence of climates of opinion is as difficult to prove as the objective existence of Freud's Eros and Thanatos or Jung's collective unconscious. Although we may feel in the very marrow of our bones that they do exist, convincing the skeptical positivist is something else.

Other intellectual historians prefer to trace the development of specific movements of thought, such as Platonism or socialism. Even on this relatively safer ground, fundamental problems arise. Can movements be studied through long periods of time, or is it legitimate to study them only in relation to certain thinkers closely interacting in space and time? Is a volume on Platonism from fifth-century Athens to twentieth-century Britain a project in intellectual history—or history of philosophy? Can one combine several historical movements—say, Lockean empiricism, Cartesian rationalism, and early modern neoclassicism—and call them "The Enlightenment"? Are there such phenomena as ideas at all, except as the articulate belief-statements of individual men and women?

This last question suggests yet another way of identifying the atoms and molecules of intellectual history. Instead of studying ideas as such, whether isolated or clustered, we may center on the thinkers themselves. Some of the most distinguished works in the field, from those of Wilhelm Dilthey to those of Frank E. Manuel, are psychobiographies. Intellectual history may also be structured as an investigation of intelligentsias: the behavior of thinkers viewed as members of social groups and classes. There is the further problem, which intellectual historians of all persuasions must confront, of whether to study the thought of elites and avant-gardes, or of intellectual middlemen, or of the popular masses. Can we risk ignoring any of these? But do we usually have adequate source materials for any but the first?

It is no doubt unreasonable to expect answers to such questions. The omniscient scholar would analyze climates of opinion and all their component ideas and idea-clusters. He would reveal their development in time, their action upon one another, and their relationship to the events of social and political history. He would psychoanalyze individual thinkers and study their thinking as expressions of group and class behavior. He would range easily through all fields of thought, from theories of physics to theories of art. He would study the function of language in the formation of ideas. He would expound the culture of elites and the culture of masses, the minds of nations and of whole civilizations, ancient and modern, Eastern and Western.

In the absence of such polymaths, intellectual history reduces in real life to a profusion of specialized studies employing many methodologies, fulfilling a variety of purposes, and based on conflicting definitions of the discipline. But the situation is not so very different in many other fields of scholarship, even those long established. A closing of the ranks behind some universally applauded model of intellectual history would perhaps do more harm than good.

In any event no one can quarrel with Felix Gilbert's observation that the forces underlying the historical process "are filtered through the human mind and this determines the tempo and the manner in which they work."[4] Without consciousness, there is no possibility of historical life; without intellectual history, in some form or other, there can be no adequate understanding of man as a historical being.

World Views

The unit of study chosen for this book is the "world view," a conception of the nature of cosmic and human reality that discloses the meaning of life. World views furnish answers to the largest questions that human beings can ask about their condition. The cultural life of all societies takes form and direction from a single, or sometimes two or three competing, world views. Individual thinkers in those societies may also elaborate idiosyncratic world views that draw upon the reigning orthodoxies and in some measure transcend them.

Notice that we are not speaking of knowledge as such. The ingredients in a world view may have cognitive significance to the thinker; he may find them true. But a world view is preeminently a structure of values, a credo responding to man's need for anchorage in life. Its ultimate source lies not in any formal system of religion, philosophy, or science, but in our ancient psychic struggle to establish a relationship to the world that binds heart and will. It functions in both the conscious and the unconscious mind. It is a surrogate for the instinctual world bond of animal life.

The concept of the world view set forth here owes much to the work of the German philosopher and historian Wilhelm Dilthey, one of the founding fathers of intellectual history. In German, a world view is a *Weltanschauung*, which Dilthey described as a conception of reality that solves the "mystery" or "riddle" of life. For Dilthey, every weltanschauung is three-layered, composed of a *Weltbild*, or "world-picture"; an understanding of life; and ideals of conduct. Through the weltanschauung, man knows, feels, and wills. In pursuing the goals prescribed by world views, he creates the historical world.[5]

Dilthey may have exaggerated the potency of weltanschauungen as forces in historical causation. His doctrine of world views itself originated in the idealist world view of modern German philosophy, which holds that reality is fundamentally mental or spiritual. But whatever one may think of the sources or powers of world views, they do exist as facts of consciousness. They possess a life of their own that may initially have little to do with "the real world"; but by virtue of their grip on the imagination of the true believer, they become part of that world.

In Dilthey's analysis, three types of world view have existed "along side each other through the centuries." The first, naturalism, apprehends reality as a physical system accessible to sense experience. The second, the idealism of freedom, takes a subjective view of reality, discovering in man a will independent of nature and grounded in a transcendental spiritual realm. The third type of world view, which Dilthey called objective idealism, shrinks from the dualism implicit in the second. It proclaims the unity and divinity of all being. Despite efforts at synthesis, the three basic types of weltanschauung have been rivals for thousands of years and remain rivals to this day.

> Each world view expresses within its limitations one aspect of the universe. In this respect each is true. Each, however, is one-sided. To contemplate all the aspects in their totality is denied to us. We see the pure light of truth only in various broken rays.[6]

A similar typology was proposed as the basis for a theory of comparative world cultures by the Russian-American sociologist Pitirim A. Sorokin. In his scheme, cultures may be described as *sensate, ideational,* or *idealistic.* The first is rooted in a this-worldly, fleshly definition of reality, the second in a spiritual definition, and the third in an organic view that seeks to integrate the other two.[7]

Both in Dilthey's work and in Sorokin's, attempts are made to show how fundamental conceptions of reality issue in corresponding conceptions of the meaning of life. The naturalist (or sensate) world view defines the good life as the pursuit of happiness or power, the subjective idealist (or ideational) defines it as obedience to conscience or divine will, and the objective idealist (or idealistic) sees it as a midpoint between the two extremes. By the same token, the naturalist (or sensate) world view tends to subscribe to a mechanistic determinism that undercuts freedom of will, whereas the subjective idealist (or ideational) upholds moral freedom, and the objective idealist (or idealistic) unites determinism and indeterminism.

These typologies are useful. But whether understood as an ideal type or as the credo of a single mind, or as the form of thought most representative of a given culture or era, the world view, let us remember, is not a product of pure reason. It is not a sequence of inevitable deductions from crystalline first principles but a cluster of options that may or may not display even the rudiments of logical consistency. Especially when peeled down to the bare formulas of a textbook definition, the world view appears as something clear and distinct. In life, it is quite otherwise.

For this reason if no other, W. T. Jones's concept of a sociocultural "syndrome" of temperamental biases is worth serious consideration as an alternative to the weltanschauung.[8] Jones complains that thought is often studied exclusively in terms of its formal content. In life, which is to say in history, theoretical works of very different "contents" may nevertheless share the same prerational preferences and hence belong together in a more fundamental way than works with similar doctrinal messages but sharply opposed biases. A logical positivist, for example, may prefer the ethics of an existentialist to those of a nineteenth-century positivist. A theist may prefer the atheism of a Nietzsche to the theism of Voltaire. A liberal may prefer Hobbes's defense of absolutism to Rousseau's doctrine of democracy. But we need not abandon the concept of the world view simply because it is too often overrationalized. We should also be rash to assume that doctrine and bias do not, ordinarily, tend to harmonize. Prerational preferences are no doubt the forces most responsible for the choice of formal belief-systems in the first place—when choice is possible and freely exercised.

In the chapters that follow, we shall conduct a survey of four world views that have dominated Western intellectual life since the seventeenth century: rationalism, romanticism, positivism, and irrationalism. Rationalism and positivism belong to Dilthey's (or Sorokin's) first type of weltanschauung, romanticism and irrationalism to their second. Rationalism laid strongest claim to the Western mind during the late seventeenth century and throughout the eighteenth. In the period from 1790 to 1840, rationalism was challenged by romanticism, which came under heavy attack from positivism, the reigning world view of the middle decades of the nineteenth century. Since the 1890s the neoromantic world view of irrationalism has struggled to prevail over a still vigorous positivism.

Formal definitions of each of these world views will appear in the chapter in which it is studied. For the moment we need only note that rationalism does not refer directly or exclusively to the rationalist methodology of Descartes; romanticism includes much more than a movement in the letters of fine arts; positivism encompasses much more than the philosophy of Auguste Comte; and irrationalism will not be limited to attacks in epistemology on the power of reason. In each instance, we are speaking of a complete weltanschauung: a picture of the world that reveals the meaning of life and the ends for which life should be lived. Further, since each of our "isms" is obviously a paradigm incorporating the lowest common denominators in the work of a broad array of thinkers, each will be significantly simpler than the world view of any of the individual thinkers involved.

At a still higher level of abstraction, Western intellectual history consists of nothing more than swings of the pendulum between the two extremes in the Dilthey and Sorokin typologies. The naturalistic or sensate weltanschauung can be traced to the Milesian cosmologists of pre-Socratic times (Thales, Anaximander, Anaximines), the rationalist physics of Anaxagoras, and the founders of atomism (Leucippus, Democritus). The work of these protonaturalists was countered by the idealist or ideational thought of Pythagoras, Parmenides, and Plato and by the eclectic systems, leaning toward idealism, of Heraclitus and Aristotle. Epicureanism revived the weltanschauung of naturalism during the Hellenistic age, but the Epicureans called on naturalism only to prove the immunity of humankind from divine power. In any event the major philosophical and religious movements of later antiquity (Stoicism, Neoplatonism, Christianity) perpetuated in their different ways the world view of idealism.

The first serious challenge to the long ascendancy of idealism came in the eleventh to fourteenth centuries with the rise of nominalism (Roscelin, Ockham, Buridan). Although the nominalists did not attack idealism frontally, their work helped prepare the way for the methodology of modern science. Finally, the Enlightenment of the seventeenth and eighteenth centuries (Galileo, Descartes, Newton, Locke, Voltaire) brought naturalism to its point of highest influence in history. Naturalism was then powerfully opposed by the romantic weltanschauung (Herder, Hegel, Goethe, Coleridge, Schopenhauer), resurrected by the positivism of the nineteenth century (Comte, Mill, Marx, Darwin, Spencer), and once again opposed by modern irrationalism (Nietzsche, Bergson, Spengler, Barth, Heidegger).

From the naturalist perspective the oscillation between naturalism and idealism emerges as the heroic progress of science from its remote Ionic origins to its triumph in modern enlightenment. From the idealist perspective the same struggle becomes a crusade to preserve perennial spiritual values against the menace of a brutalizing or robotizing scientism. There is truth in both these views of Western intellectual history. Idealism inherits the world view of prehistory, the introverted vision of reality as fundamentally spiritual—that is, analogous to human consciousness. Naturalism is an extraverted vision of reality which takes as its starting point our raw sense perception of the outside world. Idealism surrenders the world to will and desire, whether personal, tribal, or divine. Naturalism approaches the world exploitatively, as something to be measured, analyzed, predicted, and pacified. Although many "halfway" houses have been constructed between the two poles (Dilthey's "objective idealism" and Sorokin's "idealistic" value system), few of these occupy equatorial latitudes; most lie only a few degrees from one pole or the other.

The dialectical struggle of naturalism and idealism has also participated in the dialectical struggle between established and revolutionary social orders. The ancient associations of idealism with theocracy have given it a more conservative function than that of naturalism, although idealism helped to mount the attack on Rome in the sixteenth century and the programs for national liberation of the nineteenth. But throughout most of history naturalism has occupied the forward position in the march of human progress from primitivism to modernity. Idealism pulls humankind back toward its early state of dependence on nature; naturalism seeks to bring nature under human control. In this sense naturalism existed even before abstractions had been invented to articulate it, long before the Milesian cosmologists, in the minds of all those anonymous human beings who first discovered how to master fire, sow fields, work metals, and build and govern cities. Only since the Greeks have humankind's instinctual fears of offending the gods diminished enough to allow naturalism to express its values in the language once reserved for 'sacred" matters. And only in the last four centuries has secularization advanced far enough to give naturalist world views an equal share in formal philosophical discourse.

In any event naturalism in its inarticulate form had a part in developing each new mode of the exploitation of natural and human resources since the original transition to civilization in prehistoric times. In the modern age naturalism underlies most of our science and technology, and during the eighteenth and nineteenth centuries it led the ideological attack on behalf of the specifically modern system of human exploitation, bourgeois capitalism. Idealist world views were recruited at the same time to defend the feudal aristocratic anciens régimes against the encroachments of science and capitalism. More recently, now that capitalism has matured, naturalism has moved forward to help generate the next wave of social innovation, people's socialism—and idealism has begun to defend the new capitalist anciens régimes. The protean God of idealism who has successively blessed the arms of late imperial Rome, feudal Europe, Bourbon France, and Hohenzollern Prussia is now the god of the Eurocrats and darkest America.

Comparative History and the National Idea

Our task in this book is not only to follow the war of the world views but also to study their national histories. We shall explore the Anglo-French Enlightenment and its relationship to the unfolding of the rationalist weltanschauung in other Western countries; we shall look for national schools of romanticism, positivism, and irrationalism.

Comparative history is another passenger on the new wave of historical studies discussed at the beginning of this chapter, and it is one of the hardest to define. What should we compare? Is the purpose of comparison to discover uniformities with explanatory and even predictive power? Is there anything comparative history can do that such relatively venerable fields as comparative literature or comparative sociology cannot do?

These are difficult questions. All general histories of areas larger than a single country are, in a sense, comparative histories. Studies of countries that in some way conspicuously lagged behind their neighbors also venture into comparative history—answering such questions as why Russia started to industrialize so late, or why Germany was tardy in achieving political integration, or why the United States took so long to abolish slavery. But comparison is seldom the main purpose of these studies. More explicitly comparative history has been provided by the work in comparative world civilizations of Arnold J. Toynbee and William H. McNeill and by such remarkable books as Crane Brinton's *The Anatomy of Revolution* and Rushton Coulborn's *Feudalism in History*.[9]

Everything hinges on one's definition of history. Since I see history as the investigation of humankind in its existential mode of being, I am prepared to surrender to other disciplines many of the tasks that comparative historians might feel tempted to undertake. The discovery of uniformities in societies and civilizations far separated in space or time or both is a worthy scholarly enterprise, but cultural anthropologists and comparative sociologists, among others, have been pursuing it diligently for many years. Even a simple identification of what two neighboring and interacting societies have in common might be a project of doubtful validity for historians, depending on how they intended to use the results. Once the scholar becomes more interested in the production of ideal types or laws of behavior than in the explanation of concrete, historical events occurring to real men and women at particular times in particular places, he abandons the genius of history in favor of the methodology of the natural and social sciences. Once he begins looking on people or institutions or civilizations primarily as "examples" of a generalization, he is no longer a historian. In Huizinga's words, "the term 'case' does not belong in history at all."[10]

Not that historians can avoid the use of generalizations. All the abstract nouns in the language are generalizations. The concepts and theories of the social sciences provide invaluable tools for the working historian. But whereas for the social scientist these conceptual tools are end products, for the historian they are simply aids in the pursuit of an understanding of the existential. He wants to know why thus-and-such happened at such-a-time. Admittedly, his "thus-and-such" might be something as large as a whole nation or civilization, and his "such-a-time" might be a century or ten centuries. But there is a difference between viewing a nation as an example of a generalization about national behaviors and viewing a nation as a particular societal entity of intrinsic interest, as something to be understood existentially in its own place and time.

Comparative history, it follows, should leave to the social sciences the anatomy and physiology of social man and concentrate on the one thing historians do best: explaining what happened. A comparative history of fascisms would throw stronger light on the histories of France and Germany in the 1930s by showing why fascism failed in the one and triumphed in the other. A comparative history of immigration to the Americas would help explain the differences in the texture of social life in modern Brazil, Argentina, and the United States. A comparative history of Greek city-states in the fifth century B.C. would enlarge our understanding of the rise and fall of imperial Athens.

It goes without saying that the historian will also discover various "uniformities" and "similarities" as his work progresses. If there were none of these, given historical situations would not be worth studying comparatively in the first place. But the goal of comparative history is the careful identification of differences in comparable situations in order to understand each situation better. Such a procedure differs as much from comparative sociology as McNeill's *The Rise of the West* differs from Toynbee's *A Study of History*. McNeill approaches world history with the mind-set of the historian, Toynbee with the mind-set, more often than not, of the sociologist. The methodology of cognitive synthesis that would allow scholars to focus on differences and uniformities with equal acuity has not yet been perfected.

What then may the comparative historian legitimately compare? There are no limits. He may compare whole civilizations, nations, or classes. He may compare institutions, events, cultures, epochs, or ideas—so long as his primary objective is to illuminate the differences between concrete historical situations. Our special concern in this book, for example, is world views. But what we have really compared are national modes of expressing world views. We have undertaken to measure the refractive powers of national souls.

Although this chapter is already overburdened with definitions, one more exercise in semantics is needed before we can move on to our first world view. We must clarify what we mean by *national souls*, a phrase that evokes memories of ancient rivalries and a type of popular political rhetoric that has lost its magic. At the end of the twentieth century, national differences in the Western world are visibly shrinking. But they still exist, and more to the point, they did exist for several generations, both as hard facts of material life and as states of collective consciousness.

The national system originated in the fifteenth to the seventeenth centuries in western and central Europe with the consolidation of the Spanish, the French, the English, and other peoples into unified national kingdoms. The early modern monarchy, with its centralization of power and its imperial ambitions, steadily eroded regional differences; the Reformation, with its attack on the spiritual and temporal authority of Rome, accelerated the disintegration of the cosmopolitan theocratic high culture of the Middle Ages. By 1789, although the national system had temporarily collapsed in central Europe, there were at least seven well-established national states in the West (Great Britain, France, Spain, Sweden, Denmark, the Netherlands, Portugal) and another new born in North America.

The nineteenth and early twentieth centuries completed the nationalization of Europe, both politically and culturally. The seven national states of 1789 were joined by twenty others. The incipient national cultures of the early modern era were transformed into virtually self-contained cultural communities with their own school curricula, rolls of heroes, distinctive popular and serious literature, historiography, philosophy, art, and even music. That Holbein and Kepler were Germans, or that Calvin and Montaigne were Frenchmen, mattered little during their lifetimes. By the age of Wagner, Zola, and Kipling, national identity had assumed transcendent importance. Each of the major national cultures had become nearly self-sufficient in most departments of art and learning. The curve of the nationalizing process rose uninterruptedly through the generation of the world wars, 1914–45, and began to fall only after the Third Reich—the supreme political and cultural embodiment of modern nationalism—missed accomplishing the ruin of Western civilization by a narrow margin. If one must single out any period in Western history as the "age of the national system," it is obviously the period that extends from the French Revolution to the suicide of Adolf Hitler.

In large measure the national system prospered because it met the fundamental social, economic, and political needs of Western man during the industrial and democratic revolutions. The nation-state at its best was a unit of optimal size for efficient public administration, mass production and marketing, overseas imperialism, and social integration at the levels of technology prevailing in the nineteenth and early twentieth centuries. Nationalism proved an adequate temporary surrogate for the fading Christian faith and a powerful mediator in the class struggle unleashed by modern democracy.

But the national system typically justified itself by arguing that within the national body politic lived the national soul (or mind or spirit). For its defenders the national system succeeded less because of its practical virtues than because it gave expression to fixed psychosocial realities. Each people, as Gustave Le Bon wrote in 1894, "possesses a mental constitution as unvarying as its anatomical constitution. . . . Century after century our departed ancestors have fashioned our ideas and sentiments, and in consequence all the motives of our conduct." Greatness of national soul, Le Bon continued, "was the cause of the greatness of Rome in ancient times, and at the present time it is the source of the greatness of England. The moment it disappears, peoples begin to break up."[11]

The most serious early formulations of the doctrine of national souls appeared in the writings of Montesquieu, Voltaire, and Hume in the heyday of the French and British Enlightenments. Their theories stressed the role of environment and politics in shaping national character. A little later the seminal German philosopher of history Johann Gottfried von Herder put forth a protoromantic concept of national "genius" or "spirit" that dwelled on matters less tangible: language, folklore, religion, the arts. Each *Volk* had for Herder its unique genius and its appointed place to fill in the economy of world history. Each could best advance the cause of eternal humanity by cultivating its own garden. Between peoples, intimate communication was impossible since each (like the *Kulturen* of Oswald Spengler's *The Decline of the West*) was encapsulated in the thought-forms peculiar to its genius. From Herder's idea of a *Volksgeist* or national spirit it was a short step to the major theories of national differences expounded by nineteenth- and early twentieth-century thinkers: Fichte, A. W. and F. von Schlegel, Mazzini, Gobineau, Taine, Barrès, Le Bon, and many more.

Ernest Barker summed up the conventional wisdom on national souls in *National Character and the Factors in Its Formation*, his 1925–26 Stevenson lectures at the University of Glasgow. Barker divided his "factors" into two large categories—the material and the spiritual. National character was shaped by such material forces as race, geography, and economics and by such spiritual forces as law and government, religion, language, philosophy, and education. "We may define national character as the sum of acquired tendencies which a national society has built on the native basis of its racial blend, its territory, and the mass and social variety of its population—the house of thought which men have made that their minds may dwell there together." Under the conditions of modern life, he added, "the idea of the nation precedes, and tends to produce, the fact of a national existence," and "it is the nation which makes the State, and not the State which makes the nation."[12]

Certainly Barker's emphasis on the power of ideas is central to any understanding of the phenomenon of nationality in the Western world. The rough correspondence of linguistic and political frontiers, especially in Western Europe, helped suggest a basis for the doctrine of the national soul, although early prophets such as Herder had no taste for political nationalism. But once the national idea had begun to infect men's minds, it became more real than the "reality" it purported to describe. Faith in the existence of national souls helped to make them exist and went far toward creating the more or less autonomous national cultures of the late modern era.

What might have seemed preposterous a few centuries earlier became—at least to some extent—true. A Bavarian Catholic peasant might indeed believe that he shared souls with a Pomeranian Protestant shipping magnate. Both, after all, were Germans! The proprietor of a château in the Médoc shared souls with an Alsatian miner, and a Colorado cattleman with a Brooklyn rabbi. So deeply had this new tribalism rooted itself in the public mind that religious and class allegiances counted for nothing when the first universal call to arms since Waterloo sounded in 1914. Workers and intellectuals, laity and clergy, socialists and squires, all trooped obediently, even joyfully.

World views, as much as anything else, became weapons in the struggles of the national system. Although each of the great world views of the modern age—rationalism, romanticism, positivism, and irrationalism—thrived in every country, their meaning and uses varied from one national milieu to another. Rationalism and positivism originated in the interplay of French and British thought; romanticism and irrationalism originated in the German-speaking world. Each weltanschauung quickly made its way to neighboring European countries and to North America but underwent many changes en route. Each also tended to provoke a negative reaction outside its country of origin, giving rise in the next generation to an antithetical world view. The need for a symbology of national identity responsive to the vicissitudes of national history forced thinkers to enlist the world views in their service. Like siblings who choose different roles within the family to satisfy their appetite for individuality, the national cultures demanded national schools of thought that could justify and distinguish their respective "missions."

Thus, romanticism arose in response to the challenge of French hegemony in European civilization and helped create the German national "soul." Positivism was in part a French and British counterattack against the new ascendancy of German *Kultur*. Irrationalism came to fullest flower in the German-speaking world, helping to reaffirm the uniqueness of that *Kultur* and the alleged bankruptcy of Western values. Irrationalism played a comparable role in Russia where it also ignited a second positivist reaction that in turn shaped modern Soviet culture. The American experience has been somewhat different. European world views have been freely adapted to meet the need for a uniquely American identity, but without the wild oscillations of Russian intellectual history.

Despite the social uses of world views, they also have a momentum of their own that sometimes defies every external demand placed upon them. But in this book the emphasis falls by design on the external demands, especially those arising from contrasts in national experience. Five countries have been chosen for closest attention: France, Britain, and Germany, the heartlands of Western culture since the seventeenth century; and Russia and the United States, until recently cultural colonies of western and central Europe, whose histories give us another kind of insight into the comparative history of world views.

Chapter Two

Rationalism: The World View of the Enlightenment, 1650–1790

Overview

"*Sapere aude!* Dare to know! Have the courage to use your own understanding; this is the motto of the Enlightenment."[1] So wrote Immanuel Kant in 1784, and the frail philosopher of Königsberg had, characteristically, darted right to the heart of the matter. Enlightenment meant liberation from the shackles of a self-imposed tutelage, from the long centuries of man's childlike subservience to higher authority—the authority of the ancients, of the scriptures, of the gods.

The new authority, which sprang from man's own mind and spirit, was reason. In the intervening three hundred years we have heard so much about reason and sunk into such despair about this fallible faculty, that today nothing could seem more foolhardy than to invest all our hopes in it. Kant himself devoted some of his most formidable thought to the toppling of reason's claim to knowledge of ultimate reality. But here is the essence of the advanced thinking in the Western world from the revolution in philosophy proclaimed by René Descartes to the regimes of those culminating philosopher-statesmen Napoleon Bonaparte and Thomas Jefferson. The world view of the age was rationalism: the belief that nature is a reasonable system that man, by virtue of his sensory and rational powers, can know without the aid of external authority.

The indispensable corollaries of this axial faith were few and simple. The reasonableness of nature arose from its character as a mathematically and mechanically ordered creation of a Supreme Being perfectly rational in his own right, the timeless source and designer of reality. The task of mind was to disclose the structure of this magnificent cosmos; with the same dispassion and precision it could also disclose the structure of human reality, including the social order. All belonged to the same cosmos.

In one aspect the world view of the Enlightenment was as ancient as Platonism or the teachings of Confucius. It announced that the world made sense, that everything cohered, and that man could learn to attune his ways to the ways of heaven. Nothing new here. The abandonment, whether tacit or loudly trumpeted, of the need for God's revealed word might have signified only a victory for Athens over Jerusalem in the old battle between the Hellenic and the biblical forces in the medieval Western tradition. Yet in another sense everything was new. The modern Athenians began where their predecessors had wearily left off. With a fresh zeal for observation, experiment, mathematics, and hypothesis, the modern Athenians beat the ancients at their own sport and soon gained practical results and speculative frontiers barely foreseen by the best minds among the Greeks. Even more important, the new rationalism stoutly resisted petrifaction. Instead of hardening around its Platos and Aristotles, it gave rise to a bright succession of progressively bolder spirits. It inspired great enemies. And no sooner had it finally disintegrated than it returned to life in the nineteenth century, somewhat altered, as positivism.

The long reign of rationalism as the world view of Western man is broken by most historians into two parts: the Scientific Revolution of the seventeenth century and the Enlightenment of the eighteenth. First we have Galileo and Descartes, Newton and Leibniz; then Voltaire and Montesquieu, Hume and Lessing. Such a scheme wisely forces us to take notice of the important shifts in tone and substance from seventeenth-century to eighteenth-century rationalism—from an almost baroque cosmic philosophy of high ambition to the more pragmatic, critical, and down-to-earth quality of the Enlightenment.

Yet the differences should not be exaggerated. The scientific and philosophical revolution of the seventeenth century furnished the philosophes of the eighteenth with nearly all their premises and models and methods. It was like the first great blast of a volcano, followed by a steady lava flow down the mountainside into the woods and villages below. Although the philosophes, at least in France, had fewer compunctions about offending Church and state than their counterparts in the previous century, and less interest in cosmology, their world view was much the same. The lava flow inflicts more damage than the initial eruption, but no one can mistake the ultimate source of the flow.

What we are talking about, of course, is the intellectual manifestation of a much larger movement in Western and now world history that goes under the name of *modernization*. In the modernization process, an industrial economy replaces the agricultural-commercial economy of traditional societies and a radical diffusion of wealth and power displaces the elites of traditional societies, forging a new quasi-democratic social order based on ownership of capital and/or technical expertise. It is quasi-democratic because access to the new elite is relatively easy, extremes of wealth and poverty are much reduced, and yet there remains, in the Marxian sense, abundant opportunity for the exploitation of man by man.

But industrial quasi-democracy cannot be understood purely as a socio-economic process. It also involves changes in values summed up in Max Weber's term *Entzauberung*—the "de-magicking" of the mind, the gradual but inexorable withering of the sense of the supernatural, the magical, and the sacred in life, and its replacement by a perception of the world as a theater for human action and social progress. *Entzauberung* did not happen all at once, but by the middle of the nineteenth century it had fundamentally transformed the consciousness of Western man. A modernized society is also a secularized society; its religious institutions have been disestablished, in fact if not in form; its faith is in human power, not divine; it adopts worldly progress as its supreme goal.

All these things—industrialization, democratization, and secularization —go hand in hand, making it impossible to say which "causes" which or which arrives "first." In any event, the world view of rationalism met the needs of the modernizing West in the seventeenth and eighteenth centuries, just as positivism served them, perhaps still better, in the middle and latter decades of the nineteenth. Its use of mathematics and mechanical imagery fostered a climate of opinion favorable for technical innovation in industry and the rationalization of business and government. Its banishment of God from the everyday world and its indifference or hostility to both priestly and evangelical Christianity, together with its celebration of the triumphs of human reason, helped shift the loyalty of Western man from things heavenly to things terrestrial. Above all, rationalism challenged the authority of tradition. It was not guiltless of a certain arrogance of its own, but it rejected forthrightly all dependence on received opinion. The rationalist said: let us start over again and discover the truth through our own faculties. Rationalism was a movement of colossal insubordination. It thumbed its nose at the past. No gesture could have been more appropriate in an age that set for itself the task of inventing a wholly new species of civilization.

All this is not to say that rationalism actually managed to dispense with the past or that modernization itself is in all respects modern. The rationalism of the Enlightenment, as well as modernity itself, had significant origins in Greek philosophy, in the cultural renaissances of the Middle Ages, the humanism of the quattrocento, the age of Erasmus, and even the Reformation. Rationalist natural philosophy drew inspiration from almost every tradition in Western thought, not excluding the darkest mysteries of Neo-platonism. The technological breakthroughs with fertile applications in industry that are conventionally said to begin in the late eighteenth century were foreshadowed by the ingenuity of medieval and Renaissance inventors. The clock, the compass, the cannon, and the printing press declined to wait for the arrival of modern science or the Industrial Revolution. Still, the balance did not tip decisively in favor of a rationalist world view until at least the middle of the seventeenth century.

Spanning two centuries as it does, rationalism passed through several stages and enlisted minds from every country. In broad outline, it developed first and most strongly in the English-speaking world with significant French help, reached the Germanies near the end of the seventeenth century, and then became centered in France for its last seventy-five years. The British contribution is the most easily neglected, but it was decisive, both in the seventeenth century itself, which British scientists and philosophers dominated, and in the eighteenth, when the same scientists and philosophers figured as the chief mentors and exemplars of enlightened thought.

Counting a generation as twenty-five years, it took eight generations to complete the history of rationalism. Even in the oldest generation, British names were prominent (Gilbert, Bacon, Harvey) although Italy supplied the liveliest centers of learning in the sixteenth and early seventeenth centuries. Galileo was the supreme intellect of that first generation. The next generation, of thinkers born near the close of the sixteenth century, included the Frenchmen Mersenne, Gassendi, and Descartes; Herbert of Cherbury and Hobbes in England; and Grotius in Holland. By 1650, when the work of these two generations was done, the foundations of both the new science and the new philosophy had been well laid. Kepler, Galileo, and Harvey had launched the revolution in science. Bacon and Hobbes had prepared the ground for the emergence of the empiricist school in England. Descartes had developed a new rationalist epistemology.

The third generation was relatively unproductive. But in the fourth generation, born between 1625 and 1650, Britain contributed such outstanding figures as Boyle, Locke, and Newton; from France came Pascal, Malebranche, and Bayle; from Germany came Pufendorf and Leibniz; and the Netherlands produced Spinoza. The fifth generation of rationalists, with birthdates in the period from 1650 to 1675, was again singularly lacking in genius. The major British deists, Tindal, Toland, and Collins, were all of this generation as were some of the foremost popularizers and polemicists of the new world view, men like Samuel Clarke in England, Fontenelle and St.-Pierre in France, and Thomasius in Germany.

By 1725, nevertheless, British ascendancy in European science and philosophy was well established, if not yet universally recognized. Bacon, Newton, and Locke became the principal masters of the philosophes of the eighteenth century. Deism had received its classic formulations in Britain; and it was Hobbes and Locke, not the French, who founded the political philosophy of rationalism. Of all the seventeenth-century French thinkers, only Descartes wielded a major international influence in the eighteenth century.

Then came three generations of French leadership with important British contributions in each. Of the generation born between 1675 and 1700, the brightest lights were Montesquieu, Voltaire, Quesnay, and Maupertuis in France; Berkeley and Pope in Britain; and the German rationalists Wolff and Reimarus. The generation of 1700 to 1725 included Buffon, La Mettrie,

Diderot, Condillac, Helvétius, d'Alembert, and d'Holbach in France alone, not to mention the great maverick Rousseau. In Britain and North America this was the generation of Hartley, Franklin, Hume, and Smith; and in Germany of Gottsched and Kant. The last generation of the Enlightenment, consisting of men born in the second quarter of the eighteenth century, was the least impressive intellectually—Turgot, Condorcet, and Lavoisier in France; Priestley, Gibbon, Paine, and Jefferson in the English-speaking world; Lessing in Germany; Novikov in Russia. Both the American and the Russian Enlightenments were largely the work of the men of this generation.

Throughout the eight generations it is also noteworthy that the British inclined to an empirical and critical version of rationalism; the French to a purer rationalism in the Cartesian mode, even after their self-proclaimed conversion to English principles; and the Germans to an idealistic rationalism bordering at times on mysticism. The Russians, who learned much of their philosophy in Germany, adopted the same emphasis, whereas the Americans tended to follow the British lead.

In reviewing the intellectual achievements of the rationalist era, it is clear that the most fruitful work, which inspired and validated all the rest, occurred in physics, astronomy, and mathematics. The strikingly new vision of the physical order brought forth by Copernicus, Kepler, Galileo, and Newton, coupled with a veritable revolution in higher mathematics, replaced the tidy cosmos of traditional metaphysics with an infinite universe. Alexandre Koyré says it well. What had been seen as "a finite and well-ordered whole, in which the spatial structure embodied a hierarchy of perfection and value" became now "an indefinite or even infinite universe no longer united by natural subordination, but unified only by the identity of its ultimate and basic components and laws."[2] Earth and its heavenly attendants were set on an equal footing, machines constructed of the same matter, obeying the same mathematical laws. Meanwhile, Harvey and Malpighi in physiology, van Helmont and Boyle in chemistry, and many more working independently or in conjunction with the great academies that arose in seventeenth-century Europe, carried the inspirations of the new science into other fields of inquiry. Man alone, using only his natural powers, was learning how the universe operated. His new knowledge, couched in the crystalline symbolism of mathematics, displayed "such brightness and transparency, such precision," writes Ernst Cassirer, that even the truths of Christian revelation seemed vague and fragmentary by contrast.[3]

Although the results were impressive, the methods of the new science were anything but uniform, leading to deep divisions within scholarly ranks. Hugh Kearney identifies three major traditions at work in the Scientific Revolution, all ultimately derived from antiquity: the *magical* tradition welling out of Pythagoreanism and the Neoplatonists, the *organic* tradition founded in Aristotelian learning, and the *mechanical* tradition introduced into ancient thought by the atomists and Archimedes.[4] Each contributed something to modern scientific methodology. Its mathematical genius owes much to the influence of the magical tradition, its penchant for close empirical observation to the organic tradition. The mechanists triumphed in the end, but mechanistic thinking alone would not have been enough.

By the end of the seventeenth century, although the mechanists clearly prevailed in the field of natural philosophy, the situation in the other branches of philosophy was less clear. On the continent, following in the tracks of René Descartes, one group of philosophers attempted to found systems of general philosophy on reason alone. They were challenged by the English philosopher John Locke, who argued that all knowledge originated in the senses. Both the "rationalist" school of the Cartesians and the "empiricist" school of the Lockeans were upholders of the world view we have termed rationalism, but they disagreed about the uses of reason. For the Cartesians, such as Malebranche and Spinoza, the cosmos was, in effect, reason embodied. Its essence and structure were identical to the essence and structure of the rational mind, whether God's or man's: the mind could "see" the universe better than the eye because the mind, unlike the eye, was rational. Using Cartesian skepticism, it could rid itself of error and illogic and proceed on the basis of clear, distinct, and irrefutable first principles.

The Lockeans, for their part, refrained from leaping to the assumption that the universe had any structure at all. Every idea, they held, comes to us in the first instance from sensory impressions. It is the task of reason to order these impressions so that they give us a coherent understanding of the world, but reason as such is only a tool, not equatable with reality itself. In the eighteenth century most thinkers (continental and British alike) embraced Locke's philosophical program.

Yet the difference between the two approaches, fateful as it was for the later development of Western philosophy, produced less of a rift than might be imagined in the seventeenth and eighteenth centuries themselves. "There is no real chasm anywhere separating the two periods," as Cassirer notes, in comparing the "rationalism" of the age of Descartes with the "empiricism" of the age of Voltaire.[5] The basic assumption that reason and observation did not contradict one another remained intact; whether the philosopher started at one end or at the other, with general principles or sensed phenomena, he finally arrived at the same place, always providing that his methods were sound. The truths of deductive and inductive reason were one, pointing to a single, ordered, knowable universe.

It is also something of a myth, invented by philosophers rather than historians, that the thinkers of the eighteenth century (except Hume and Kant) were intellectual lightweights by comparison with the titans of the seventeenth century. The exponents of the rationalist world view in the eighteenth century carried on the work begun in earlier generations with the same fervor and seriousness of purpose displayed by their philosophical forebears, and as Peter Gay observes, they were no less learned in mathematics and the "hard" sciences.[6]

The profoundly rationalist impulse of the avant-garde thought of the seventeenth and eighteenth centuries was nowhere more visible than in its religious ideas. A strict empiricism would have counseled caution and skepticism. But the majority of enlightened minds were anything but doubting Thomases. If they ignored or discarded some of the more arbitrary articles of the Christian faith, they adhered firmly to those which they found reasonable. Never mind the quality of the sensory evidence! For Descartes, God's existence was demonstrable by deduction from the existence of the thinking self, and the laws of nature could be deduced from God's perfection. His disciple Malebranche took many pains to show that God was a logician, whose design for the universe and for humankind alike was wholly rational, and who could not act otherwise than rationally himself. In more radical terms the great Dutch philosopher Spinoza expounded the same doctrine, obliterating the distinction between laws and lawmaker, and stripping God of will and personhood. John Locke insisted, in a book of that name, on *The Reasonableness of Christianity*. His rival Leibniz derived a rigorously rational theology from a rigorously rational metaphysics that represented the universe as the self-sufficient harmonious creation of a God who was reason personified.

The common thread running through all their work was a willingness to submit the supreme questions of religious faith, or at least some of them, to the test of pure reason. As Bishop Bossuet sternly warned in a letter to a Cartesian philosopher in 1687, the moment a Christian decided not to believe what he could not understand, "he invests himself with a right to accept or reject which ends in his discarding Tradition and boldly adopting whatever conclusions he, as an individual, may happen to come to."[7] Rationalism would lead to spiritual anarchy.

Bossuet's warning did not prevent the wide diffusion of rationalist views in the eighteenth century. The "deism" of the Enlightenment, which originated in England at the turn of the century, reduced Christian faith to a few simple axioms that could be found, so the deists affirmed, in the heart of every man, in all places and times, because they were evident to the reason that every man possessed from birth. The existence of God, his function as designer and creator of the world-machine, a code of common morality, the intrinsic goodness of the human race, the immortality of the soul, and a scheme of rewards and punishments in the life hereafter were all rationally demonstrable in the view of most deists. From Toland, Pope, and Tindal in early eighteenth-century England to Voltaire, Lessing, and Franklin, deism proclaimed a rational religion that needed no help from churches or holy writ. Even Bishop Butler in his famous defense of Christian orthodoxy, *The Analogy of Religion*, had to resort to rationalist arguments in endeavoring to prove the rationalists wrong. At the other end of the spectrum, the firebrands of the French Enlightenment who melted deism down into a simple ethical naturalism, thinkers such as Julien LaMettrie and the Baron d'Holbach, nonetheless managed to cling to a thoroughly rational view of the cosmos with Mother Nature in effect substituting for Father God. In all events, nature, reason, and goodness were different faces of the same ultimate reality.

Rationalism exerted an equally powerful influence over most political theory in the period from Grotius to Paine. The key idea was natural law, whether defined prescriptively or descriptively. As nature was governed by certain immutable laws, so the human body politic was or should be governed by the laws of nature peculiar to itself and discoverable by reason or by a mixture of reason and scientific observation of political behavior. Modern natural law theory had its origins in the thought of Althusius and Grotius in Holland early in the seventeenth century. Thomas Hobbes carried the work forward in *Leviathan* with his concept of the state as a machine contrived by human art, whose laws should be based on the law of nature, "a precept or general rule, found out by reason, by which a man is forbiddden to do that, which is destructive of his life, or taketh away the means of preserving the same." Hobbes allowed his assumptions to drive him to a reasoned defense of absolutism, but his successors advanced from similar premises, and a more optimistic view of human nature, to similarly reasoned defenses of a mixed form of government after the English example (Locke and Montesquieu) or of enlightened despotism (Pufendorf and the young Voltaire).

The form of government prescribed by reason, however, is less important here than the fact that reason did prescribe. Just as the bees cooperated by instinct, wrote Voltaire, so God "endowed man with certain inalienable feelings; and these are the eternal bonds and the first laws of human society." When men allowed themselves to act rationally, consulting the laws written on their hearts, they created good societies and wise polities. Only when they yielded to ignorant passions, unregulated by the quintessentially human faculty of reason, did they go astray.

The empiricist element in the world view of the Enlightenment was far from silent, despite the obvious power of Cartesian deductive logic and the doctrine of innate ideas in its religious and political philosophy. In psychology, for example, the eighteenth century largely abandoned Cartesian principles. Except in Germany, the prestige won for empirical method by the natural sciences and the secularizing impulse that permeated all Enlightenment thought persuaded the philosophes to see the mind no longer as a self-contained reasoning machine, a terrestrial analogue of the divine mind, but as a target for sense impressions. Reason was powerless to act without the raw material furnished by the bodily organs of sensation. The philosophes also pondered seriously the role of will and emotion both in the knowledge-seeking process and in human behavior generally. The inconsistency of sensationalist psychology with the methods in everyday use by Enlightened thinkers did not go unnoticed, but they could not purge it from their thought.

In two other areas empiricism made deep inroads: historiography and aesthetics. Cartesian philosophy could take no notice of the primary data of historical experience since they consisted exclusively of the sense impressions of observers and participants; no one could hope to know the sequence of events in the phenomenal world by inspecting the structure of his mind. But in Locke's epistemology, which at one point he described as the "historical plain method," the primary data of the historian were identical with those of the scientist or any other knowledge seeker. Like the scientist, the historian developed his picture of reality from particular observations. He had reverence, not contempt, for the bits and pieces of information brought to him by the senses although he was forced to rely on the senses of others much more than the scientist. Lockean empiricism helped mightily to make historical research more respectable in the eighteenth century.

As Cassirer reminds us, however, the beginnings of a new historical method are traceable to Locke's contemporary, Pierre Bayle.[8] Instead of ignoring history or searching for a rational plan in its inner workings, Bayle saw it as "an enormous heap of ruins," a mass of facts that the scholar could little by little lay bare, once he had sifted through the errors and superstitions of the centuries. Bayle's skeptical, critical, and empirical approach found many followers in the next century, from Montesquieu and Voltaire to Hume and Gibbon. Each of them put historical learning to "higher" uses, but their methodological starting point was empiricist.

In aesthetics, empiricism prevailed somewhat later and only after a bitter struggle with the Cartesians and the neoclassicists. The orthodox conception of beauty from the late seventeenth to the late eighteenth centuries was rigorously rational. Beauty and reason were equated, although writers and artists more often extracted their vision of rationality from the Greeks and Romans than from Descartes or Newton. Classical columns, unimpassioned couplets, and well-proportioned marbles typify the age. But by the third quarter of the eighteenth century, thinkers of the rank of Diderot, Hume, and Lessing had submitted radically revised ideas of beauty that did away with Descartes's flinty condemnation of feeling and imagination. The subjectivity of aesthetic experience was acknowledged at last, and a purely rational philosophy of beauty became difficult for good minds to defend. Even then, creative work continued for some years to adhere chiefly to classical models; a major revival of classical values occurred in the visual arts, and in music an approximation of classical style appeared for the first time.

But it is important to emphasize once more the historical, if not the logical, compatibility of Cartesian rationalism and the new empiricism. Throughout most of the eighteenth century, despite the paradoxes involved,

Cartesian and Lockean principles mingled in the same minds. Everywhere reason was recognized as the highest faculty of humankind. Everywhere the underlying mechanical rationality of the world was taken for granted, and prophets loudly proclaimed the need to rationalize whatever was irrational in human institutions.

Only near the end of the eighteenth century did the breaking point arrive. The tension between the disparate elements in Enlightened philosophy grew intolerable, a tension aggravated by the decay of the ancien régime in France, by the first stirrings of democracy and industrialism, and by a deep-in-the-bone weariness with the endlessly repeated formulas of rationalism. The emergence of national feeling played its part as well, especially in Germany.

Norman Hampson splits the Enlightenment of the eighteenth century into two halves, an early Enlightenment that insisted on the fundamental harmony of reason and experience and a later Enlightenment that opted for harsher views. In the second half the universe was seen either as inscrutable or so deterministic that it reduced men to automatons suitable only for cosmic or social engineering.[9] In the early Enlightenment the password was harmony—the benevolence of a divinely supervised world order in which all truths reinforced one another and all things worked out for the best. In the later Enlightenment philosophers subjected reason to the acids of a critical rationalism that exposed reason's own limits as a way of knowing the world and opened up a logical chasm between reason and experience. At the same time deism was giving way to atheism or a resurrected evangelicalism, the theory of enlightened despotism to Rousseau's cry for democracy, and the idea of eternal laws to doctrines of evolution, development, and progress. Psychology and aesthetics turned increasingly to a consideration of the inner self. National cultures sprang up to challenge the old cosmopolitan Latin culture of the Renaissance. The Enlightenment, so to speak, blew up. As in politics, so in thought: the later eighteenth century was an era of change and conflict coming on the heels of an era of stability and consensus. When rationalism finally collapsed as the world view of Western civilization, its own internal contradictions were not the only cause of its passing.

Reason and Experience: Great Britain

For a thousand years, writes Friedrich Heer, from the ninth century to the nineteenth, there was a single European civilization, exhibiting "a remarkable degree of unity in form and spirit."[10] Christian, Latin, aristocratic, this monolithic culture fed on the very heresies that threatened to consume it. Only the "modernizing" process of the last two hundred years finally brought it down.

Heer makes a good case, which works particularly well for Austria, his own country, but he exaggerates the unity of European civilization and the persistence of its medieval heritage into early modern times. The closer we approach the present era in Western history, the sharper are the contrasts between the separate national cultures. Each goes its own way, and the ways veer off from one another at steadily widening angles until quite recently. As early as the seventeenth century, the differences were already substantial. The Enlightenment of which historians speak so glibly, including this historian in the pages just written, was actually many Enlightenments— French, German, English, Scots, Italian, Dutch, Spanish, North American, Russian, and several others. One may gloss over the differences, emphasizing areas of general agreement, as I have done above. But the facts remain. The Enlightenment did not start everywhere simultaneously; some countries had a larger share in its making than others; each adapted the Enlightenment to its own needs and circumstances. This was also the case with the rationalist world view that lay at the center of Enlightenment thought. In no two Western cultures did rationalism mean quite the same thing, and from their various understandings sprang many later cultural differences.

In the case of British rationalism, what stands out above all is the close interaction between the empirical sciences and the rest of thought, an interaction that made the British the most empirically minded of Enlightened thinkers, and in relationship to the Christian and classical heritage, the most radical. It can also be argued that in the seventeenth century Britain was the focal country in the development of the rationalist world view, a position held through much of the eighteenth century as well.

That British thinkers should have contributed as much to the evolution of rationalism as French, and perhaps more, is not surprising in light of British history from its beginnings. The self-image of the British as practical folk with no head for abstract speculation, a conceit they share with North Americans, is not entirely false. The highly successful commercial, industrial, and imperial exploits of the English-speaking peoples in modern times may have conspired to give them less time, in the aggregate, for the cultivation of the mind and the senses than some of their rivals on the European continent. Certainly those exploits have made for an unusual degree of integration between intellectual and practical life. Pure science and philosophy and art have suffered in proportion.

But wealth and power also create the leisure for segments of the population that are not necessarily wealthy or powerful to devote themselves to the life of the mind. If the life of the mind holds little value in a culture and has no roots in its history, the opportunities opened up by affluence may go unseized. Such was not the case in the British Isles. Despite their distance from the centers of ancient learning, they began to participate actively in the making of European culture as early as the fifth century, when the conversion of the Irish was completed by St. Patrick. The English accepted

Christianity in the seventh century. Irishmen and Anglo-Saxons such as Pelagius, Bede, Alcuin, and Erigena were among the greatest thinkers and scholars of early medieval Europe.

British intellectual life continued to flourish all through the rest of the medieval millennium. No British center of learning could equal Paris, but British monasteries, cathedral schools, and universities played a central role in medieval thought. During the intellectual renaissance of the twelfth century, Adelard of Bath and John of Salisbury contributed significantly to the development of scholastic philosophy. Oxford, the second oldest university in Europe outside Italy, became a principal center of scholastic learning in the middle of the thirteenth century. Robert Grosseteste, Roger Bacon, and John Duns Scotus taught there, followed early in the fourteenth century by William of Ockham: all things considered, perhaps the most brilliant sequence of minds in medieval Christendom. England also figured prominently in the Northern Renaissance, with scholars such as John Colet and Sir Thomas More. The English and Scottish Reformations failed to produce theological work of the first magnitude, except for Richard Hooker's *Laws of Ecclesiastical Polity*, but there was as much religious ferment and controversy in the British Isles as elsewhere in Europe throughout the Reformation era. At no time, from the early Middle Ages down to the time of Shakespeare, did the British stand outside the mainstream of European intellectual life.

Whether this wealth of scholarship prior to the seventeenth century in any way presaged the character of British thought in the era of rationalism is a more difficult question. Historians sometimes make the claim. The two Bacons are linked because of their common interest in experimental science. Ockham's nominalism is described as a direct precursor of British empiricism. The temperate, reasonable tone of the Anglican Reformation seems to foreshadow the modern British love of "common sense" and "compromise."

But when all the evidence is weighed in, the case for a distinctively English or British school of thought in premodern times is not conclusive. During the High Middle Ages, British schoolmen were if anything more conservative than their French counterparts, preferring Augustinian orthodoxy to Aristotelian innovation. Thomism, that most reasonable and finely balanced of all medieval schools of philosophy, won few followers at Oxford. When the medieval British mind did come forward with powerfully original thought, as in Scotism and Ockhamism, it cut in both directions, forward to a more secular and empirical theory of natural knowlege, yet back to Augustinian views in theology. In any event the more "modern" of the two, Ockhamism, enjoyed only a short reign in England. Its influence was more sustained in the universities of France and the Empire. Nor were the British immune to the appeals of Neoplatonism, mysticism, and the most fanatical varieties of Calvinist and radical Protestantism. The seventeenth century itself was a time of passionate extremes in British life and thought, against which the new empiricist-rationalist philosophy asserted itself only with great effort.

The question still remains, why did the new philosophy finally prevail and prevail with special authority and vigor in Britain? Was there anything in the history, medieval or early modern, of the British peoples that prepared them to assume the intellectual leadership of the Western world in the seventeenth century?

In this case, I think we are safe to answer in the affirmative. It may be true that even in Tudor times British thought still lacked a definite national orientation. But certain tendencies in the development of the economic and political life of England were already beginning to push the intellectual class toward the world view that it would espouse for the next two centuries. Not rich, large, or powerful in medieval times, England nonetheless enjoyed several advantages over its continental rivals that permitted the steady, disproportionate growth of its wealth and political influence.

The first basis of English wealth was the richness of England's soil, always better than the hinterlands left to the Celts by the Anglo-Saxon invaders. The wool trade was another asset. For many years wool was England's chief export. But other countries had comparable blessings. A more distinctive advantage lay in the early unification of the country by the Normans, who gave it strong central government without at the same time feeling any need to obliterate the habits and institutions of local self-government. Thus the English were doubly fortunate. The freedom and initiative of burghers, gentry, and nobility were not sacrificed for national unity, and national unity was not sacrificed for the sake of local privilege. Of equal importance, English society was less rigidly structured than most continental societies. A certain amount of upward and downward mobility permitted the estates of the realm to mingle their blood and wealth, and the cross-fertilization that occurred worked to the nation's advantage.

To explain, in turn, why the English monarchy could afford to provide strong central administration without crushing local initiative and why English society was unusually mobile would take us beyond our proper business, but one point at least deserves to be made. England, and later the United Kingdom, seldom faced any serious threat of foreign military invasion. Like Japan in its relation to the Asian mainland, England was close enough to the centers of European civilization to participate fully in its commercial and cultural life but had the protection of the Channel from overland aggressors. Although it was not spared occasional bouts of feudal anarchy, civil war, and conflict with its Celtic sisters, as well as prolonged campaigning on the continent, English life was less disrupted by warfare and less shaped by military exigencies than life in Europe generally.

By the sixteenth century the result of all this was a society whose gentry and aristocracy could afford to direct an unusual proportion of their energies to peaceful pursuits. A relatively unwarlike landowning elite is an elite less hostile than others to urban values. It invests its wealth more willingly in agricultural improvements and commercial ventures. At the same time the English crown was not so hard-pressed by problems of national defense that it felt compelled to take the drastic measures adopted by many continental rulers in the late medieval and early modern centuries. It could allow for more local political initiative, and it could tolerate the continuing existence and power of a national parliament. The townsmen, for their part, did not have to maintain a fearful and isolated existence behind high walls but were able to cooperate much more freely both with the landowning class and with the crown. That the sons of landowners regularly represented British boroughs in the House of Commons is an obvious measure of that cooperation.

The turning point for England came in the middle of the fifteenth century. The Black Death had by then done its worst, the Hundred Years War with France was over, and a long period of remarkably effective national government had begun with the accession of Edward IV in 1461. In another generation the opening up of America initiated a revolution in trade that brought many economic advantages to the Atlantic nations. England's per capita wealth, which had grown relative to that of the continent throughout the later Middle Ages, grew still faster in the sixteenth century. The incorporation of Wales, Ireland, and finally Scotland into the kingdom added to England's power while simultaneously bringing many of the best minds of Celtic Britain into the mainstream of English life. By the age of Elizabeth I, England was a major force in world affairs with only one-third the population of France and one-fourth that of Germany.

During the seventeenth and eighteenth centuries, England's fortunes rose even more spectacularly. It built a vast overseas empire, came abreast of France in the volume of foreign trade, surpassed France as Europe's chief industrial power, acquired a long lead in the modernization of agriculture, and doubled its population. By the middle of the eighteenth century, the United Kingdom had the highest per capita income in the world.

The impact of affluence, seafaring, political stability, and interclass cooperation on the intellectual life of the British peoples was profound. Worldly success generated, as it had done before in Renaissance Italy, massive confidence in human power to know and master the universe. The practical needs of navigation and industry helped to stimulate work in the natural sciences: a good example of the interplay is William Gilbert's studies of magnetism, inspired in part by an English seaman's investigation of the manufacture of compasses and in part by mathematical research that a group of London merchants endowed in hopes of improving navigational techniques. The fact of interclass cooperation, coupled with soaring affluence, was also a boon to the intellectuals in that it provided a relatively larger public and thus more freedom for scholars and writers. British towns-

men were not such urban bumpkins as many of their continental equiva-
lents. Ideas flowed rapidly up and down the social ladder, creating a national intellectual culture and a national public that made British literati the
first in Europe to achieve financial independence from ecclesiastical or
princely patronage.[11] In the more relaxed political atmosphere of Britain,
especially after the Restoration, there was far less governmental censorship
than on most of the continent, which further encouraged British minds to
strike out boldly on their own.

As for the empirical bent of British thought in the age of rationalism,
nothing could be less strange. When the Industrial Revolution began in
England late in the eighteenth century, more than half the British population was already occupied in commerce, manufacturing, and seafaring, a far
higher percentage than in France or the German-speaking world. Wide-
spread participation in local and national politics on the part of the educated
classes was, at the same time, encouraged by the unique character of the
British constitution. In a relatively mobile and open society, scholars and
writers stood much closer both to business life and to public affairs than they
did on the continent. They were drawn as if by instinct to a world view that
deemphasized the abstruse problems of metaphysics in favor of a utilitarian,
optimistic, extraverted philosophy founded not on reason alone or the
promptings of the spirit but on observation of the sensorially "real" world.
It was no coincidence, perhaps, that the founder of British empiricism,
Francis Bacon, was also a lawyer and statesman of highest rank, or that John
Locke was a physician and close friend and adviser of one of the leading
politicians of his time, the first Earl of Shaftesbury. Thomas Hobbes, Bishop
Berkeley, David Hume, and many other luminaries among the British intelligentsia participated in public affairs in various capacities. By contrast, a
goodly number of continental thinkers, especially in the seventeenth century, were virtual recluses.

Thus there developed among the British intellectual class of the seventeenth and eighteenth centuries a peculiarly British world view, whose
starting point was the empirical philosophy of Bacon and the practical
scientific achievements of such eminent British savants as William Gilbert,
William Harvey, Robert Boyle, and the incomparable Sir Isaac Newton.
Hobbes contributed his own unique combination of deductive logic, materialist metaphysics, and hedonistic psychology, an eclectic but modern-minded philosophy from which theology was effectively banished. Locke
resolved many of the contradictions in the philosophies of Bacon and
Hobbes with his empiricist theory of knowledge and his no less radically
empiricist ethics. At the same time, both Hobbes and Locke produced
seminal theories of politics.

In letters, however, the British lagged a full generation behind their
French rivals in making the transition to a rhetoric and subject matter
attuned to the rationalist world view. Not until at least the 1670s did the

baroque art of the age of Milton begin to yield to a simpler style that joined classical taste, modern wit, and the linguistic economy enjoined by the new philosophy. The presiding genius was John Dryden (himself a member of the Royal Society). He was soon followed by the literati of England's so-called Augustan Age, including the essayists Joseph Addison and Richard Steele, the novelist Daniel Defoe, and Newton's poetic admirer Alexander Pope.

In the eighteenth century British thought continued on course with George Berkeley's empiricist refutation of materialism, the neo-Lockean attacks on revealed religion of such "deists" as John Toland and Matthew Tindal, and the sensationalist psychology of David Hartley. Adam Smith's systematic science of political economy offered a carefully reasoned defense of British commercial capitalism. The most astute of eighteenth-century British philosophers, the Scotsman Hume, brought the empiricist tradition nearly all the way up the skeptical heights it would scale two centuries later and did more than any other thinker of his age to undermine the logical integrity of the rationalist weltanschauung. The second half of the century also produced the truculent figure of Dr. Samuel Johnson, the unsentimental novels of Henry Fielding, and (at long last!) a native British art. The dean of British artists, and a strict academic rationalist, was Sir Joshua Reynolds; a classical revival in architecture was led by Robert Adam.

In much of this varied cultural activity, the line between what is specifically British and what belongs to the mainstream of European rationalism is not always easily drawn. But there was a clear tendency in British thought to see reason as an instrument only, a way of forcing sensory data to disclose the nature of things, which happened to be rational or, in the case of humankind, susceptible of rationalization. The keyword is *happened*. For many British thinkers nothing predetermined such rationality. When Newton could not account for all observed planetary movements, he appointed God to act as the repairman of the cosmic clock, whereas the equally devout Leibniz, a more consistent rationalist, insisted on its perfection and sought ways of rendering the divine repair service unnecesssary.

Actually, if one must choose between British and continental thinkers on the basis of acuity of critical faculties, it is the British who triumph. Inferior as system builders, they excelled at using reason critically and analytically. Although Britain hardly figures as the motherland of radical atheism in the early modern period, British thought was by implication and influence the least Christian in Europe, since it departed the furthest from the ancient conception of the world as a necessarily coherent system embodying the divine Logos, a system that man knows because the Logos in some measure also resides in him. To stand in awe of a Lockean blank tablet, or compare it to the mind of God, is difficult. There is somehow less majesty in knowledge that begins with sensory data than in knowledge that begins with

Cartesian "clear and distinct" ideas or Neoplatonic intuitions. The British version of rationalism was a homely one, built of bricks rather than marble slabs. Yet as no less a critic than David Hume wrote, in contrasting English and French civilization, "the English are, perhaps, greater philosophers."[12]

Mother of Lights: France

In the same passage where Hume praised English philosophy, he took pains to observe that the French had made a greater total contribution to European civilization. "The French are the only people, except the Greeks, who have been at once philosophers, poets, orators, historians, painters, architects, sculptors, and musicians."[13] Even in intellectual life alone, after we skim the few indubitable master philosophers off the top, the magnitude of the French achievement during the Age of Rationalism is astonishing.

Against British acuity must be set not only the systematizing genius of the French mind, but also the sheer numbers of Frenchmen. Before the nineteenth century France was the most populous country in Europe and has always been one of the richest and most powerful. Between the reigns of Louis XIV and Napoleon Bonaparte it had no equal. Nor has any European city north of the Alps ever surpassed Paris as a cultural and intellectual center since the founding of its university in the twelfth century. When Latin ceased to be the lingua franca of the Western world, the French language for a time took its place as a matter of course.

Although France must share with Britain the credit of having conceived and formulated the modern rationalist world view, rationalism was more fully foreshadowed in French intellectual history than in British. The tradition of France as the great rationalizer of Europe dates as far back as the Carolingian Renaissance of the eighth and ninth centuries. Charlemagne set himself up as the defender of theological orthodoxy, sound classical learning, and the unity of Christendom. With the help of such able Anglo-Saxon scholars as Alcuin of York, the Carolingian court struggled resolutely to overcome the protoromantic mysticism of the Irish monks, the powerful residues of folkish paganism, and all the other forces in the early medieval world that fought against imperial law and order. Indeed, the Carolingian enterprise, although it was by no means exclusively French, helped to shape the whole future of France. It established France as the new Rome of the West, above all in the life of the mind.

The next great era in French thought began early in the twelfth century with the gathering of a distinguished band of Neoplatonist scholars at the cathedral school at Chartres. There, and soon after in Paris, occurred the most advanced speculative thought in Europe for the better part of two centuries. The University of Paris, the first university to be founded outside

Italy, dates from the middle of the twelfth century. It quickly became and long remained the leading center for theological and philosophical studies in Europe and the home of scholasticism.

Every tendency in medieval thought competed for allegiance at Paris and throughout France, but the prevailing spirit was clearly rationalist. Even in the eleventh century such singular figures as Berengar of Tours and Roscelin, abbot of Compiègne, asserted the dignity of reason against the claims of tradition. Roscelin may have been the first nominalist, contending that reality resides in things, not in the universal qualities abstracted from them by the mind. His position, later elaborated by Ockham, was one of the chief philosophical sources of modern empiricism. The Neoplatonists at Chartres rejected nominalism but stressed the role of reason in understanding divine truth and explained the Trinity by analogies drawn from geometry. A further step toward rationalism was taken by Peter Abélard, who lectured at Paris in the early twelfth century. More fully than any other thinker of his time, Abélard affirmed the independence of philosophy, showing that reason could arrive at universally valid knowledge without succumbing to the extremes of nominalism on the one side or mysticism on the other.

The climactic years for Paris came in the mid-thirteenth century, when for twenty years Aquinas taught there, and at about the same time, Roger Bacon, Siger of Brabant, Albertus Magnus, and St. Bonaventure. Few of the major figures were French themselves, not even Aquinas, but in the battle over the limits of human reason, centered on the rediscovered teachings of Aristotle, rationalism won the greatest number of converts among French scholars. Later, in the middle of the fourteenth century, Paris turned to the still more radical views of the Ockhamists. Some of the most original scientific work of the late Middle Ages was done at Paris under Ockhamist inspirations by Jean Buridan and Nicole Oresme.

France had its share of Renaissance humanists and Reformation theologians, and again reason found able champions, ranging from the liberal and skeptical rationalism of Montaigne to the theocratic rationalism of Calvin and the Jansenists. As Friedrich Heer notes, Calvinism for all its insistence on human depravity exerted a strongly secularizing influence on Western culture. Calvin himself was very much a child of French scholasticism, with a mind that was both keenly analytical and broadly systematic. His *Institutes of the Christian Religion* bears comparison, in form if not in substance, wth the *Summa Theologica* of Aquinas. More to the point, Calvinism saw the world as "a battlefield that must be conquered." Both nature and society were to be organized and disciplined ruthlessly for God's glory. Nothing earthy escaped the exploitative genius of his chosen children: "Calvinism developed a new, matter-of-fact way of treating things, weapons, commodities, and men, which was unthinkable both in the magical cosmos of archaic society and in the sacramentally linked world order of Catholicism."[14] The logical outgrowth of both Calvinist and Jansenist teaching was the rationally ordered, bureaucratic modern state that France herself became in the seventeenth century.

All the tendencies of premodern French thought except its empiricism coalesced in René Descartes, who imparted to the rationalist world view a characteristic brittleness and arrogance that clung to it throughout the late seventeenth and eighteenth centuries. Under his influence, deeper than the French themselves often realized, the heritage of medieval scholasticism was transmitted to the modern world. The organizing, systematizing impulse of French thought was further strengthened. With little direct influence from the world of science and philosophy and at about the same time, a neoclassical movement emerged in letters and the fine arts that complemented the rationalism of the Cartesians. Its prime movers were close contemporaries of Descartes, the painter Nicolas Poussin and the playwright Pierre Corneille. Poussin's followers eventually lost their battle with the disciples of Rubens, and French art wandered for nearly a century through the luscious trivialities of rococo, a style that might best be characterized as watered-down Rubenism, but in literature Corneille's example was followed by the playwrights Molière and J. B. Racine and the critic and poet Nicolas Boileau. In view of the tyranny of rationalism in literature and philosophy and the relative scarcity of major French experimental scientists until the eighteenth century, it is surprising that empiricism ever deeply penetrated the French thought-world at all.

The penetration was nonetheless real. Voltaire led the way with his *Letters on the English* in 1732. Pierre-Louis de Maupertuis, admitted to membership in the Royal Society of Great Britain at the age of thirty for his contributions to Newtonian physics, did much to convince the French scientific community of the fundamental correctness of the Newtonian world picture, a work continued by Jean Le Rond d'Alembert and others. Locke's theory of knowledge and mind was transported to France by E. B. de Condillac, with important elucidations from Maupertuis and Claude Adrien Helvétius. Like Hartley in England, the French psychologists insisted that all human mental activity was reducible to sensation. The most complex feats of the mind started from simple sensory experience, and ethics itself, as in the system constructed by Maupertuis, became nothing more than a technique for calculating what acts would produce the greatest number of the most pleasurable sensations. In religious thought the French enthusiastically endorsed British deism. They also adopted the insistence in British thought, derived from Bacon, on the need to apply knowledge to the solution of practical problems. Descartes himself had applauded Bacon's utilitarianism, although he died before he could show the relevance of his own philosophy to human progress.

Another example of Anglicization in the eighteenth century was the blossoming of the natural sciences in France. Apart from mathematics, the French contribution to the Scientific Revolution of the preceding century

had not been impressive. Then, under the stimulus of the British achievement, French scientists took the lead. The work of Réaumur, Maupertuis,
Buffon, Lagrange, Lavoisier, and many others gave France unrivaled emi-
nence in several fields of scientific inquiry in the age of the Enlightenment.

But was all this, in fact, Anglicization? Even as empiricists and natural
scientists beholden to Newton and Locke, French thinkers remained remarkably faithful to the Cartesian ideals of order, precision, and clarity.
They talked of forming their principles, in the words of the *Encyclopédie*,
from "an infinity of particular observations." Yet in practice they jumped
to vast generalizations that were either unsupported by empirical evidence
or not dependent on the evidence adduced. Their most characteristic essays
and treatises—such as Maupertuis on moral philosophy, Montesquieu on
the spirit of the laws, Helvétius on man, François Quesnay on political
economy, the Marquis de Condorcet on progress—bristle with self-evident
truths and their deductive consequences. The mechanistic materialism of
Julien La Mettrie and Baron d'Holbach, influential in the final stages of the
French Enlightenment, was still more Cartesian in its inspiration. Even
Rousseau used an almost purely rationalist methodology in constructing the
otherwise antirationalist political philosophy of *The Social Contract.*

The same strictures apply to French science in the eighteenth century.
It owed much to the experimentalism of Boyle and certainly went much
further in the direction of empirical method than before, but on the whole
it still inclined to a Cartesian abstractness. Mathematics remained its forte.
The great names in mathematics and the mathematical sciences of astronomy, mechanics, electricity, and magnetism, as Hugh Kearney points out,
were nearly all French and Swiss. Only in the area of technological innovation did the British excel in the eighteenth century.[15] The metric system, by
no coincidence, originated in France, and it is at least symbolic of Anglo-
French differences that the English-speaking countries should be the last to
adopt it.

Also significant is the lack of moderation in eighteenth-century French
thought. The homely common sense that Voltaire displayed on so many
occasions is not really typical of the philosophes, perhaps not even of
Voltaire himself. Although they preached tolerance, they were themselves
much given to intolerance and an intellectual extremism and purism that
smacked more of Descartes or Calvin than of Locke. Even French empiricism was more extreme (at least in theory!) than the native British variety.
Enlightened France, not Enlightened England, was the natural home of
anticlericalism and atheism in the eighteenth century, of democratic and
socialist theory, of the first doctrinaire defenses of free enterprise, of a
mechanistic physics more Newtonian than Newton, and of empirical psy-
chologies more Lockean than Locke. The British intellect, better versed in
empirical methods, tended to see shades of gray where the French saw only
blacks and whites.

In literature and the arts, too, the French adopted a much purer classicism than their British counterparts. The neoclassical theater of Corneille and Racine has already been noted; in the eighteenth century Voltaire contributed many great plays and poems in the same vein, and there were smaller fry by the dozen. At the end of the eighteenth century, France even served as one of the principal centers of yet another classical revival in the arts. The painting of J. L. David and his most gifted student J.-A.-D. Ingres, the sculpture of Jean Antoine Houdon and Antonio Canova (an Italian who often worked in France), and the architecture of Claude-Nicolas Ledoux helped to keep the classical ideal before French eyes long after romanticism had arrived to challenge its authority.

The peculiarities of French rationalism seem less mysterious when one calls to mind the peculiarities of the French historical experience. In many ways France and Britain followed similar courses throughout the medieval and early modern centuries, and in many ways their versions of the rationalist world view were also similar. Both were countries with an abundance of rich soil, which supplied most of their wealth in medieval times. During the early modern period, both developed great commercial interests and overseas empires, thanks in part to their location on the Atlantic seaboard, and by the eighteenth century the volume of their foreign commerce was about equal. Although a far smaller percentage of Frenchmen was engaged in manufacturing than Englishmen, France was nevertheless Europe's leading industrial nation during the age of rationalism, not overtaken by Britain until at least 1780. Like Britain, France had one great central metropolis with a population vast by eighteenth-century standards. Both London and Paris numbered about 500,000 inhabitants in midcentury. Lyons, Marseilles, and Bordeaux were also major cities of the age. All in all, the French bourgeoisie counted as one of the most affluent, literate, and sophisticated in the world, and the same may be said of its upper aristocracy, tamed and urbanized by Louis XIV. In such a country, so blessed, the appeal of an extraverted, confident world view is obvious.

But there are important differences from the British experience. If the smaller threat of foreign invasion and the smaller degree of military involvement in continental wars helped to make the British aristocracy less bellicose and more business-minded, the larger part played by warfare in French society had the predictable effect of helping to keep the social gulf between landowners and burghers wide. Aristocratic acceptance of the bourgeoisie was slow in coming; even in the eighteenth century, although social mobility was higher than in central Europe, the blue bloods of Bourbon France preserved a deep contempt for the middle classes and for any of the bourgeoisie who happened to buy their way into fashionable society.

To the social disunity of the kingdom was added, from the beginning, the problem of size. France had about three times the population of England throughout the medieval and early modern periods, and after the fifteenth century it had three times the land area. The complexity of the medieval kingdom, with its many disparate regions, its local and provincial representative assemblies, its system of high courts, its virtually autonomous towns, and its constant wars, compelled the French crown to seize the initiative early in French history and unify the country by crushing local and regional centers of power, imposing a huge royal bureaucracy on the nation, and rendering itself financially and politically independent of the national parliament. The process began in the twelfth century under Philip Augustus. It continued under Louis IX in the thirteenth, and after the disasters of the Hundred Years War and the Black Death, resumed in earnest with the regimes of Charles VII and Louis XI in the fifteenth century. The administration of Louis XIV was only one landmark in a long history of ever-increasing centralization and rationalization of government in France. Even then royal power and national unity were something less than total. The Revolution and its creature Napoleon Bonaparte added the final touches. At every stage along the way, the apparatus of national government in France was more massive and complex than its British counterpart.

Paris also played a major role in the shaping of the French national state and its culture. The favorable geographical situation of Paris made it the natural center of a vortex of commerce, industry, politics, and cultural life in the northern half of Europe during the Middle Ages and throughout modern times. The magnetism of Paris and its great population helped pull the nation together and attracted many of the best minds of Europe. In the seventeenth and eighteenth centuries, Paris shared this power of attraction with its close royal neighbor, Versailles, as it had once done with another illustrious town in the Seine basin, Chartres.

For the quality of the French mind, the importance of these differences between the historical situations of Britain and France is easily seen. The prosperity and sophistication of French and especially of Parisian life ensured that French thinkers would be relatively more socialized than those of central Europe. But the disdain of the ruling classes for bourgeois callings, together with the political inexperience of all classes in the Bourbon monarchy, tend to give the French intellect a sense of remoteness from everyday affairs that contrasts sharply with the worldly pragmatism of the British. The sense of remoteness, in turn, instilled a respect for abstract ideas that satisfied the intellect even if they bore little relationship to the confusions of the real world.

Meanwhile, the efforts of the crown to impose bureaucratic order on the many warring provinces and estates of the French national organism further encouraged, and were themselves further encouraged by, the rationalist tradition in French thought. The model of public order that the Bourbons sought to provide was—quite unlike the British model—authoritarian, imperial, legalistic and gravely Roman. The spirit of Charlemagne permeated all of it and even more fully permeated the administrative and legal reforms of the Revolution and the Napoleonic regime. Despite the relative distance of the intellectuals from the inner circles of public life, they could not avoid being influenced by the shape and texture of that life, either as men who merely attempted to make it better or as dissidents and revolutionaries seeking to replace it with something new. British political ideas exerted their appeal, but only superficially.

When the dam finally broke in 1789, the France that had experienced no political revolution comparable to the English revolutions of the seventeenth century and no church reformation comparable to the Anglican and Puritan upheavals turned in both thought and deed to a radicalism that swept away the past far more thoroughly than had ever happened in Britain and yet retained the distinctively French mode of thinking. The Revolution was a triumph of the rationalist world view. For a quarter-century Frenchmen sacrificed themselves proudly and splendidly on the altars of their cold goddess, Reason. The Declaration of the Rights of Man, the metric system, the revolutionary cults, the constitution of the First Republic, the division of the nation into departments of roughly equal size, the new calendar, the clean sweeps of the Terror, the Code Napoleon, and the whole imperial system were monuments to its power.

The Claims of Spirit: Germany

Once Britain and France are given their due, there is not much left to say about the Enlightenment. Nearly all the highest achievements of rationalism were the work of British and French minds. Italy's contribution came early, chiefly in the form of scientists, and then the country of Galileo fell into an intellectual slumber from which not even an occasional Vico or Beccaria could rouse her. Spain slept as well. Such philosophes as it produced were only pale copies of the northern originals. The Dutch made a good showing in the seventeenth century, under mixed British and French influence, but the decline of Dutch commercial power was accompanied by a marked decline in cultural life in the eighteenth century. We shall have something to tell of Russia and the American colonies in the next section of this chapter.

The only other country from which a great deal might have been expected in the age of rationalism was Germany. Our faithful analyst of national differences, David Hume, remarked in 1748 that if Germany were united, "it would be the greatest power that ever was in the world."[16] Hume perhaps exaggerated. As of 1748 the German-speaking peoples had not yet overtaken the French in population, much less in wealth or power or *Kultur*. That Germany did eventually unite and did eventually measure up to Hume's expectations was due to circumstances that the Scottish philosopher could not have foreseen in more than the fuzziest outlines.

In any event, the German potential was not realized during the age of rationalism. The Enlightenment penetrated the German world fully, but during most of the period Germany was almost—like Russia—a cultural colony of the West. When Germans of obvious genius did emerge, they adopted a perspective rather different from the French or British. Indeed, by the time the Enlightenment had reached its high point in Germany, it was already undergoing rapid conversion into something else, a movement in which the rationalist world view metamorphosed into its dialectical opposite, the world view of romanticism. The greatest intellects of late eighteenth-century Germany—Kant, Herder, and Goethe—no more belonged to the Enlightenment as we have defined it than the scores of Beethoven belonged to the "classical" period in music. They were half inside it, but half (the better half) was outside and beyond it.

The German Enlightenment, the *Aufklärung,* originated in the late seventeenth century, one or two generations after its start in the West. The first major German *Aufklärer* were members of the same generation as Locke and Newton in Britain or Pascal and Malebranche in France. Samuel Pufendorf, an exact contemporary of Locke, continued the work of Grotius on international law and skillfully argued the case for enlightened absolutism. Leibniz, four years younger than Newton, was Germany's most eminent philosopher until he was superseded by Kant. Modern rationalism first entered the German academic world through the inspired teaching of Christian Thomasius at the universities of Leipzig and Halle.

After these formidable champions, the Germans had to settle for figures of less heroic proportions in the middle decades of the eighteenth century: the likes of J. C. Wolff, Leibniz's heir and chief interpreter for many years at Halle; J. C. Gottsched, who used his chair at Leipzig to preach the glories of the classical style in literature, in open imitation of French models; and yet another professor, Samuel Reimarus of Hamburg, who scandalized Germany with his posthumously published deist manifesto, *Apology for the Rational Worshippers of God.* The one giant among the Aufklärer of midcentury was the man who rescued Reimarus's manuscripts from oblivion, G. E. Lessing, a humane philosopher of history, religion, and aesthetics, and a playwright of the first rank. But already in Lessing we see the stirrings of romanticism. He was not wholly of the Enlightenment, and by the year of his death (1781) the Sturm und Drang movement had worked a transvaluation of values in German literature, Kant had published his first critique of reason, and Herder had begun to construct his folkish philosophy of history. Rationalism had died an early death. Only in architecture and in the realm of music—in the neoclassical spirit that permeated the graceful and supple scores of Christoph Gluck, Franz Josef Haydn, and W. A. Mozart—did rationalism of a sort thrive vigorously in late eighteenth-century German culture.

The most distinctive feature of the German Enlightenment is its conservatism. In the German context, conservatism seems an odd word, but by contrast with developments in the West, the Aufklärung was deeply conservative. The German illuminati were by and large abstrusely academic, devout, politically loyal, and unreceptive both to British empiricism and to French materialism. The Aufklärung stripped the rationalist world view to its barest essentials: a faith in the rationality of man and the universe, an allegiance to the powers of reason, a plea for freedom of conscience. The idea that sense impressions were the ultimate source of knowledge met with icy rejection. Nor did the natural sciences, for the most part, thrive well in Enlightened Germany. There was little enthusiasm even for Newton, whose achievements in mathematics were equaled and whose physics and theology were strongly challenged by the great Leibniz.

The philosophy of Leibniz functioned in the German thought-world much as that of Descartes had served the French. Leibniz was a thinker of many parts, a theologian, a cosmologist, a philosopher of history, a mathematician, an apostle of Christian ecumenicism, a propagandist for the Holy Roman Empire. What marked his philosophy in particular was its organic conception of the world—a world composed not of matter in motion, but of an infinite number of unique immaterial atoms or "monads" culminating in the supreme monad, God himself. Leibniz's scheme was eminently rational, but founded in intuition rather than observation. It proclaimed the intrinsically spiritual and thus divine nature of reality. It also put forth a doctrine of mind that stressed its affective and conative, as well as intellectual powers. The mind was no passive receptacle, but a vital agent in the pursuit of truth.

In all fairness it must be said that German thought had its utilitarian aspect—a pragmatism that almost counterbalanced the introverted and mystical tendencies well illustrated by the monadology of Leibniz. German thinkers were professorial, but German universities were conceived by their princely and municipal patrons as useful institutions. So had universities always been conceived: the notion of the "ivory tower" is fairly recent. In Germany, however, universities counted for relatively more in the early modern period than they did elsewhere. A greater percentage of the intellectuals flourished within their walls, and their chief function was to train clergymen, civil servants, and teachers.

In the seventeenth century the universities had fallen behind the times in Germany as they had everywhere in Europe, but under the leadership of men like Thomasius strong efforts were made to modernize their curricula. Theology and the classics were not abandoned, but the University of Halle pioneered in giving extensive instruction in modern languages, modern philosophy, law, science, and other subjects relevant to the needs of the growing bureaucratic establishments of the German states. Thomasius was the first professor to lecture in German instead of Latin; he took the perhaps equally bold step of refusing to wear traditional academic garb in the classroom. The other pace-setting institution of higher learning in eighteenth-century Germany, the new university of Göttingen in the electorate of

Hanover, revived classical learning, but also offered advanced work in such fields as history, law, and mathematics. The German universities quickly became the best in Europe.

At the same time, German thinkers took a lively interest in government. Pufendorf, Thomasius, J. J. Becher, and many others issued highly abstract, yet far from impractical defenses of enlightened despotism, religious tolera-tion, rationalized public administration, mercantilist economics, and the growing corpus of international law. "Even Leibniz," as W. M. Simon observes, "spent most of his time at the court of Hanover composing politi-cal tracts and treatises intended to exert a very practical effect on public affairs."[17] If the German philosophes were not conspicuously radical in their politics, it can hardly be said that they all lived exclusively in a world of abstruse speculation. In their way, they were involved.

But the German way was different from the French or the British way. German intellectuals played a comparatively small part in politics and a still smaller one in the world of trade and industry. No large, sophisticated bourgeoisie existed to support a free-swimming intelligentsia, and Germany had no cosmopolitan magnet like Paris or London to draw great numbers of thinkers and poets together. The revolutions that had transformed Britain and would soon transform France were still far away. If German thinkers, by British or French standards, appeared timid, conservative, and introvert-ed, with a world view closer in spirit to medieval Christianity than to modern physics, it was only because Germany herself had not fully entered the modern era.

German backwardness in the age of rationalism stemmed, in the final analysis, from the failure of the German states to form a single coherent polity during the Middle Ages. At first, German prospects had looked bright. Much of western Germany had belonged to the Roman Empire, and Charlemagne's empire was German as well as French. He chose as his capital city not Paris but Aachen, in the Rhineland. In the tenth century Otto the Great inherited Charlemagne's imperial claims and founded the Holy Roman Empire. During the "Ottonian Renaissance" learning and commerce thrived in Germany as never before, and Germany gave every indication of becoming the new Rome.

Yet by the thirteenth century, the imperial experiment in Germany had failed disastrously. The persistent efforts of the German emperors to rule Italy as well as Germany, together with the sheer size of the German-speaking world, made success impossible, given the limits of medieval sys-tems of transport and communications. Geography also militated against German unification. The German landscape was crisscrossed by rivers flow-ing in different directions, providing both north-south and east-west trade routes that helped to prevent any single city or principality from gaining a central position in German economic and cultural life. The Rhine, which might have served as a spinal cord for the country, became a major waterway only in the far west; the Danube only in the far southeast. There were many German cities but none comparable to Paris, London, or even Amsterdam.

With the country divided and exposed to easy invasion from the west, north, and east, it naturally became the arena for all kinds of ruinous wars, which made for an exceptionally fierce aristocracy, a nervous and impotent bourgeoisie, and a fatalistically docile peasantry. All the class differences that impeded the integration of French society afflicted German society still more acutely. Burghers were more completely shut out of state and church affairs, the nobility was correspondingly more arrogant and aloof, the princes more autocratic. Intellectuals could expect little patronage except from princes and churchmen and scant tolerance of heterodox ideas. Loyal acceptance of the established order was in effect the only posture that thinkers could adopt. It was hard enough for the many separate German principalities and free towns to survive at all in late medieval and early modern times; they needed no further trouble from contentious intellectuals. The intellectuals, for their part, readily withdrew into the contemplative life or faithfully served state and church in modest stations.

German backwardness was a matter of economics as well as politics. Through much of the medieval period the Germans had been as prosperous as any nation in Christendom. German commercial development surpassed that of France or England in the fourteenth and fifteenth centuries, when the cities of the Hanseatic League and major south German cities such as Nuremberg and Augsburg, the home of the Fugger family, were at their peak. But in the sixteenth century, the economic initiative passed to the Atlantic countries. Although at first Germany experienced no decline in absolute terms, it fell into a period of stagnation, followed by the national disaster of the Thirty Years War. While England, France, and Holland were reaping the benefits of the opening of America and East Asia, not to mention the commercial advantages of national unity, the German states suffered massive economic dislocation, the ruin of many of their towns, the collapse of their financial leadership, and severe depopulation. The German people, twenty million strong at the beginning of the seventeenth century, numbered only thirteen million in 1648.

It took a full century for Germany to recover from the shock of the war. When one state—Prussia—did emerge from the cataclysm as a potential unifier of the German-speaking world, it was one of the most militaristic, economically backward, and conservative polities in Europe, a remote kingdom beyond the pale of Carolingian Christendom in Germany's wild east. Had Bavaria or some Rhenish principality led the way instead, the whole course of German history would certainly have been altered. Under Prussian hegemony the German states pulled steadily further and further away from Western influence.

From the point of view of intellectual life, the chief immediate impact of the misfortunes of the sixteenth and seventeenth centuries was to accentuate all the most conservative tendencies in the German tradition. The bourgeoisie, nearly wiped out, could exert no leadership in national life; it would have been difficult for the burghers to exert leadership under the best of circumstances in view of the extreme rigidity of German society and the relative smallness of the German cities. (As late as 1800, only Vienna, Berlin, and Hamburg had more than 100,000 inhabitants.) But the war made matters much worse. The intelligentsia, as one would expect, gravitated almost exclusively to court, church, and university.

Even in the Middle Ages the German intellectual climate had been less hospitable to naturalism and rationalism than the English or French. When Paris and its offspring, Oxford, were fostering scholastic philosophy in the thirteenth century, there was not a single university on German soil. Of the major scholastics, only Albertus Magnus, the teacher of St. Thomas, was a German. As princely particularism grew in the later Middle Ages, and commercial wealth along with it, small universities sprang up throughout Germany and the Empire, the first in Prague in 1348. But they were the creatures of their princely patrons, intellectually timid, preoccupied with the training of loyal German clergymen and court officials. The most original German thinkers of the late Middle Ages—men such as Eckhart, Tauler, and Nicholas of Cusa—were mystics, profoundly suspicious of the claims of reason, and (except for Nicholas) unworldly refugees from affairs of state. What Friedrich Heer calls "the first German movement," the mysticism of Eckhart and his disciples, "washed its hands of politics and society. By this abdication it handed over all possible aspirations for religious and political renewal to the princes and *their* Church."[18]

When religious and political renewal did occur in German society in the age of the Reformation, the leading German reformer was Martin Luther, one of the most thoroughgoing antirationalists in intellectual history. Although he rejected the mystical heritage, Luther also rejected scholastic philosophy and every trace of the old Pelagian confidence in human power. At the same time he entrusted the business of Caesar to the caesars of his day, the princes of Germany, admonishing his followers to obey their every command (so long as the princes, for their part, abandoned their hellish alliance with Rome!). Luther's faith, unlike Calvin's or Erasmus's, was a faith rooted in despair for human effort and fearful resignation to God's will. Not every German became a Lutheran, but Luther's influence clearly helped steer the German mind away from Western rationalism. During the Scientific Revolution it is also noteworthy that Germany's only significant contribution was the work of Kepler, a Lutheran and a mathematical mystic who stood closer in spirit to Pythagoras, Euclid, and Plato than to his Anglo-French contemporaries. The mechanistic and empiricist tendencies of Western natural science gathered little support in Germany.

Thus the German Enlightenment, when it did come, was inevitably later in arriving, quicker to fade, and more conservative than the Enlightenment in the West. Its foremost exponents accepted the rationalist world view up to a point. But they were much more concerned to show that it harmonized with the teachings of theology. They could not endorse the Cartesian or Newtonian visions of the world as mere machinery and inclined instead to the protoromantic organicism of Leibniz. By the same token, they could not accept the passive and mechanical conceptions of mind put forward by Locke, Condillac, and Hartley. The mind, as viewed by Leibniz and Wolff, was more than a blank tablet, more than a computer. As defined in the aesthetics of Alexander Baumgarten and Lessing, the arts, too, had their own sphere, far beyond the purely rational imitation of a purely rational nature prescribed by some Western philosophers.

In short, the Germans agreed that human affairs should be ordered in a reasonable way. Men should be reasonable. But the matter-of-fact, business-like, reductionist quality of Anglo-French thought, which seemed to leave no place for heart or spirit, which transformed men into nothing better than pleasure-seeking, pain-avoiding animals equipped with brains, never really captured the German imagination. The Aufklärer were too much impressed by Western achievements to produce a complete alternative to Western rationalism in the seventeenth and eighteenth centuries. Nevertheless, the rationalism they espoused did not require the radical rupture with tradition-al faith implied and sometimes demanded in modern Anglo-French thought. The German Enlightenment may have done a better job of echoing the idealist past and anticipating the romantic future than it did of articulat-ing the values of rationalism.

The Frontiers of Reason: Russia and North America

The "backwardness" that embarrassed Germany in the age of rationalism was as nothing compared to the socioeconomic and cultural situation of the countries on the far fringes of Western civilization. In the remote east, Muscovite Russia had begun the phenomenal expansion that would soon make it the largest and most populous of Christian powers. But it shared only superficially in the Enlightenment. In the remote west across the Atlantic, the British colonies of North America were undergoing compar-able growth with the help of a vigorous stream of European immigrants and European ideas. Rationalism had a deeper impact on American life, but the American contribution was slight.

Russia and North America in the seventeenth and eighteenth centuries were similar in many ways. Both stood at a great distance from the centers of European civilization. Both had sparsely peopled frontiers that absorbed much of their energy. Both depended on western Europe for their further cultural development. In both, intellectual life was dominated to an unusual degree by religion: Russia by its own Orthodox Church, constructed on the Byzantine model, and North America by the Protestant Reformation, which thrived superbly in the soil of the New World long after it had sickened and withered in Europe's.

Both countries were also far from wealthy during the age of rationalism. Russia, with few towns and fair to poor agricultural land, lagged well behind Germany in its economic development. Only 3 percent of its people lived in cities at the beginning of the eighteenth century when its total population stood at 12 million. As late as 1790 only two American cities had more than 20,000 inhabitants, and the astonishing affluence of later times was still unknown. But both countries grew spectacularly during the eighteenth century. Russia shot up to 29 million by 1800, and the North American states rose from a population of 325,000 in 1713 to 4 million at the time of the first national census of 1790.

The differences between Russia and America were also very great and dictated radically dissimilar responses to the challenge of the European Enlightenment. Russia, with its mixture of Byzantine, Mongol, and Prussian absolutism, had a closed society in which all wealth and power centered in the crown and the aristocracy. The minuscule bourgeoisie counted for little, and a serfdom, more grinding than anything known in western Europe for centuries, engulfed the peasantry. America, by contrast, was a society of farmers and merchants (except for the planter-slave economy of the Old South) with a high degree of social mobility, by European standards, and extensive opportunity for citizen involvement in politics and enterprise. The structure of Russian society encouraged an inward-turning, mystical view of life, whereas the structure of American society promoted an outgoing, optimistic, exploitative view.

The chief influences on Russian and North American thought further strengthened these differences. After the Byzantine example, the Russian Church left politics to the secular power and served the czars loyally as a virtual department of state: its real interest was the life of the spirit, where it had long followed the mystical, Platonizing bent of Eastern Christianity. In North America the single strongest religious influence came from the Calvinists with their theocratic activism. America's Calvinists had no doubt that the world, and the New World in particular, was a building site for God's temporal kingdom. Like their European brethren they attached high value to work and thrift, little value to the contemplative life.

Russian introversion and American extraversion were also intensified by the countries through which Russians and Americans made contact with the thought-world of the Enlightenment. For Russia the teacher was its near neighbor Germany. German thinkers had a much deeper influence on Russian thought than those of France and Britain, and if a young Russian went abroad to study, it was almost invariably to a German university. Russian thought took on a German coloration. The Americans, of course, were mostly of British origin and learned the Enlightenment from British thinkers; French thinkers had a lesser impact, and German least of all.

One may ask whether the Russian Enlightenment was an Enlightenment at all. Certainly a process of national education took place. Intellectual contacts opened up with the rest of Europe through correspondence, the translation of western books, visits paid by western thinkers, study abroad by Russians, and so on. The first Russian colleges and universities were founded. Peter the Great established an Academy of Science in his new capital, staffed with foreign savants. The first Russian philosophers and scientists appeared, and men like N. I. Novikov introduced Russians to book publishing and journalism along western lines.

But the world view of the Russian Enlightenment was another matter. The nascent Russian intelligentsia found it much easier to borrow the forms of Western thought than the substance. When Russian thinkers did borrow the substance, they preferred what was furthest removed from rationalism in Western culture: the mysticism of Eckhart, German Pietism, British Freemasonry, the vitalist and protoromantic aspects of the philosophy of Leibniz. Locke and Voltaire were read, but few Russian thinkers of the eighteenth century adopted their world view. Even more emphatically than in Germany, empiricism, materialism, and mechanistic theories of the universe met with coldness and mistrust. In a sense the Russian Enlightenment amounted to little more than a partial secularization of an already deeply embedded Christian mystical world view. Thinkers strove to harmonize or reconcile the essentials of Christian faith with the stock ideas of the Western Enlightenment. The dramatic polarities of later Russian thought could hardly have been foreseen.

The Russian Enlightenment (like the North American one) also came very late. Nearly all of it can be fitted into the seventy-five years that followed the death of Czar Peter in 1725. His Academy of Science, inspired by the Royal Society of London, was founded in that year. The first institution of higher learning not exclusively theological in its studies, the Kharkov Collegium, dates from 1727, and the first university was established in Moscow in 1755.

These same years gave rise to a generation of at least superficially westernized Russian intellectuals—chiefly of aristocratic blood, speaking French and German, and including two or three thinkers of real distinction. Among these were G. S. Skovoroda, the father of Russian philosophy, a wandering ascetic who denounced worldliness with the passion of a Meister Eckhart, and M. V. Lomonosov, who studied in Germany and helped to disseminate the scientific thought of Leibniz and Wolff in his native land. Lomonosov, alone among eighteenth-century Russians, made major original contributions to both theoretical and experimental physics. He was also a poet and a grammarian and the founder of the University of Moscow. Incredibly, he had started out in life as a poor fisherman, one of the few men not of noble lineage to penetrate the upper layers of Russian society in his time.

The liveliest period of the Russian Enlightenment took place during the reign of Catherine the Great (1762–96). German by birth, French by predilection, the czarina made a considerable to-do about the thought of *les philosophes*, corresponded with Voltaire, patronized Diderot, and presided over a court that she transformed almost overnight from half-barbaric quaintness to Gallic sophistication. But most of the outstanding intellectuals of her reign were no more Gallic at heart than their counterparts in Germany. The gallomania of courtly fashion disgusted them and called forth a kind of incipient Russian nationalism by way of reply.

The great publisher and journalist, N. I. Novikov—perhaps the most representative of the philosophes of Catherine's era—is a case in point. We remember him best as the Voltairean satirist who ran afoul of the censors because he exposed the condition of the serfs, but he inveighed against Western, i.e., French thought, as well. He found its atheist and materialist tendencies repulsive, praised the Russian people for being steadier than the shallow French, and preached a sentimental, humanitarian mysticism derived from Freemasonry. A similar line on gallomania was adopted by his contemporary, the playwright D. I. Fonvizin.[19] Catherine's still better known literary opponent, A. N. Radishchev, whose masterpiece *A Journey from St. Petersburg to Moscow* (1790) earned him banishment to Siberia, was another child of the German Enlightenment. Educated at Leipzig, he championed the thought of Leibniz and Herder. In French letters, Radishchev took his inspiration not from Descartes or Voltaire but from the harbinger of romanticism, Jean-Jacques Rousseau.

Russia was unresponsive to the full range of Western rationalist thinking for the same reasons that Germany held out against it. In effect Russia was a more "German" Germany—further removed than the Germans from the mainstream of European life, with poorer land, less commerce, a smaller and more isolated bourgeoisie, less well defined natural boundaries, fiercer enemies, more need for autocracy in order to survive at all as a state. Anything short of an intensely conservative spiritual-intellectual orientation as Russia finally entered the European world in the seventeenth and eighteenth centuries would have been surprising.

As V. V. Zenkovsky points out, even theology was somewhat alien to the Russian tradition since medieval Russian churchmen had felt little need or challenge to explicate their faith in systematic form. There was nothing like the intimate contact with ancient philosophy that existed in Western Europe during the medieval period with its universal Latin learning and its organic links with Rome, the Islamic world, and Byzantium. Ironically, Western Europe enjoyed closer ties with Byzantium than Byzantium's own Slavic offspring; it is no coincidence that when the old Eastern empire began to disintegrate during the Turkish onslaught, the Greek scholars fled to Italy and the West, not to Russia. Theology and philosophy were also less needed in traditional Russia because the schism between state and church power that stimulated so much controversy in the West failed to occur in Russia. Nor did "leftish" heresies or a Protestant Reformation erupt in the Russian experience to test the wits of Russia's prelates and monks.[20] Russian religious feeling ran deep, but the scholasticism that schooled Western clergymen to avail themselves of the powers of reason, and thereby helped to make rationalism such a seductive world view later on, had no real analogue in premodern Russian cultural history.

The American colonies participated more actively in the Enlightenment and drank directly from its purest waters, the leading philosophers of England, Scotland, and France. In one sense the new polities of the New World were laboratory experiments in the social physics of the Enlightenment. Certainly many admiring Europeans so regarded them, and in no part of the Western world in the eighteenth century did such an intimate connection exist between Enlightenment philosophy and the ruling class. The roster of American illuminati reads almost like a roster of its greatest politicians and revolutionary leaders: Benjamin Franklin, Thomas Jefferson, Ethan Allen, John Adams, and Thomas Paine were all thinkers as well as men of action and affairs, and all revealed in their writings the profound impact of the Anglo-French Enlightenment on the American mind.

At the same time there was another America, an America of divines and professors ensconced in churches and colleges very much like the intellectual class in the German-speaking world, who struck on the whole a somewhat more conservative note. In the absence of vast cosmopolitan cities or glittering courts, this other America did much to establish the spirit of colonial intellectualism.

The parallel with Germany in the eighteenth century is not far-fetched. As in Germany, academic centers were abundant. By 1776 the colonies boasted ten university colleges, and twelve others joined them during the next quarter-century. A remarkable array of thinkers earned degrees in these colleges, and some went on to teach there. Cotton Mather received his M.A. from Harvard, where his father was president. Jonathan Edwards was a Yale graduate who stayed on to teach at Yale for three years before taking a church in Massachusetts. The idealist philosopher Samuel Johnson taught at Yale also and later became the first president of King's College, New York (forerunner of Columbia University). The champion of Scottish realism in America, John Witherspoon, was a president of the College of New Jersey (later Princeton), one of whose early graduates, Benjamin Rush, contributed important work in the fields of medicine and psychology. The statesmen, too, maintained close ties with academe—Jefferson, who studied at William and Mary, founded the University of Virginia; Hamilton was a brilliant student at King's College; Franklin helped found the University of Pennsylvania; Adams earned his degree at Harvard. In colonial America the' rapport between government, education, religion, and intellectual life could scarcely have been more intimate.

American thought in the age of rationalism ranged widely. Historians of colonial philosophy identify several well established "schools," from the deism of Harvard and the Berkeleyan idealism of Yale to the scientific materialism of Philadelphia and the South. Whatever their school, most American philosophers were celebrants of reason. The deists and idealists, reacting vigorously against the denigration of human power in seventeenth-century Puritanism, saw God as a benevolent intelligence presiding over a reasonable world. The scientific materialists centered their attention on studies of nature but clung to much the same idea of God. In their political and legal thought, the fathers of the new republic leaned heavily on the rationalist politics of Locke and Montesquieu with a generous admixture of seventeenth-century English democratic radicalism. The constitutional structure they designed was like a piece of Newtonian cosmic machinery brought down to earth: self-regulating, superbly balanced, and set forth in crystalline prose.

There were, of course, eccentrics beyond the pale such as the formidable Jonathan Edwards, a mystic who bears comparison with his Russian contemporary, G. S. Skovoroda, and who carried to one possible conclusion the alliance of Platonism and Calvinism first negotiated by Peter Ramus in sixteenth-century France. Although the Enlightenment touched Edwards, it did little to shape his mind. But the archetypical figures of the American Enlightenment were everything that one could expect of colonial philosophes, both in the content of their thought and in its temperateness. They assimilated Anglo-French rationalism without severing their Protestant roots or accepting the more extreme implications of rationalism uncovered by the avant-garde in Britain and France.

Thus, men like Franklin and Jefferson could expound deism, undertake important scientific work, found academies and universities, hobnob with the keenest minds of France, sire a successful revolutionary republic, and still remain well in the rear of the rationalist line of march. Their academic colleagues, if anything, lagged even further behind. In only one sense could the North Americans claim to be more advanced than the Europeans. Intellectual life and practical life were more fully integrated, and even here the difference was one of degree only.

In fact colonial North America teemed with contradictions: a society of aggressive yeomen and frontiersmen and businessmen unburdened by European feudalism welded to a slaveholding society reminiscent of late Rome; a society under the direct influence of the most emphatically modern thinkers of Europe, but at the same time a society in which the Reformation remained hot and militant; a society of glorious intellectual amateurs that was also thickly populated with clergymen and academicians actively involved in the making of the public mind. To confuse matters even more, it was the Roman and aristocratic South (along with Philadelphia) where the Reformation sat most lightly and the socioeconomically modernized North where the clerical and academic establishment flourished above all. Materialism and free thought had, in the main, an easier time among the gentry of Virginia and the Carolinas than among the farmers and burghers of New England. Depending on where one looks and what one looks for, the colonial Enlightenment can appear almost purely British, at least half French, remarkably like the Aufklärung, or a close analogue of the Russian Enlightenment. A distinctively North American mind had yet to emerge.

Summation

For considerably more than a hundred years, then, from the middle of the seventeenth to the close of the eighteenth centuries, rationalism was the prevailing world view of Western civilization. It furnished much of the structure and substance of what we call modern consciousness. Whether in alliance or rivalry with the Christian and Hellenic sources of Western culture, it enabled the Western mind to liberate itself once and for all from subservience to the thought-world of antiquity. It proclaimed that the universe, and everything within it, conformed to reason. It proclaimed that man, as a rational being, could understand how the world-machine operated and from his knowledge design a simple, natural, reasonable social order purged of the superstition and tyranny of past ages. The manifest triumphs of natural science in the seventeenth century, which had the effect of overthrowing both biblical and Hellenic tradition, gave the claims of the rationalist philosophers a credibility that little could shake.

At the outset rationalism was more a British than a French invention. Britain played a decisive part in the march of natural science in the seventeenth century, and her greatest minds—Bacon, Hobbes, Locke, Newton— did more than anyone, with the possible exceptions of Descartes and Leibniz, to prepare the way for the thought of the eighteenth century. Rationalism in the British context took a distinctively empirical turn, defining sensory experience as the ultimate source of all human knowledge, and through shrewd critical analysis that brings to memory the Scotist and Ockhamist movements in medieval British philosophy, sharply delimiting the epistemological claims of pure reason. Nevertheless, the universe as viewed by British thinkers was a thoroughly reasonable place in which to live. Such strictly rationalist movements as deism and the science of political economy made great progress in Enlightened Britain, and those who saw furthest beyond rationalism, like David Hume, remained loyal to its spirit and objectives.

France contributed relatively little at first to the Scientific Revolution, but the long reign of Paris as the capital city of scholasticism, the powerful neoclassical movement in seventeenth-century French letters, and the general prosperity of the age all helped to make the French receptive to the new rationalism. Guided by the thought of René Descartes and his disciples, France had become, by the death of Louis XIV, the cultural and intellectual heartland of Europe. Although self-proclaimed converts to Lockean and Newtonian empiricism, French thinkers dominated the Enlightenment of the eighteenth century. In practice French rationalism was a mixture of Descartes' brittle philosophy of pure reason and the empiricism of Locke, with the Cartesian component usually more powerful. The differences between British and French society ensured that the spirit of Descartes would not be so easily dispelled.

In Germany rationalism came late, unable to assert itself until the wounds inflicted on central Europe by the Thirty Years War had healed. German social and economic backwardness, in any case, determined that when rationalism did reach Germany, it would take on a more introverted quality than in the West. From the beginning German thinkers accepted from Western philosophy its conception of the cosmos as a rational order, but they reinterpreted reason to exclude the claims of empiricism and to insinuate a quasi-mystical view of the way in which reason works. Even the Western idea of the universe as a machine offended German sensibilities. The chief mentor of the Aufklärung, G. W. Leibniz, may be described as a rationalist. Yet the theological and protoromantic aspects of his thought harked back, on the one hand, to a Christian past that survived more vigorously in Germany than in France or Britain and looked forward, on the other hand, to a nativist intellectual movement that would produce a defiantly anti-Western and antirationalist vision of reality even before the end of the eighteenth century. In Germany rationalism came late and left early.

Finally, we looked at the ways rationalism penetrated the Russian and North American thought-worlds. Here, rationalism arrived still later, in the opening decades of the eighteenth century. Neither Russia nor the American colonies made a major contribution to rationalist philosophy, as one might expect of countries far removed from the political and economic centers of Western civilization in this period, but both ingested heavy doses of rationalist thought from European tutors. The Russians learned most from their German neighbors, and the North Americans from the British. Because of the German influence and because of Russia's own national tradition, the Russian Enlightenment followed a conservative course, so much so that one can ask whether it deserves the label of "Enlightenment" at all. The North Americans, on the whole, accepted rationalism much more enthusiastically. But the mighty grip of Protestant scholasticism and the Puritan conscience on the colonial mind helped to set limits to its tolerance of the full range of rationalist teaching.

In summary, the world view of modern rationalism gained its most advanced formulations in Britain and France, with the British seizing the initiative early in the seventeenth century and the French early in the eighteenth. French rationalism, thanks in part to the greater instability of French society under the ancien régime, tended to arrive at positions more extreme than those taken by the pragmatic British, but in some ways British thought broke more cleanly with Christian and Hellenic tradition. Germany, Russia, and North America brought up the rear, and of the three perhaps only the Americans truly empathized with the new world view. The Germans and Russians were reluctant rationalists; in the end, after having traveled part of the way on a turnpike built from imported materials,they entered the modern age by circuitous mountain detours of their own making. What they created was the romantic world view, and to it our attention must now shift.

Chapter Three

Romanticism: The World View of the Age of Revolution, 1790–1840

Overview

"Do not all charms fly," asked John Keats, "at the mere touch of cold philosophy?" Reason would clip an angel's wings, conquer all mysteries, unweave a rainbow. "O sweet Fancy! let her loose; every thing is spoilt by use."

In these few lines (from "Lamia" and "Fancy") Keats transports his readers to a thought-world in which the values of the Age of Enlightenment are rapturously reversed. Philosophy, the rationalism and empiricism of the now expired eighteenth century, falls under attack for its prosiness. It may have its sphere, but what can it tell us about angels? Reality, the life of everyday experience, falls under attack for its unfailing tiresomeness. Only in the inmost fastness of the mind, the poet's imagination, can we discover a truth that will endure. With a certain rough justice the Harvard neoclassicist Irving Babbitt once defined romanticism as "the pursuit of strangeness." In its early nineteenth-century form, at least, he found it denying worldly reality in favor of the overheated reality of the madhouse.[1]

But romanticism is not so easily dismissed. What makes an equation, a deduction, or a day of honest bookkeeping more "real" than a reverie? Is man a computing machine or a spiritual being? Do we exist in the scientist's theoretical constructs or in the changing states of our own consciousness? The central ontological insight of romanticism was the subjectivity of the real. As Sir Isaiah Berlin notes, through all the great romanticists ran the "common notion ... that truth is not an objective structure, independent of those who seek it, the hidden treasure waiting to be found, but is itself in all its guises created by the seeker." Truth, then, is man-made. We invent—we do not discover—the answers to the great questions.[2]

The ethic of romanticism was also, in its way, more "realistic" and less "escapist" than the static morality of rationalism. The philosophes had urged their followers only to obey the reasonable law of Newtonian nature, in short, to be what they already were. They preached conformity to a preconceived and eternally valid rational model. Romanticism, for its part, enjoined struggle. Because truth and being were subjective, a man achieved authenticity only by thinking, feeling, and acting in obedience to himself. The measure of his goodness was not an external ideal but a dynamic and indwelling force, whether conscience, will, faith, or heart's desire. "He only earns his freedom and existence," as Goethe's Faust told Mephistopheles, "who daily conquers them anew." In Fichte's dictum, being free was nothing, but becoming free—the act of liberation—was heaven itself. If struggle yielded nothing better than madness, still it was morally superior to a thousand years of clockwork toil. For the proof of life's worth was in the living.

So ran the writ of the new world view that took possession of the Western mind in the tumultuous half-century that followed the outbreak of the French Revolution in 1789. None of the political, economic, or social events of that half-century was any more revolutionary, or wielded a wider influence on Western civilization, than the romantic movement. Romanticism conquered the arts, letters, and music; won strategic footholds in philosophy, science, and scholarship; invaded religion, education, and politics. It left nothing untouched. Nor was the disintegration of self-consciously romantic schools of thought and expression by the middle of the nineteenth century accompanied by the collapse of romanticist influence in Western culture. The influence has persisted, in various ways, down to the present time.

For that matter romanticism may have reached more deeply into the Western psyche than the rationalist world view. Rationalism shared the stage with a literary and artistic neoclassicism that did not always act in concert with it. The art, architecture, poetry, and theater of the late seventeenth and eighteenth centuries owed far more to Greece and Rome than to Cartesian logic or Newtonian physics. But the romanticist world view inspired the arts fully as much as it inspired systems of thought. The inspiration was so obvious and so direct that for many scholars the term *romanticism* properly denotes the literary and aesthetic movement and applies only metaphorically (if at all) to contemporary developments in the world of ideas. Since words mean whatever we choose to make them mean, there is nothing intrinsically wrong with such an approach except that it may help to conceal the psychospiritual bond that obviously exists between art and thought in the Age of Revolution. The same world view appears in its most characteristic philosophy or political theory as in its most characteristic literary works and, by implication or programmatic statement, in its art and music. Although "romanticism" was initially used only in reference to literature, it makes as good a term as any for the world view that sustained nearly all the highest-level cultural enterprise of this half-century.

A formal definition is now in order. Let us define romanticism as the world view which holds that reality (or so much of reality as we can know) is fundamentally mindlike, in process of organic development through time, and best reached by direct intuitive perception rather than by measurement and analysis. Romanticism saw the world in terms of mind. Its approach was deeply anthropomorphic. It belongs to what, in our first chapter, we called the "idealist" family of world views, whose chief manifestations in premodern times were Platonism and Christianity. Perhaps more completely than any medieval or early modern world view, it fused the Platonist definition of reality with the existential and historical consciousness of Christian faith. This fusion of opposites gave it the possibility of being both worldly and otherworldly at the same time, of uniting the eternal and the temporal, the general and the individual, the realms of imagination and action. But by its very nature, it attempted too much. The peculiar vice of the romanticist was always to overreach himself: Faust, Prometheus, Lucifer were his models. To hold the conflicting elements of the romantic synthesis in equilibrium proved too great a strain on nerves and will.

In any event romanticism called forth prodigious effort. It originated in the universal wave of revulsion against the established orders of the eighteenth century that swept the whole Western world between 1789 and the middle of the next century. It was the counterpart in cultural life of the political upheaval that assailed the ancien régime (although the revolutionists of 1789 borrowed most of their political ideas from the philosophes) and also of the violent reaction that sought to undo the work of the French Revolution. By instinct the romanticists were outlaws, desperadoes of thought and expression, condemned to lives of alternating ecstasy and despair.

The hectic quality of romanticism corresponds to the hectic quality of life in general during the post-1789 era, but if one wishes to ferret out its spiritual and intellectual sources, the place to begin is obviously the eighteenth century itself. With or without the cycle of political earthquakes that shook Europe after 1789, the times were ripe for cultural revolution. Rationalism and neoclassicism had dictated thought and taste for more than a century, and the formulas of both had grown dull with repeated rehearsal and application. A steady deterioration was notable in the quality of their work in the last decades of the eighteenth century. Their devotion to reason had in any case left little scope for the play of imagination, the storms of passion, or the claims of faith and piety. Much of the Western cultural heritage, indeed the larger part of it, had been deliberately suppressed or reinterpreted almost beyond recognition by the philosophes and their neoclassicist colleagues.

The second half of the eighteenth century was also a time of destructive internal criticism for the rationalist world view. In the most penetrating philosophical inquiries mounted in those years, reason turned upon itself and devoured its own flesh. The great empiricist David Hume exposed the logical fallacies in the Enlightenment doctrines of natural law and natural religion, rejecting the necessity of any link between experience and reason. The great rationalist Immanuel Kant argued that pure reason could tell us nothing more than the structure of the phenomenal world, the world as it appears to the senses. The real world, of ultimate truth, moral imperatives, and the divine will, was accessible to us only through conscience and faith. The upshot of both philosophies was to rupture the conventional rationalist alliance between science and human action, between fact, however ordered, and the whole realm of values. Learning more about the sphere of reality visible to the natural sciences added nothing to our knowledge of how we should live. Science was a game that people played with phenomena, not the holy of holies. Reason could not replace sentiment (for Hume) or conscience (for Kant). Although the influence of both Hume and Kant was somewhat limited in the eighteenth century itself, the mere fact that philosophers of their magnitude, who moreover belonged heart and soul to the Enlightenment, could arrive at such devastating critiques of its world view showed how exhausted rationalism had become.

There were other indications. Throughout the century its leading thinkers had grappled with the paradox that nature was, according to their world view, reasonable and well-ordered, yet humankind confronted a world rich in suffering, crime, and folly. Even without subjecting natural law to close philosophical analysis, moralists could hardly fail to observe that man, and sometimes nature itself, experienced incredible difficulty in obeying it. Why so? The clash in the ethical thought of the late Enlightenment, as between Diderot and Helvétius, or between the optimism of Adam Smith and the pessimism of the Marquis de Sade and Parson Malthus, confirmed the inability of rationalism to resolve the paradox. Voltaire himself was agonized by it. The crisis in ethical theory accelerated the collapse of deism and all notions of a "natural" religion. By the late eighteenth century most advanced thinkers in the rationalist camp had become either atheists or believers in a God who transcended reason.

The antihistorical thrust of the rationalist world view also failed to meet vital tests. In early rationalism the universe was a machine that never changed. It could not be a process of development, and therefore any progress observable in it must have occurred, as it were, by accident, by fortuitous victories of reason over unreason. Yet as the eighteenth century wore on, scientists and philosophers and historians departed more and more from the static world-machine of Descartes and Newton. Men such as Buffon and Kant speculated about the evolution of the solar system and life on earth. Some, including Turgot and the versatile Kant, promulgated doctrines of general and necessary progress. Others adopted dynamic, transformist concepts of the natural order, well illustrated by Diderot's *Thoughts on the Interpretation of Nature*, with its frontal assault on the rationalist dogma of the uniformity of nature throughout all time.

Aesthetics underwent an even more dramatic change. The belief that good art conforms to eternal rational principles yielded, inexorably, to the belief that art and science must go separate ways and that beauty is subjective. Some of the most important steps in the transformation of aesthetics were taken by thinkers whose credentials as men of the Enlightenment can be challenged only with the greatest difficulty: Hume, Diderot, Lessing. Kant summed up the whole process in his *Critique of Judgment* in 1790.

In all these ways the children of the Enlightenment had already advanced to the brink of romanticism by the closing decades of the eighteenth century or had at least broken with some of the central doctrines of rationalism. At the same time other seminal and creative minds less readily identifiable with the Enlightenment had appeared on the scene whose work just as clearly foreshadowed the romanticist revolution. A few of them, such as Rousseau, Herder, and Burke, deserve to be called romanticists in their own right, heralds and fathers of the new world view, filling places not unlike those of Bacon, Galileo, and Descartes in the development of rationalism.

Three preromantic movements merit special notice: the cult of sentiment in eighteenth-century art and literature, the rise of new varieties of religious faith diametrically opposed to the rationalist world view, and the beginnings of modern historicism. In each instance we are speaking of movements that span most of the eighteenth century or may be traced even to the late seventeenth century.

The cult of sentiment was the last of the three to make its mark. Its own origins are complex, but it can be seen as an early emotional backlash against the coldness and formalism of the eighteenth-century aesthetic ideal. Novelists such as the Abbé Prevost in *Manon Lescaut* (1731) and Samuel Richardson in *Pamela* (1740), poets such as James Thomson, and painters such as Jean-Baptiste Greuze were among the first in a long line of popular eighteenth-century "sentimentalists" who elevated feeling above reason, rejoicing in man's capacity for kindness and sympathy and finding new beauty in the simple contemplation of nature. The cult of sentiment reached its literary apogee in the writings of Rousseau, Laurence Sterne, and the young Goethe. *The New Héloïse* (1761), *A Sentimental Journey* (1768), and *The Sorrows of Young Werther* (1774) may work with a more limited emotional palette (and plumb fewer depths) than the masterpieces of the romantic era, but they stand closer to romanticism than to rationalism in their view of life. Drawing the line between "preromantic" and "romantic" sensibility is often more a matter of chronology than of substance.

In a very real sense the cult of sentiment was only the worldly counterpart of the sectarian religious movements that sprang up to challenge the ascendancy of rationalism in its years of greatest influence. From the Lutheran Pietism of P. J. Spener and A. H. Francke to the Methodism of the Wesleys and the mysticism of Swedenborg, the new sects stressed elements in the Christian tradition that were most alien to the rationalist world view: salvation through Christ, inner piety, God's love, and the Bible. Like the sentimentalists, the new sectarians made much of feeling. Theirs was a warm faith that valued subjective religious experience over the rational learning and the cold dogmas of the established churches. It turned back to Christian tradition, but it also prefigured the religiosity of romanticism.

Meanwhile, the eighteenth century was discovering another source of truth about the human condition in the labyrinthine processes of history. The study of history had always been considered an avenue to human understanding but only because men and women of all eras presumably partook of the same universal humanity. A work of history was like a fable by Aesop, with its timeless lessons for contemporary life. But in the eighteenth century, as we have noted, many thinkers in the rationalist camp began to venture beyond the confines of the Newtonian cosmos to interest themselves in the problems of natural history and human progress. Suppose —and this is the germinal idea in what Friedrich Meinecke later called *Historismus* or "historicism"—things had not always been as they were today? What if, to paraphrase A. J. P. Taylor, Julius Caesar had not been simply the Earl of Chatham in a toga? Historicism was the discovery, not completed until the nineteenth-century revolution in historical scholarship, that history is an organic process of change and development in which every event is unique and can be understood only in terms of its own unique temporal context.

If the philosophes themselves did much to deepen historical consciousness, still more was accomplished by thinkers outside the rationalist mainstream in the eighteenth century. One maverick, Giambattista Vico, who published his *Principles of a New Science* in 1725, took issue with the mechanistic politics of his generation and maintained that different ages required different forms of government because every age had its own spirit, needs, and values. Human beings were not machines, but irrational creatures molded by culture and faith. Although Vico's book fell on deaf ears in his own time, its reputation grew steadily thereafter. Among its readers was a German thinker cited in our first chapter as the discoverer of the "national soul," J. G. von Herder. In his magnificent and far-ranging studies of history, contemporary with the work of Kant, Herder found that the path of human progress lay in the historical unfolding of distinctive national cultures. The uniformity of human nature was for him a rationalist illusion: on the contrary, human nature was "a molding clay which assumes different forms in accordance with different conditions, needs, and pressures.... Every human perfection is national, temporal, and ... individual." Humanity did not exist in the crystal formulas of a philosopher's treatise—humanity happened.

Herder was a transitional figure, partly of the Enlightenment, in greater part a pioneer of romanticism. The same deep feeling for history and its vital processes suffused the thought of his British contemporary, Edmund Burke. Men of letters began to seek out the medieval sources of their national literary culture. Herder himself performed this service for German and Slavic folk literature. Other landmarks in the recovery of the medieval heritage were the Ossianic poems of James Macpherson and Thomas Percy's collection of old English ballads. The classical ideal suffered further setbacks in the first tentative revivals of Gothic architecture and in the new appreciation of Shakespeare, especially by German critics. A whole new past opened up to Western eyes: a world of gigantic passions, mystery, rough beauty, even wisdom, grounded not in reason but in the deeds and blood of national forefathers.

Since nearly all of this had taken place before 1789, it is clear that romanticism did not originate as a response of thinkers and poets to the French Revolution and its sequels in Western history. Nothing could have prevented its coming in one form or another. But the events of the Age of Revolution made their contribution, to be sure. The new regimes, installed with such drama and fanfare, swung from one extreme to another, winning ardent admirers and generating massive hostility and disillusionment. Romanticists could be found to applaud each new government as it arose, while other romanticists turned away in rage or disgust from the Revolution, from the Empire, from the Restoration, and finally from the new bourgeois politics that brought the Age of Revolution to its inglorious end in the 1850s. Had the ancien régime managed to limp on into the nineteenth century, chaning gradually from within, romanticism might well have spoken with a softer voice and adopted positions far less desperate. Certainly the swift flow of events, and the mighty changes they effected, did much to convince Western minds of the processive nature of reality. The career of Napoleon, the upsurge of the German national movement, the collapse of old elites and the rise of new ones, and the early progress of industrialism in England refuted Newton's eternal world-machine with a logic all their own. The romanticists knew well, and noted often, that theirs was a time of crisis in human affairs, of levelings and liberations without precedent in the experience of mankind. To see the march of events as a model of reality was only natural for men of their epoch.

If the eighteenth century had been a time of steady expansion for the Western world, the years from 1789 to 1848 witnessed even more growth at a much accelerated pace. Behind the political drama a still greater social and demographic drama unfolded that quickened the whole life of Europe and America. The British population nearly tripled, the North American increased sixfold. On the continent, except for the Latin West, populations doubled, all in the space of just two generations. The people, mute and powerless for so long, gathering in the new urban agglomerations, hearing the siren songs of Rousseauians and Jacobins and Nationalists, awoke to self-consciousness. Although many of the early romanticists were aristocrats, and most of the rest bourgeois, Friedrich Heer rightly observes that in one sense romanticism represented a dark uprush of forces from the popular and pagan underground.³ These folkish forces, long suppressed by the heavy weight of classical and Christian antiquity, broke free and began increasingly to determine the shapes of Western culture.

So in the end one must agree, too, with Jacques Barzun that the romanticists were preeminently creators. They were men and women who confronted the disarray of the Enlightenment and the ruins of the old order and concluded that civilization had to make a fresh start, drawing on a fuller range of powers and resources than the philosophes had accepted into their systems.⁴ In creating, the romanticists only furthered the same process of modernization that the rationalists before them had sought to advance. Few among them dreamed of a literal restoration of any past order. Few among them doubted progress, or at least change and evolution, in human affairs. In their rebelliousness the romanticists were the heirs of those same philosophes who had long before, with stupendous egoism, challenged the conventional wisdom and put forward their own recipes for human reconstruction. Under the lash of romanticist criticism and romanticist idealism, Western civilization moved further along the highroad to a new, distinctively modern consciousness. In some respects the culture they struggled to build may have been less modern than that of the Enlightenment. But in others, it was more so. In its very nervousness, its characteristic manic-depressive mixture of enthusiasm and melancholy, it seems much closer to twentieth-century sensibilities than rationalism. At all odds the culture of romanticism cannot be charged with infertility. None has ever been more powerfully creative in almost every sphere of literary, aesthetic, and intellectual life.

Romanticism rose and fell in a much shorter time than its predecessor. A scattering of founding fathers (Rousseau, Burke, Hamann, Herder, Jacobi, Lamarck, Goya) were contemporaries of the last rationalists, but the first full generation of romanticists was born between 1750 and 1785. The Germans led the way with Goethe, Schiller, Jean-Paul, the Schlegels, Hölderlin, Novalis, Hoffmann, and Kleist in letters; Fichte, Hegel, Schelling, and Oken in philosophy and science; and such seminal figures in other fields as Beethoven in music, Friedrich in painting, Schleiermacher in theology, and Savigny and Müller in political thought. The first generation of British romanticists included, in literature, Blake, Burns, Wordsworth, Scott, Coleridge, and Southey; and in the fine arts, Turner and Constable. In France romanticism arrived some ten years later with the philosophy and social thought of Maine de Biran, Fourier, Sismondi, and Lamennais and a few outstanding literary personages—de Staël, Chateaubriand, Sénancour. Russian romanticism began with Karamzin, American with the later work of Irving and the novels of Cooper.

A second full generation, consisting of men and women born between 1785 and 1815, reached its creative zenith in the second quarter of the nineteenth century. This was the golden age of romanticist music, the generation of Weber, Schubert, Schumann, and Wagner in the German-speaking world and of Berlioz in France. German philosophy carried on, less illustriously, with Schopenhauer and Stirner, literature with Uhland, Eichendorff, Rückert, Heine, and Lenau, art with Overbeck and the Nazarenes. In British letters the second generation numbered in its ranks Byron, the Shelleys, Carlyle, and Keats and also the greatest mind in nineteenth-century Catholicism, Cardinal Newman. The Gothic revival in architecture was championed by Pugin in England, Viollet-le-Duc in France.

In addition to Berlioz and Viollet-le-Duc, the second (and by far the greater) generation of French romanticists included Lamartine, Vigny, Dumas, Hugo, Sand, Nerval, Musset, and Gautier in literature; Géricault, Corot, Delacroix, and T. Rousseau in painting; and Lamennais, Cousin, Thierry, Enfantin, Michelet, and Proudhon in thought and scholarship. Russian romanticism culminated in the work of Pushkin and Lermontov, Khomyakov and Herzen. Nearly all of American romanticism also belongs to this second generation: the Transcendentalism of Emerson, Fuller, and Thoreau; the historiography of Prescott and Motley; the prose and poetry of Hawthorne, Longfellow, Poe, Whitman, and Melville; the art of Doughty and Cole. The romanticism of the other European cultures dates from the same years: Oehlenschläger, Atterbom, Andersen, Wergeland, and Kierkegaard in Scandinavia; Manzoni and Leopardi in Italy; Kollár, Mickiewicz, and Krasińsky in western Slavdom.

But even as these later romanticists pursued their labors, they collided with the first generation of positivists, spokesmen of a world view that challenged romanticism almost as fundamentally as romanticism had challenged rationalism. The brief ascendancy of the romanticist world conception came to an end by the middle of the nineteenth century. Never fully discredited by the criticisms of the romanticist epoch, science and reason enjoyed something of a renaissance of influence. Even letters and the arts turned away from the full romanticist gospel, incorporating fragments of it, but upholding a new, more prosaic, more realistic view of life. Reacting fiercely against the cloudy raptures of idealism, some philosophers vaulted to a defiant materialism that even in the Enlightenment had attracted only marginal support. The new positivist culture, unlike romanticism, embraced the practical virtues of a rapidly industrializing society and set itself to bring humankind into attunement with its hard realities. But romanticism, although it could not avoid taking notice of industrialization, had originated and flourished for the most part in a preindustrial age. The Europe and America of the period after 1848 were as different, certainly, from the Europe and America of the Age of Revolution as both differed from the world of the ancien régime. Needs changed, and world views changed with them.

The Quest for Identity: Germany

In the end every major country in the Western world produced romanticists of the first magnitude; but in the beginning romanticism was chiefly a German phenomenon, with serious competition only from the British. The romantic era coincided with a national revival in the German lands that did as much to shape late modern German culture as rationalism had already done for Britain and France. In large measure the German national revival was made possible by romanticism. The two were inextricably linked. Through romanticism Germany found an identity both true to her past and open to a wider future.

The romanticist movement in the German-speaking world ranged through every field of cultural endeavor, and with spectacular results, especially in the first generation. Starting with Goethe and Schiller and leading on to Hölderlin, Novalis, and Kleist, there has never been a brighter constellation of literary genius, before or since, in any Western country. All but a little of the philosophy, theology, and science of the romanticist movement was German, from Herder and Fichte to Oken and Schopenhauer. The same is true in music. No painters clung to the romanticist vision more faithfully than Friedrich and the Nazarenes. The Germans were also the great trailblazers in the modern discovery of the Middle Ages, of ethnicity, and the historical foundations of law and community. They were the first apostles of nationalism, the most deeply romantic of all politial idelogies. Even the use of the word "romantic" to apply to a movement in letters was at first confined to the German-speaking world. But of course the romanticism of which we speak in this chapter covers much more ground than any of the self-styled romantic schools of the period, German or foreign.

German romanticism was in effect the model for all the other Western romanticisms, and it was the only national movement to articulate the new world view comprehensively and rigorously in the language of philosophy. Anglo-French philosophy made little creative use of romanticist ideas until the closing decades of the nineteenth century. This fact in itself helps to distinguish German romanticism from the other national versions. It was more explicitly philosophical and thus more self-conscious. In addition, it was more Christian. All the romanticisms were marked by fresh serious interest in the core teachings of the Christian religion, but faith exerted the strongest influence on thought and art in Germany. The philosophy of German romanticism owed more to the still considerable power of the Christian tradition in central Europe than to anything happening in the internal history of philosophy itself. It owed even less to the progress of physical science.

A further idiosyncrasy of German romanticism was its intense historical consciousness, and above all its medievalism. Forced to choose between the two extremes of individual and community, the Germans usually opted for community, for the order of reality rooted and structured in historical experience. The lonely ego seeking definition in terms of itself was not an unfamiliar figure in Germany, but it appeared more often in other countries during the romantic age. Nor did the Germans exhibit the devotion to wild nature so characteristic, for example, of English romanticism. Of all the countries where romanticism flourished, it was most serious, most constructive, and perhaps even most heartfelt in Germany.

Romanticism could not have come at a better time. By the second half of the eighteenth century, the German states had fully recovered from the devastating effects of the Thirty Years War. Prussia had joined Austria as one of the Great Powers of Europe. Populations rose, cities grew. Yet Germany, as such, was still a political nullity, divided against itself, fought over, excluded from the sea lanes and the scramble for overseas empire. In its cultural life it had adapted the Anglo-French Enlightenment to German habits of thought without establishing a firm cultural identity of its own. In some ways, the Aufklärung was only French spoken with a thick Teutonic accent. As the Enlightenment progressively disintegrated from within, it became even more rapidly unacceptable to the Germans in their search for an identity better than that of ersatz Frenchmen or Englishmen.

Soon, of course, Germany's condition deteriorated still further. The French Revolution unleashed on Europe a new imperial power more dangerous to Germany than the Bourbons. French armies marched at will over the German landscape. The Revolution itself threatened the survival of the institutions of the German ancien régime. At just the time when the Germans were engaged in a desperate struggle to define themselves, France sought to engulf and gallicize all of Europe. Already, in 1789, the greatest power on earth and the cultural arbiter of modern civilization, France now aspired to Roman grandeur. It was too much. Wavering between a lofty cosmopolitanism and incipient nationalism, young Germany bolted to nationalism. Torn between the Aufklärung and incipient romanticism, young Germany hesitated no longer, and embraced fully the romanticist world view.

As Eugene N. Anderson has observed, the German decision constituted a "counterrevolution," a conscious leap into the past.[5] After being ashamed for so long of the backwardness and provincialism and insignificance of Germany, the German intelligentsia resolved to mount a rebellion against modernity. French civilization, once so seductive, now seemed false and cheap. The wit, the coolness, the smartness, the sophistication of France lost their power to bewitch German hearts. Germans turned to their own past for inspiration, and not so much to the recent past, corrupted by foreign influence, but to older and purer times, to the Germany of the Reformation, the Germany of the Middle Ages, even pagan Germany. They celebrated German law, German art, German piety. Like so many other ethnic groups who were later to rebel against the West—the Russians, the Spaniards, the

Irish, the Arabs, the Indians, the Africans—they proclaimed that German culture was rooted in the dark soil of a living history, not in the shallow sophistries of modern thought. Germany had a soul; France, and perhaps England, too, only a brain.

Ironically, much of the stimulus for the German counterrevolution came from abroad, from Westerners who themselves in various ways rejected the compulsive up-to-dateness of Western culture. The greatest teacher of the first generation of German romanticists was no doubt Jean-Jacques Rousseau. In Rousseau they found the perfect model of the Outsider, a humorless sentimentalist in an age of scoffing rationalists, a lover of small-town naïveté in an age of cosmopolitan elegance. Rousseau shocked the philosophes by blaming the woes of civilization on civilization itself. A poor historian, he nonetheless saw goodness in the relative simplicity of an arcadian past before men had learned the fine arts of exploitation and despotism. What could have been more welcome to German thinkers in the last third of the eighteenth century than a French philosopher who undertook to demolish the foundations of French philosophy and who rallied to the defense of something very much like the "backwardness" that had for so long been their principal shame? Backward indeed! The more backward, the better!

Another foreign influence exactly contemporary with the major writings of Rousseau came in the form of two epic poems allegedly translated from the Gaelic by a little known Scottish writer, James Macpherson. Attributed to the third-century Irish bard Ossian, *Fingal* (1762) and *Temora* (1763) were instant literary sensations, poems of almost Homeric or biblical quality that carried Europeans back to a world of barbaric adventure idealized in steamy, sonorous verse by a skillful forger. How much of Macpherson's work was based on Gaelic oral tradition, how much was Irish and how much Scottish, and how much originated purely and simply in the fecund imagination of James Macpherson, is still impossible to determine with any degree of accuracy. But of one thing there can be no question. *Fingal* and *Temora* took Europe by storm. The Germans, including Herder and the young Goethe, were especially fascinated. Again the romance of a simpler, wilder past, even if it was not a German past, spoke with eloquence for values and passions remote from those extolled by the philosophes. The same service was supplied by the English antiquarian Thomas Percy's *Reliques of Ancient English Poetry*, a collection of medieval ballads first published in 1765. In short order German scholars were delving into the folkish sources of German literature and discovering an antiquity no less romantic than the world of King Fingal.

A way back to the Middle Ages was also opened by the revival of the works of Shakespeare in the second half of the eighteenth century. For some time the major figures in that revival were German. Wieland, Lessing, Herder, and Goethe led the critical chorus, and Shakespeare's characters—romantics before their time—soon filled the German stage.

Many other examples of foreign influence could be cited: Vico's influence on Herder, Hume's on Kant, Burke's on Savigny and Adam Müller. Clearly the Germans learned more from their fellow Europeans than the rationalism and classicism of the Enlightenment. But native influences were still more decisive in the shaping of German romanticism. Even the Aufklärung, as we noticed earlier, departed at many points from the Western model. Leibniz was not simply a German Descartes, nor Kant a German Hume. In aesthetics, in epistemology, in religious thought, in natural philosophy, the leading German minds of the Aufklärung differed significantly from their Anglo-French counterparts in ways that usually foreshadowed the romanticist weltanschauung.

Behind the nascent romanticism of the German Enlightenment lay the whole unique course of German history in medieval and early modern times that we explored in Chapter 2. The prominence of mysticism in the late Middle Ages in Germany and the virulent antirationalism of the German Reformation had obvious long-term implications for German thought. Of more immediate relevance is the religious history of Germany in the seventeenth and eighteenth centuries. In no part of western Europe did the Christian faith live on with such warmth and intensity, even among the educated classes, as in Germany. The disasters that repeatedly overwhelmed the German lands, their depressed or lagging economies, and their social and political conservatism furnished an ideal setting for the thriving of piety.

The keynote of German religious thought in the seventeenth and eighteenth centuries was, indeed, piety. Under the surface of the official Reformation orthodoxies and later the deism of the Aufklärung flourished a series of mystical and pietistic movements that insisted on the priority of feeling in religious life, on heartfelt devotion and inwardness as the touchstones of faith. From these movements emanated the most powerful Christian thought of the time. It had its effect on the Aufklärer themselves and even more strongly influenced the founders of romanticism.

The beginnings of the new piety in Germany can be traced to the mystics of the late sixteenth and early seventeenth centuries, men such as Valentin Weigel and Jakob Böhme. Taking up the already well-established themes of the mystical tradition, Weigel and Böhme viewed the visible and established church as an empty shell. Its creeds, its rites, its priests could not bring God into the hearts of men. The way to salvation could be found only in the inner world of the spirit, which Böhme linked in the tradition of Paracelsus with all of creation. Little known at first, the teachings of these post-Reformation mystics spread slowly but surely throughout Germany. At the same time Johann Arndt, in his widely read *Four Books on True Christianity* (1606), achieved an ingenious fusion of Lutheran orthodoxy and mysticism that helped to dissolve the barriers between the two and brought mystical influence into the bosom of the church.

Arndt was in some respects the founder of what came to be known as Pietism. With little exaggeration Friedrich Heer dubs Pietism "the most powerful movement of modern German intellectual history."[6] It became a recognized sect of Lutheranism in the late seventeenth century under the leadership of P. J. Spener, who spoke from pulpits in Frankfurt, Dresden, and Berlin and wrote many devotional works, of which the best-known was *Pia Desideria* (1675). The writings of Arndt had been a major force in his religious education. He was followed in the eighteenth century by his disciple A. H. Francke, who made the University of Halle the leading center of Pietist learning in Germany, and by Count Zinzendorf, the organizer of the Church of the Moravian Brethren at Herrnhut in Saxony.

In brief the Pietist gospel was one of love, spiritual commitment, and the nurturing of inner piety. Believers were bound to a severe rule of daily life. Devout, penitent, evangelistic, they took their "religion of the heart" into many corners of Germany and the world. Pietism spread to Scandinavia, the Baltic provinces, Great Britain, and North America; a Moravian preacher in London launched John Wesley on the spiritual pilgrimage that led to the founding of Methodism. Wherever they went, the Pietists brought the message that the Christian life demanded rebirth, a change from within that transcended all doctrine, all institutional structures, all the works of man and reason. Pietism was a second Reformation, fueled by the same passions as the first.

Although Pietism lost much of its momentum in the second half of the eighteenth century, especially within the church, its effect on German thought grew rather than diminished as the century wore on. Many of the thinkers and poets of the Age of Revolution were raised in Pietist homes, educated in Pietist schools, or inspired by mystic and Pietist books. Few of the rest could have avoided being influenced indirectly. A figure so central to the emergence of the romanticist world view as Immanuel Kant, for example, had devout Pietist parents and for more than eight years attended a Pietist Latin school. The leading religious thinker of the romanticist movement, Friedrich Schleiermacher, studied at a Pietist school, a Pietist seminary, and later, the University of Halle. The philosopher J. F. Fries, an important critic of Kant, was also a product of Pietist schooling. J. H. Jung-Stilling, whose memoirs of a Pietist youth remains one of the great works of eighteenth-century German literature, became a political and religious prophet of wide influence among the early romanticists. The young Goethe was powerfully moved by the writings of the Pietist savant Gottfried Arnold. Schelling and Hegel learned much from Böhme, as did the Bavarian mystic and romanticist Franz von Baader.

What Pietism and all the other antiestablishmentarian, antirationalist tendencies in German religious thought in the eighteenth century meant for romanticism is nothing mysterious. Despite the heroic efforts of the philosophes (like the medieval schoolmen before them) to rationalize the Christian faith, it claims an intractable core of truth that reason can never assimilate. It is a truth of passion, of inwardness, of ecstasy beyond the grasp of everyday consciousness. The German religious underground, with Pietism as its strongest voice, kept insisting throughout the century of Enlightenment that this faith beyond reason was the only authentic faith. To the truth of reason, it opposed the truth of revelation and mystical insight. To the faith of intellect, it opposed the faith of the heart and a world view little different from that of romanticism.

This is not to say that German romanticism focused most of its energies on overtly religious themes and problems. Quite often the religious impulse operated only in a secularized form. Certainly Christian values were not ascendant in the first wave of romanticist literature and philosophy that arrived in the 1770s. In letters this was the decade of the Sturm und Drang, the "storm and stress" movement, of special importance because it introduced to Europe the genius of Johann Wolfgang von Goethe. It took its name from the subtitle of a play by Friedrich von Klinger, one of the angriest of its angry young men. His hot-blooded dramas illustrate as well as any the influence of Shakespeare on German literature at this time. But the supreme figure was Goethe, first for his play *Götz von Berlichingen* (1773), a romance of the sixteenth century, and then for his sentimental novel *The Sorrows of Young Werther* (1774). The Sturm und Drang epoch came to a glorious close with the first three plays of a still younger writer, no less a Shakespearian and romanticist, Friedrich von Schiller. Disrespect for classical forms and unities, coupled with a feverish striving for emotional impact, characterized all the works of the Sturm und Drang. They have not, for the most part, worn well.

Goethe and Schiller became close friends in the 1790s. Even before this they had begun to veer away from some of the enthusiasms of their youth. They discovered the power of Hellenism, the virtues of self-discipline, and the strength of humanistic and cosmopolitan values. The last works of Schiller, who died prematurely in 1806, and the middle period in Goethe's career, spanning the years from *Iphigenia in Tauris* (1787) to his writings of the early 1800s, belonged to the Aufklärung as much as to romanticism. But even as classicists, Goethe and Schiller were poets of fervent idealism and profound faith in the power of art. They continued to adhere to the great romanticist vision of the subjectivity of truth. Schiller's aesthetic philosophy, inspired by Kant, and Goethe's nature-philosophy, wholly in the romanticist tradition, further demonstrated their rapport with the new world view. As for that remarkable work of Goethe's final period, *Faust* (1808–32), it was no less an epitome of romanticism than Beethoven's Ninth Symphony or Hegel's *Phenomenology of the Spirit*.

As literature turned to new orientations in the 1770s, so did philosophy. The Sturm und Drang itself might never have materialized without the impetus it received from the thought of Herder. Goethe met Herder in

Strasbourg in 1770 and learned much from him, including his exalted ideas of poetry and the creative task of the poet and his appreciation of the beauties of folkish and medieval culture. The collection of essays *On German Character and Art* (1773) that became in effect the manifesto of the Sturm und Drang movement contained two pieces (on folk poetry and Shakespeare) by Herder. The young philosopher went on to attack the Enlightenment frontally in his first major treatise on the philosophy of history, published in 1774, and after 1776 joined Goethe at Weimar, where he died in 1803 after producing a body of work that in its first collected edition ran to forty-five volumes.

But there were other voices. Kant, who outlived his younger contemporary by two months, published his critiques of rationalism in the period 1781–90. Both Kant and Herder profited immensely from their friendship with another and far more radical foe of the Enlightenment, Johann Georg Hamann. Heer calls Hamann "the first priest of the night. He began the great sanctification of force and of the chaotic and demonic in man."[7] His quasi-theological writings in this period (he died in 1788) celebrated the priority of faith, action, and passion in conscious defiance of the cool religiosity of rationalism. He could almost have been a Pietist divine although in fact he earned his bread working as a bureaucrat in Baltic custom-houses. The last significant member of the philosophical generation of Kant and Herder, Friedrich Jacobi, was also an intimate of Hamann. Jacobi taught a philosophy of "feeling," whose central tenet was the eminently romanticist idea that only immediate experience by the mind of things-in-themselves could offer us truth. Neither the senses nor abstract reason gave access to reality: consciousness alone could reveal it.

The ground was thus fully prepared for the next major crop of romanticists, who began coming to light in the middle and late 1790s. The new men were all quite young, and for the first time the word "romantic" was employed as a party label. The original "romantic" school consisted of men of letters, centered at Jena, where in 1798 the brothers August and Friedrich von Schlegel founded their influential journal, the *Athenaeum.* Around the Schlegels gathered a circle of writers united by their love of Shakespeare, the Middle Ages, language studies, and to quote their French admirer Mme. de Staël, "the interior existence . . . that mystery of mysteries." The circle included Ludwig Tieck, novelist, playwright, and critic; and Novalis (the pen name of Friedrich von Hardenberg), poet and prophet of a new Catholic Middle Ages of "eternal peace." Standing apart from the Jena school, but today regarded as one of the greatest lyric poets in German history, was Friedrich Hölderlin. His brief career ended at the age of thirty-six in 1806 when he became incurably insane.

A second romantic school based in Heidelberg flourished for several years in the mid-1800s. The founders were Clemens Brentano and Achim von Arnim, folklorists and poets who together edited *The Youth's Magic*

Horn (1805–8), a popular collection of German folk poetry dedicated to Goethe. Soon the group had its own periodical, the *Journal for Hermits*, and a brilliant new collaborator in Joseph von Görres. It broke up as quickly as the Jena circle, but it did much to promote German cultural awareness at a time when the survival of Germany seemed in doubt. The romanticist movement in letters continued for at least twenty more years with the plays and novellas of Heinrich von Kleist, the fantastic tales of E. T. A. Hoffmann, the folklorism of the Grimm brothers, the ballads of the Swabian poet Ludwig Uhland, the love lyrics of Heinrich Heine, and much more.

In the realm of ideas, the period from the mid-1790s to the mid-1820s saw the blossoming of German idealism. J. G. Fichte produced all his chief philosophical works between 1792 and 1806; Friedrich Schelling began writing in 1795 and published little after 1803; G. W. F. Hegel's most important books appeared between 1807 and 1821 except for his great Berlin lecture series of the 1820s, published posthumously in editions compiled mostly from student notes. To follow the stages in the thought of each philosopher, their vigorous disagreements with one another, their relations with other thinkers and writers, and their influence during the Age of Revolution is hardly possible here, but of their allegiance to the romanticist world view no serious question can be raised. All three agreed that reality is ultimately spiritual, akin to or identical with consciousness. All three sought to fuse epistemology, metaphysics, and ethics into a single system that hinged knowledge on acts of will and intuition rather than sensation and abstract reason. All three held a dynamic view of the world, seeing it as a process of evolution or historical unfolding. Of the three, Schelling— who in early life interacted with the Jena circle and in later life turned to a religious mysticism inspired by Böhme—seems to have been the most complete romanticist, Hegel the least. But their differences pale next to their similarities. Even Hegel's bureaucratic passion for structure and order, which as W. T. Jones observes, "is the chief surviving trace in his thought of the old Enlightenment Syndrome,"[8] did not prevent him from adhering to the most crucial articles of the romanticist faith.

Romanticism lost no time in penetrating other fields of thought. Its champions in religion included the Catholic writers Baader and Görres and, in Protestant theology, the lofty figure of Friedrich Schleiermacher. Romanticist religion meant, essentially, a religion of experience. The believer felt God acting within himself, and for him this was proof enough of God's existence, which reason could do nothing to improve. Under the influence of the metaphysics of idealism, which equated God with the spiritual ground of this-worldly being, God lost his transcendental and personal qualities to become a force acting within history not unlike Spinoza's God. For that matter Spinoza's pantheism was on the mind of virtually every German philosopher and theologian in the romantic era. The Dutchman's methods may have been Cartesian, but his God was nothing like the

divine absentee landlord of the deists. For both Spinoza and the romanticists, God belonged in the world, not outside it: indeed, in a sense, God and
the world were the same. Here, as in so many ways, romanticism took on
a decidedly secularizing character, perhaps in spite of itself. Although it
deplored the prosaic, mundane consciousness of the Enlightenment, it fixed
most of its attentions on the affairs of this world. In the sphere of religion
it called for spiritual experience here and now and faith in a God who
pervaded the whole world-process here and now. Its transcendentalism was
a call for the transcendence of matter and mechanism, not for flight from
this world into eternity.

The romanticist transcendence of matter and mechanism was nowhere
more apparent than in its scientific thought. Newtonianism had never won
much of a following on German soil, and the romanticists objected strenuously to every effort to reduce nature to a machine, a merely material
system, or a dead and static phenomenal order. Not content to oppose the
prevailing scientific wisdom of the West, they came forward with their own
science. A celebrated instance is the work of Goethe, who made extensive
contributions in such fields as optics, botany, and morphology. From the
first he had found Western scientific ideas repugnant. As a young law
student in Strasbourg in 1770, he had tried to read d'Holbach's new book,
The System of Nature, and left it unfinished, not so much shocked by its
atheism as baffled and amused by its corpselike dullness. There was no life
in its pages, no breath of freedom, no spirit. Goethe and his friends, he wrote
in his autobiography, "did not understand how such a book could be dangerous," and for some time thereafter maintained a proud contempt for all the
branches of philosophy.

Goethe's contempt was short-lived. After the fireworks of the Sturm und
Drang, he became deeply involved in scientific research and theory. Some
of his work, especially in morphology (a science that Goethe himself founded), was of great value. Some of it, including his attempt to disprove Newton's theory of light, led nowhere. Through it all Goethe clung to a
distinctively romanticist view of nature as a single, continuous system,
comprehensible in its organicity only through the self-aware and empathetic
powers of human minds conscious of their own participation in its processes. His lead was followed by Schelling, by Lorenz Oken, and several
others, who developed a characteristically German school of "nature-philosophy" that found its spiritual roots in the teachings and methods of
Paracelsus, Böhme, and Leibniz. The nature-philosophers, in Stephen F.
Mason's summation, argued that the universe was permeated by the same
free psychic activity as the human mind, "and so the processes of nature
were to be interpreted by analogy with the inner movement of the mind,
not in terms of the pure externality of matter in motion." The new science
contended "that the laws of spirit are no different from the laws of nature;
but that both are transcripts or likenesses of each other."[9]

German nature-philosophy scored its greatest triumphs in biology. Evolutionary theory, embryology, and cytology all advanced with its help during this period. Even in physics nature-philosophy had its effect, most dramatically in the discovery of electromagnetism in 1820 by Hans Christian Oersted, a Danish follower of Schelling.

The main thrust of the political thought of German romanticism has already been indicated earlier in this chapter. It developed in obvious response to the need of the German peoples for a cultural and national identity of their own, and its development between 1789 and the revolutions of 1830 followed a predictable course. After a brief flirtation with some of the more cosmopolitan values of the French Revolution, German political thought turned defiantly to nationalism, an ideology that one may argue the German romanticists invented. Nationalism maintained that the natural polity was the folkish state, the political expression of an ethnic community whose members are united by a common language, folk culture, and history. The philosophy of Herder and Burke's *Reflections on the French Revolution* (1790), translated into German by Friedrich Gentz in 1792, played a decisive part in the growth of nationalism, but it did not emerge as a full-fledged political ideology until late in the first decade of the nineteenth century, when Germany was threatened with incorporation into Napoleon's Gallic version of the Roman Empire. The romanticists rallied, for the most part, to the national cause. Schleiermacher lectured on natural resistance in Berlin, Kleist pamphleteered on behalf of the idea of a German national state, Friedrich von Schlegel cried for German regeneration under Austrian leadership, Ernst Moritz Arndt became the poet laureate of the new ideology, and the philosopher Fichte expounded its theory of education in his Berlin lectures of 1807–8, *Addresses to the German Nation.* The capstone was furnished by F. L. Jahn's half-mystical tract *German Folkdom* (*Das Deutsches Volkstum,* 1810).

Yet German nationalism had difficulty in identifying its goals. Some early nationalists opted for a more modern national state ruled from Vienna, others for a Greater Prussia, still others for a liberal and constitutional confederacy of the German lands. It would be two long generations after the fall of Napoleon before a true German state appeared in Europe, in part because the Germans could not agree on what form it should take.

But political romanticism dealt with other issues besides national unification. Among its principal concerns, as in the political philosophy of any age, was the definition of statehood itself. Here the romanticists closely followed the historicism of Burke. A major figure was the Prussian convert to Catholicism, Adam Müller, who contended in the Burkean vein, with influence also from counterrevolutionary French thought, that the state could never properly be seen as a matter of utility or convenience. It was the synthesis of human life, a sacred union of families extending far into the past, without which the private individual amounted to little more than a beast. The

Western notion that states could be manufactured to order by reason or revolution lowered them to the level of mere merchandise, an idea that might suit the rootless bourgeois but had no place among those fortunate peoples who trusted in the historical wisdom of their Christian homelands. On a higher plane of abstraction, no less a political philosopher than Hegel offered the same doctrine. The state, in his *Philosophy of Right* (1821), was a moral entity, God's will in earthly form, to which all subjects owed service and unswerving fidelity and in which alone they could find true freedom.

The conservatism of German romanticist political thought may seem to foreshadow fascism, as perhaps it does, but it responded to the needs of the time. The divine right of states was not, in the context of the early nineteenth century, a doctrine of totalitarian nationalism but a defense of German institutions against a foreign invader, and not even an unqualified defense. Few political thinkers wished for a continuation of the ancien régime in all its creaky confusion: they sought in various ways to make the German states more Christian, more ethically responsible, more efficient, and more respectful of due process and established law. The Hegelian idea of the just state, as George H. Sabine writes, can be "summed up in the aphorism 'a government not of men but laws.'"[10] It combined in its very German way the absolutism of Louis XIV with the constitutionalism of Hanoverian England. But it justified itself in terms of the transcendental logic of history, which it chose to identify, as German idealism identified everything, with the will of God.

German art and music made the transition from Aufklärung to *Romantik* somewhat later than either literature or philosophy but with results well worth the delay. Prompted by the aesthetics of Ludwig Tieck and W. H. Wackenroder, who appealed in the 1790s for a return to the inspirations of medieval Christian art, a new self-consciously German school of painting arose in Dresden in the next decade headed by Philipp Otto Runge. At about the same time, Runge's friend Caspar David Friedrich turned to the production of the strangely disquieting landscapes that have persuaded twentieth-century critics to rank him as the best German painter of the romanticist movement. Friedrich's canvasses typically offer solitary human figures confronting vast stretches of wilderness (somewhat as in classical Chinese art), suggesting both the kinship of man with the cosmos and also the terrible majesty of nature—or, in theological terms—the love and the awesomeness of God. "It is the unflinching directness of Friedrich that is most disturbing," as Morse Peckham remarks, "for he unites, even better than Wordsworth, terror and beauty in a single image."[11]

Elsewhere, at the Vienna Academy, Johann Friedrich Overbeck and his followers organized a circle of young painters in 1809 known as the Brotherhood of St. Luke, or more popularly, the Nazarenes. Believing that all art should serve religious ends, the Nazarenes, like Runge, cast back to the medieval masters for spiritual guidance. For nearly twenty years they lived as a quasi-monastic community in Rome, painting religious frescoes. In art as in literature romanticism furnished Germany with its greatest achievements since the Renaissance.

Music presents a somewhat different picture, since the German lands had already overcome the old leadership of their Latin rivals: the superb baroque art of Bach and Handel and the classicism of Gluck, Haydn, and Mozart were, in the language of show business, hard acts to follow. Nevertheless, romanticism soon penetrated even here, a process easily traced in the works of Beethoven from the Mozartian buoyancy of his first piano music to the hammerlike power of the Third and Fifth Symphonies (1804, 1808) to the dense, complex, and soulful syntheses of the Ninth Symphony (1824) and the last quartets. Like other romantic artists, Beethoven envisaged himself as a seer and prophet. Music, he proclaimed, "gives the feeling, it carries the inspiration, of heavenly sciences; and that which the mind perceptibly draws from it is the incarnation of spiritual knowledge. . . . Music is that electric ground in which the spirit lives, thinks, and discovers." After Beethoven had demolished the dikes of classicism, romanticist impulses virtually flooded the musical world. From the 1820s to the 1870s, Germany and Austria astonished Europe with a seemingly endless succession of romantic masters: von Weber, Schubert, Mendelssohn, Schumann, Liszt, Wagner.

But this latter-day movement in music was not accompanied by work of the same high value in other areas of culture. The period of late romanticism in Germany wears a melancholy aspect. Just when the French romanticists were at their peak of exuberance, the Germans had begun to lose the faith. Between 1831 and 1834, Hegel, Goethe, and Schleiermacher died; Schiller, Novalis, Kleist, Fichte, and Friedrich von Schlegel had already gone; and the new men were of different quality, less heroic, less Promethean, and, with few exceptions apart from music, less brilliant. The only philosopher of first rank, Arthur Schopenhauer, pursued romanticism into a cul-de-sac of despair and world-weariness. The greatest of an otherwise mediocre crop of poets, Heinrich Heine, turned against the romantics in his later years and began the debunking process that culminated in the bitter polemics of midcentury materialism and realism. Hölderlin lived on, insane and unable to write; Tieck became a grand panjandrum of literary criticism in Dresden and Berlin, purged of the enthusiasms of his youth; Schelling published nothing, retreating into a religiously oriented philosophy out of touch with all the tendencies of post-Hegelian thought. Romanticism flourished after 1830 in Germany, but (always excepting music) both its golden and its silver ages were by then clearly over.

Fellowship with Nature: Great Britain

Although Britain is conventionally paired with Germany as a homeland of the romantic movement, the situations of the two countries during the

Age of Revolution could not have been more different. So, too, were their experiences of romanticism. In both romanticism came early, but for Britain there was no national identity crisis and no urgent need for cultural renascence. The French had never succeeded in gallicizing their neighbors across the Channel. Romanticism generated less excitement in Britain than in central Europe, and—the gospel taught in every literature classroom in the English-speaking world notwithstanding—it achieved far less. Romanticism inspired many volumes of great poetry, but in every other field, from philosophy to theater, the British contribution was uneven or negligible. Yet these were years of national power and wealth, unprecedented demographic expansion, and no dearth of genius. Some of the best minds and outstanding writers of the Age of Revolution in Britain were not romanticists at all—the philosophers Jeremy Bentham and James Mill, the socialist prophet Robert Owen, the economists T. R. Malthus and David Ricardo, and the novelists Jane Austen and Thomas Love Peacock.

The emphases of romanticism in Great Britain also differed significantly from those of German romanticism. There was much the same historical-mindedness, the medievalism, the sense of continuity with good old days, but the British romanticists felt an affinity with wild nature even more strongly, which for them functioned as both the Ego and the Absolute of German idealism. Along with nature-worship went a deep veneration of village and rural life, rustic simplicity, home and family.

At the same time, the British romanticists lacked the religious fervor of their German counterparts. Methodism and Anglican evangelicalism, akin to the Pietist and mystical tendencies in German religious life, wielded less influence on thought and letters and in any event were noticeably more pragmatic in their aims. Immorality, slavery, and heathen ignorance overseas aroused their concern as the agonies of poets and philosophers could never do. By the same token the great empiricist tradition in British philosophy from Bacon to Hume had no organic relationship to romanticism, quite unlike the impact of philosophy on romanticism in Germany. As a result British romanticism seems curiously mindless. It floats above British life in a half-distracted state, gentle, eccentric, unhappy with the drift of modern life, searching ineffectually for ways to bring it under the tutelage of old wisdom or fleeing to the ingenuous charms of lakes and hills.

The absence of high tension in the romanticist rebellion in Britain can best be explained by relating it to absence of high tension in British life generally since the civil wars of the seventeenth century. Unlike Germany, Great Britain had not experienced economic backwardness or political weakness and division in the past two centuries. Unlike Germany, Britain had not been denied outlets for her expansive energies in Asia and America. Unlike Germany, Britain had not felt herself culturally overwhelmed or physically crowded and (in Napoleonic times) crushed by the French colossus. Since Britain had done as much as France to originate the culture of the Enlightenment, romanticism could hardly become, for her, an opportunity to revolt against "the West." Moreover, class conflict had been powerfully mitigated by the institutions of British law, society, and politics so that the British had a sense of continuity with their own past that made radical change seem unnecessary.

Why, then, did romanticism arise at all in Great Britain? Obviously, some British thinkers and writers were as weary as any Europeans with the long reign of rationalism and felt the need for a world view that would give more scope to the demands of the heart. Having lived under the authority of rationalism for so many generations, they were among the first to look for alternative weltanschauungen. But a stronger impetus for the romanticist rebellion came from the uneasiness generated by the pressures of rapid change in British life during these years. The French menace, less ominous than it was to central Europeans, remained nonetheless a menace, stirring fears of revolution at home and invasion from the continent. Meanwhile, the Industrial Revolution was transforming the whole texture of British society. A country of eight million people in 1770 had grown to a country of twenty-one million by 1850. Urban blight, industrial pollution, the decay of rural influence and the yeoman farmer, the rise of a restless proletariat and a bourgeoisie of Gradgrinds—all this was new, and in large measure still unique to Britain. Men could see great changes afoot with more to come, involving every aspect of British life. A world view celebrating historical continuity, the joys of community, and the beauties of unspoiled nature could be seductive indeed in such times.

There can also be some question of just how deeply the rationalist world view had penetrated British culture. Some parts of it manifestly reached deeper levels of the British collective psyche than others. The pragmatism of the British Enlightenment, its theory of knowledge, its associationist psychology, its rational theology, and much of its political and economic doctrine won broad acceptance. But the British variety of rationalism had never gone as far as the French in systematically subjecting all areas of life to reason's dominion. Side by side with the rationalism of mainstream British philosophy during the Enlightenment flowed other currents that helped to prepare the way for romanticism even if they did not exert much concrete historical effect upon it.

In aesthetic and moral philosophy, especially, British philosophers of the eighteenth century tended to escape altogether the course charted by rationalism. Lord Shaftesbury's Neoplatonist idea of beauty, adopted by several British thinkers throughout the century and influential in Germany as well, ignored both the Cartesian and the Lockean schools. Burke's aesthetics of the "sublime" (*A Philosophical Enquiry into the Origin of Our Ideas of the Sublime and Beautiful*, 1757) carried its argument a step further. Shaftesbury also founded a movement in ethics, to which the Scottish philosophers Francis Hutcheson, Adam Ferguson, David Hume, and Adam

Smith belonged, that derived knowledge of the good from intuition or feeling rather than rational calculation. Bishop Berkeley's home-grown subjective idealism further illustrates the transrationalist quality of much of eighteenth-century British thought, and in its way looked forward to the idealism of Fichte. Nor can it be without significance that in French letters neoclassicism had completely carried the day, whereas in England the fame of Dryden and Pope never eclipsed that of Shakespeare and Milton.

At any rate the cultural historian can find evidences of a protoromantic sensibility in Great Britain long before 1789. James Thomson's cycle of nature poems, *The Seasons*, often regarded as the beginning of the naturist tradition in English verse, was published in 1726–30, when the poet was still in his twenties. Edward Young's lugubrious *Night Thoughts* first appeared in 1742–45; he earned Pope's censure for his lack of "common sense," but his work reached a large public and attracted much sympathetic attention in Germany. Young's friend, the novelist Samuel Richardson, also published his popular sentimental novels *Pamela* and *Clarissa* in the 1740s. None of this was quite romanticism, but it broke decisively with classical models and aesthetic principles.

Foreshadowings of romanticism continued into the second half of the century in the verse of Thomas Warton and Thomas Gray, the sentimental novels of Henry Mackenzie and Laurence Sterne, the Gothic and oriental romances of Horace Walpole, William Beckford, and Ann Radcliffe. The Ossian poems of the 1760s and Percy's *Reliques* helped stir interest in the Middle Ages. Walpole's country house, Strawberry Hill, was built in a quasi-Gothic style between 1749 and 1776, initiating the Gothic revival in architecture. In the graphic arts a protoromantic movement formed in the 1770s around the bizarre figure of the Swiss-born painter John Henry Fuseli. Michelangelo and Shakespeare were Fuseli's heroes; his sensuous works in turn helped to fire the imagination of William Blake.

If one adds in Hume's critiques of reason, the aesthetics of Burke, and the intuitionist ethics of the Scottish moralists, it is clear that by the time of the French Revolution the rationalist world view had already suffered a considerable battering. The romanticist challenge arrived promptly. Burke's *Reflections* (1790) unfolded a philosophy of history and politics more effective than any other single work of romanticist social thought. Then came the first great wave of poets—William Wordsworth, Samuel Taylor Coleridge, Robert Southey, all in their prime in the late 1790s, closely followed by Sir Walter Scott, who began publishing his verse in 1805. Scott turned in the following decade to the writing of historical novels, a genre in which he soon established himself as undisputed master throughout Europe. Also of this first generation were the Scottish poet Robert Burns and the versatile English poet and artist Blake.

Each of these great originals pursued his own version of the romanticist view of life, specializing, as it might be, in the worship of wild nature, in mystical or metaphysical ecstasy, in the evocation of a golden past, or the joys of love. The priority of the subjective vision, of eye and heart, is their common denominator.

Close on the heels of the first generation came a second. It began with a meteor shower of young poets, Lord Byron, Percy Shelley, and John Keats, the literary heroes of the decade after Napoleon's downfall, and included two oddly matched intellectuals who did not find their public until the 1830s and 1840s, Thomas Carlyle and John Henry Newman. Mary Shelley, the mother of modern science fiction, was of this generation together with the great neo-Gothic architect, Augustus Pugin. England's most gifted romanticist painter, J. M. W. Turner, although actually a contemporary of Wordsworth and Coleridge, did not arrive at the swirling, dreamlike style of his finest canvasses until after 1830.

The intellectual leaders of British romanticism, leaving aside Burke, were first Coleridge and then Carlyle. Well versed in the literature and philosophy of German romanticism, they functioned in the absence of an indigenous school of romanticist philosophy as the bearers of the new light from the East. In such works as Coleridge's *Biographia Literaria* (1817) and Carlyle's *Sartor Resartus* (1836), the tender-minded Englishman and the flinty Scotsman came to remarkably similar conclusions about the meaning of life. Together they rejected the Lockean conception of the mind as tabula rasa: on the contrary, all higher knowledge came to man through acts of creative intuition in which truth was not so much found as made. The vaunted Lockean world of sense was in truth nonsense, a formless mass devoid of value.

In its wrestling match with reality, mind encountered or, one could almost say, merged with God. Behind sensory appearance, visible to Coleridge's "eye of the spirit," lay an order simultaneously natural and divine, the Absolute of German idealism, the God of traditional theology. As Carlyle wrote in his journal in 1833, the philosophes had sunk the supernatural to the level of the natural, but he, Carlyle, would raise the natural to the level of the supernatural. Unbelief would be met and conquered on its own ground. "The Church is dead?—then worship in the temple of the universe; Heaven is a fable? but Infinitude remains; miracles are discredited? but Nature is a miracle; the Bible is incredible? but History is a Bible; Revelation is a fairy-tale? but the true Shekinah is Man and in worshipping Heroes we are acknowledging the godlike in human form."[12]

Coleridge and Carlyle agreed, more or less, on the best way to restore human society to the health it was losing under the assaults of revolution, bourgeois materialism, and atheism. The way forward lay not through the ballots of ignorant citizens or the calculations of grasping businessmen but through a reconstituted aristocracy. The Anglican Coleridge envisaged a neomedieval order of benevolent barons and wise priests, the Puritan Carlyle preferred an aristocracy of genius and energy, heroes on the scale of

Cromwell or Frederick the Great, who could govern humankind by sheer force of character. But in both political philosophies the state was endowed, as in Fichte or Hegel, with a majesty that far transcended anything allowed to states in the teachings of the philosophes. Organic, hierarchical, ethical, it was the sacred vessel of God's will on earth. It had nothing to do with mere happiness, mere convenience.

But of course the medium of the Coleridgian and Carlylean gospels was a prose more like poetry than like the treatises of German philosophy. To systematize their thought is to inflict upon it more than the usual violence associated with systematizing. In the end perhaps all British romanticism reduced to poetry, Wordsworth's "spontaneous overflow of powerful feelings ... modified and directed by our thoughts," or Shelley's "something divine ... the centre and circumference of knowledge." The British romanticists had fire in their pens. They meant to burn away the errors of rationalism and make a better world, but they engaged too little of Britain's national energies for too short a time to command the authority they sought.

The Revolutionary Ego: France

In a thoughtful essay in *The Kenyon Review*, Edwin Berry Burgum observes that the romanticisms of Germany, England, and France differed according to the readiness of each country for revolution. German romanticism stressed the medieval heritage because Germany was unready for the socioeconomic changes overtaking industrial England and the sociopolitical changes overtaking the France of 1789. Revolution was premature in Germany, as the German romanticists instinctively knew. English romanticism emphasized the beauties of nature because England had no further need of revolutions but did require a stabilizing, tranquilizing world view that would help it adjust to the challenges of industrialism and at the same time resist the radical doctrines emanating from France. But for the French themselves, the Revolution came at the right moment. Romanticism took from Rousseau the cry of the rising artisans and bourgeoisie for individual liberty, social equality, and fraternity with the masses against the despotism and privilege of the ancien régime.[13]

There are shortcomings in Burgum's argument: it fails to explain the prevalence of rationalist and classical themes in French culture in the 1789–1815 period, and it fails to explain the antirevolutionary zeal of the first generation of French romanticists. But Burgum does direct us toward an understanding of the special character of romanticism in France. Its interest was, indeed, centered on the social order, above all in relationship to the problem of individual freedom. Whether for or against each new turn of the wheel of fortune in French politics, the French romanticists were acutely conscious of the disintegration of the old regime and what it meant for the position of the individual. They hoped to discover how society could be restructured, or transcended, through the powers that all romanticists extolled: passion, intuitive perception, religious faith, tradition, will and ego. Nothing in nature, nothing in theology or metaphysics, nothing in the Middle Ages could mean so much to Frenchmen of their epoch as the disorienting effect of the periodic explosions in Paris.

By one system of political accounting, France experienced eight revolutions between the storming of the Bastille and the middle of the nineteenth century. The first was the Revolution of 1789, the second was the Revolution of the Jacobins, the third was the Revolution of the Directory. Then came Napoleon's revolution, the Bourbon counterrevolution of 1814–15, the Orleanist revolution of 1830, the Revolution of 1848, and finally Louis Napoleon's protofascist coup d'état of 1851. Each new regime brought with it a somewhat different distribution of political and economic power in France. Each came as a shock to the national nervous system. Although France experienced comparatively little demographic growth (from twenty-five to thirty-five million people in half a century) and lagged well behind Great Britain in industrial development, its political upheavals were more traumatic than anything happening elsewhere in Europe during the Age of Revolution.

But French romanticism did not always align itself with the forces of the Left. In its first generation, the generation of Chateaubriand, it tended to support the counterrevolution. In its second, the generation of Lamartine and Hugo, it shifted allegiance to liberalism or republicanism, or despaired of political solutions altogether. Throughout, the romanticists were consistent in their inability to accept established orders. They began by opposing the Revolution of 1789 as the embodiment of the sterile rationalism of the eighteenth century; they ended by opposing the Restoration of 1815 and the Orleanist constitution of 1830 as schemes of the reborn ancien régime to perpetuate the power of landlords, priests, and the haute bourgeoisie. Either way, the French romanticists could represent themselves as enemies— which they were—of the eighteenth century.

The grip of that century on the French intellect was not easily or quickly broken. The Revolution of 1789, although it would evoke romantic feelings of the deepest intensity in later generations of Frenchmen, had in itself little to do with romanticism. Apart from the influence of Rousseau's preromantic populism on the Jacobins, "its style and thought," as Jacques Barzun insists, "remained thoroughly classical. Not only were its doctrines derived from the philosophes, but its imagination was cast chiefly in the molds of classical antiquity and abstract reason."[14] The same may be said of the age of Napoleon. Many of the leading minds of the time, such as the philosophers Condorcet, Cabanis, and Destutt de Tracy, the scientists Monge, Laplace, and Cuvier, and the artists David and Gros, belonged wholly to the Enlightenment and its world view. Well into the post-Napoleonic period, romanticism encountered stubborn resistance from the academies, the universities, the liberal press, and the Orleanist political establishment. Neoclassicism continued to rival romanticism in the fine arts, thanks in good measure to the brilliance of David's student Ingres. Romanticism also failed to make much headway in French philosophy and scientific thought.

All the same, it is difficult to agree with J. J. Saunders that "French Romanticism was an importation from Germany and England and proved a short-lived phenomenon."[15] In fact very little of it was imported from any other country, and it lasted almost as long as anywhere else, with the usual reverberations on through the late nineteenth and twentieth centuries. As in Germany or England, two generations of romanticists can be identified with the difference that in France romanticism emerged several years later and the second generation was far more impressive than the first. German and British romanticism reached their highest levels between about 1790 and 1810, but the period of maximum achievement in France was more like 1820 to 1840.

The way to romanticism in France was prepared in the late eighteenth century not by Hume, Kant, Burke, or Herder, and not by the revival of medieval folk literature or Gothic architecture or Shakespeare, but by the solitary figure of J.-J. Rousseau. Already in Rousseau, the characteristic outlines of French romanticism assert themselves: brooding introspection, utopian politics, the primacy of sentiment. The interaction of self and society was his abiding concern, in the context of a profoundly irrationalist view of human nature. "For us," he wrote, "to exist is to feel; and our sensibility is unquestionably prior to our reason."

Rousseau harbored a candid scorn for the views of his brother philosophes on the blessings of modern civilization. The first generation of romanticists were all, in their several ways, hostile to modernity and to the Enlightenment, although most could not accept the democratic implications of Rousseau's politics. But this first generation was a far from homogeneous group. It did not found a self-consciously romanticist movement, nor did its members work together. They were also—like Rousseau—writers of prose, producing treatises, novels, and essays rather than poems and plays.

The best known of their literary men, François René de Chateaubriand, belonged to the émigré royalist nobility. Returning to France in 1800, he published his most seminal work in the next two years: the short novels *Atala* and *René* and his prose epic *The Genius of Christianity*. Mediocre as they may seem today, these early books were the literary sensations of Napoleonic France. The character of René gave the French their own version of Goethe's young Werther: a melancholy romantic hero cursed by a forbidden passion, who spent his last days "gazing at the fires of sunset." At the same time, Chateaubriand supplied his readers with sentimental appreciations of nature, the noble savage, and Catholicism, a bouquet of sensuous images appealing more to the eye than to the intellect. There was religiosity in Chateaubriand, a longing for faith that anticipates the Decadents of the late nineteenth century, but little real conviction. Not surprisingly, Chateaubriand was unhappy with every new regime that came to power in Paris, although the Bourbon restoration suited him best. Under Louis XVIII he even served briefly as the French ambassador to Great Britain and as minister of foreign affairs. During his official stay in London, his chef allegedly created the steak that still bears his name and perhaps does more to keep it before the public than his writings.

Chateaubriand's success in the early 1800s did not lead to the appearance of a great flock of like-hearted writers. One of his few interesting contemporaries was Etienne Pivert de Sénancour, also an émigré, who returned to France in 1803 and published his only major work, *Obermann*, in 1804. The hero, a tortured soul living like a hermit in the mountains of Switzerland, suggests Chateaubriand's René, and the book is full of Rousseauian influence. But it did not seize the imagination of the French public as fully as Chateaubriand's novels. Only after 1833, when it was reprinted with an introduction by the romanticist critic Sainte-Beuve, did *Obermann* receive the attention it deserved.

After Chateaubriand and Sénancour the only other luminary of the first generation of romanticist litterateurs was Germaine Necker, better known as Madame de Staël. Her first work, *Letters on Rousseau* (1788), established her credentials as a Rousseauian. In her novels and criticism she responded, as J. Christopher Herold argues, "to the emotional climate of Rousseau's ideas, rather than to the ideas themselves."[16] She could not go as far as he in rejecting modern society, but she shared his passions. Her highest achievement, *On Germany* (1810), was an exhaustive inventory of romanticist predilections cast in the form of a survey of modern German culture. It introduced Frenchmen to the concept of romanticism and offered it as a respectable alternative to the Enlightenment. Enraged by de Staël's praises of German and English civilization, the Emperor personally ordered the suppression of the book, but it enjoyed a great success after its publication in London in 1813. The future came to life in its pages.

Romanticism began to penetrate other aspects of French culture in these same years, although its progress was hardly spectacular. Many elements of the romanticist world view are present in the political thought of Joseph de Maistre, the high priest of émigré counterrevolution, who insisted on the hopeless irrationality of humankind and the necessity of a new Middle Ages, a new order of Christian monarchs recognizing the supreme authority of the Pope. The same medievalism appears in the writings of the Vicomte de Bonald and, with more affinity to the romanticist world view, in those of Pierre Simon Ballanche. Charles Fourier published his first book in 1808, an exposition of utopian socialism saturated with romanticist ideas; he did not begin to attract followers until the mid-1820s, but in essence his thought belongs to the first romanticist generation. In philosophy, Maine de Biran—a former follower of the neo-Lockean Cabanis—put forward a theory of knowledge not unlike Kant's, which represented perception of self (the *sens intime*) as the gateway to the understanding of ultimate reality. Finally, mention should be made of J. B. Lamarck and his *Zoological Philosophy* (1809). Lamarck attributed progress in organic nature to an inner force that impelled adaptive change, much like the striving of the World Spirit described by the romanticist nature-philosophers in Germany. Important as it would be later on, Lamarck's work was not accepted by most of his fellow biologists at the time, and the romanticist world view wielded little authority in French scientific circles.

Until the 1820s, then, French romanticism remained little more than a possibility, a few scattered voices proclaiming a new world view with a collective impact perhaps no greater than that of Rousseau or even of Goethe, whose *Werther* had already passed through fifteen editions in France before the turn of the century. France was for years the last redoubt of the Enlightenment. Only after the final crashing fall of the Empire at Waterloo did matters begin to change decisively.

Various dates are offered for the coming of age of French romanticism. The exhibition of Théodore Géricault's "Raft of the Medusa" in 1819, the publication of Alphonse de Lamartine's *Poetic Meditations* in 1820, and the founding of the Cénacle by Victor Hugo and Charles Sainte-Beuve in 1827 marked its rapid progress. The *annum mirabile* was 1830. Hugo's romanticist play *Hernani* touched off a war between the adherents of classicism and romanticism at the Théâtre Français which ended in triumph for Hugo and his comrades of the Cénacle. In the same year came Lamartine's election to the Académie Française and Berlioz's "Symphonie Fantastique." Thereafter, for more than a decade, romanticism unequivocally dominated French cultural and intellectual life.

It was an astonishing period, comparable in some aspects to the best years of German romanticism. Its Goethe and Schiller were Lamartine and Hugo, both deeply involved in republican politics, poets and novelists of humanistic passion who earned enormous popularity during their lifetimes, as did their Rabelaisian friend, the playwright and historical novelist Alexandre Dumas. But for twentieth-century readers, some of the other romanticists of the second generation may cast stronger spells. More introspective than Lamartine and Hugo, less committed to the arguing of public issues and the quest for political solutions, they tended to dwell on the plight of the individual at a time when politics, if still important, had lost some of its power to enthrall and the artist was challenged to take stock of his own soul. I refer now to poets such as Alfred de Vigny, Pétrus Borel, and Alfred de Musset; to Gérard de Nerval, whose deranged and macabre imagination fascinated the Decadents; and the mocking aestheticism of Théophile Gautier. Estrangement afflicted all of them. "The people who have passed through 1793 and 1814," Musset wrote, "nurse wounds in their hearts. That which was is no more; what will be, is not yet. Do not seek elsewhere the cause of our malady."

The two greatest novelists of the second generation, Stendhal and Honoré de Balzac, despite some early affinities with romanticism, were not really part of it and came into their own at a later time. Meanwhile, in music and art nearly all the supreme figures were swept into the romanticist movement. The operas of Daniel Auber and Giacomo Meyerbeer took Paris by storm, works such as Auber's *La Muette de Portici* (1828) and Meyerbeer's *Robert le Diable* (1831). Romantic in the brisk, elegant manner of Rossini, they were soon overshadowed by the still greater talent of Hector Berlioz. No one more closely approaches the complete romanticist than Berlioz. The music of Beethoven, the theater of Shakespeare, the novels of Scott, and the poetry of Byron and Goethe were his inspirations. In the "Symphonie Fantastique," a musical self-portrait of the artist as a love-mad young man, and "Harold in Italy," a symphony for viola and orchestra based on Byron's *Childe Harold*, the romanticist doctrine of the subjectivity of truth was perfectly translated into sound. In each, as in the best of Beethoven, the composer depicted his own mind and spirit in its confrontation with the inscrutable universe.

Classicism in the fine arts, especially powerful at the turn of the century under the leadership of J. L. David, received its first major rebuff in the work of his former student Louis Girodet-Trioson. A typical canvass of Girodet-Trioson's maturity, "The Entombment of Atala" (1808), taken from an episode in the novel by Chateaubriand, shows classical technique in the service of romanticist pathos. The more formidable art of Géricault and Eugène Delacroix appeared in the 1820s, an art of baroque power and drama, and in the 1830s came the Barbizon school of landscape painting. Some of the Barbizon painters, especially Théodore Rousseau and Camille Corot, captured the beauty and mystery of nature with the sure instincts of a Wordsworth. There was also a major Gothic revival in French architecture after 1840, championed by the restorer of the fabulous walled city of Carcassone, E. E. Viollet-le-Duc.

Only in the spheres of formal thought and scholarship did romanticism prove less than vigorous during the second generation. Borrowing heavily from the psychology of Maine de Biran and the idealist metaphysics of Schelling and Hegel, the court philosopher of the Orleanist monarchy, Victor Cousin, led the most important movement in academic philosophy, the so-called Eclectic school. His system was a poor thing at best despite its wide influence in French educational circles. In political, social, and religious thought the reactionaries of the Restoration yielded center stage to a variety of enthusiastic liberals and radicals. Félicité de Lamennais, the most brilliant religious writer of the period, turned in the 1830s to an intransigent populism imbued with the romanticist spirit that provoked his expulsion from the Church by Pope Gregory XVI. The Fourierists were active in several parts of the world; their master lived on, still writing, until 1837. In the 1830s another party of socialist prophets, the followers of Henri de Saint-Simon, veered off from the fundamentally positivist orientation of Saint-Simon himself to a romanticist cult of love and brotherhood that took up the familiar cry for a new Middle Ages. The Saint-Simonians, led by "Father" Enfantin, also adopted from romanticism its idea of artists and poets as the moral mentors of humanity, desperately needed to regenerate the atrophied heart of modern man.

Some of the greatest romanticists of all were the historians. At the turn of the century, the Swiss historian Johannes von Müller had set a seductive example for later scholars with his colorful and astonishingly successf'l narrative history of Switzerland. Romanticist historiography was marked by intensity of feeling, a strong dramatic sense, and empathic identification with remote eras, but it tended to play fast and loose with primary sources. It also became readily embroiled in partisan causes. Of the leading French romanticist historians, Augustin Thierry acted as a spokesman for the liberals and Jules Michelet spoke for the left wing of French nationalism, proclaiming Revolutionary France as the redeemer of Europe. Their literary styles were those of Chateaubriand and Scott, their passion for history nothing short of mystical. Michelet attributed his special merit as a historian not to brilliance or profundity but only to the fact that he "loved more." So he did. No one has ever written history with more exuberance and affection.

Michelet's love affair with France, its people and its past, typifies the orientation of French romanticism. The revolutionary or, in the first generation, the counterrevolutionary ego confronts society, accepting this, rejecting that, but always defining itself in relation to a social environment. The dialectic of self and society appears in nearly all the romanticists. But for France, the most intensively socialized of Western countries in the eighteenth and early nineteeth centuries, where the struggle for order and the struggle for freedom were waged over and over again in the streets of Paris, that dialectic became absolutely the central fact of cultural life.

Thus the French could not allow themselves the deep involvement in theology and metaphysics, in the worship of nature, or in the quest for a magical Middle Ages that circumstances encouraged in Germany and Great Britain. They could not allow themselves to participate fully in the romantic movement at all until after Waterloo. The France of the Revolution of 1789 was the same France where the Enlightenment had reigned with the greatest éclat during its last two generations: the Revolution was its child. Even after the collapse of 1815, not a few die-hard rationalists and classicists tried to persuade their countrymen that espousing romanticism was un-French, an act of treason to the national genius.

But when France finally did admit romanticism into its heart, it had to be a romanticism of social conscience, tuned to French needs. Chateaubriand's René in his Louisiana, Madame de Staël rhapsodizing about her Germans, de Maistre invoking the wrath of God against rebellious man, Hugo's hunchback in his bell tower, Vigny's martyred poet Chatterton, Berlioz's tormented lover marching to the scaffold, Michelet trembling with ecstasy as he recreates the glories of 1789, Musset's confessions of a child of the century, Delacroix's voluptuous yet heroic Liberty leading her people out of bondage—all are images of the ego struggling to find itself in a social universe racked with confusion.

The Coming of Age: Russia and the United States

For the colonial cultures of Romanov Russia and the new American republic the Age of Revolution was a time of national liberation. Romanticism helped both to burst the shackles of their adolescent dependency on the thought and art of Europe. They remained closely aligned to European civilization, and in some ways their development continued to lag, but by the middle of the nineteenth century they had established identities of their own. They had also begun to produce creative work of worldwide importance. Colonialism was on the wane, if not yet entirely dead.

In both Russia and the United States, the growth of population and wealth went unchecked during the half-century. With 73 million people in 1858, Russia became the largest country in the Western world, and the United States, with 23 million in 1850, had at last overtaken the mother country, Great Britain. The proportion of Russians living in cities doubled between 1800 and 1850. Steady progress was recorded in trade, manufactures (chiefly on the domestic system), and standards of living. American economic growth was much more spectacular. Hundreds of factories sprang up in the Northeast, westward migration occurred at a dizzy pace (not paralleled in Russian history by eastward migration until the 1880s), and the movement to the cities became a veritable stampede. Boston, New York, and Philadelphia, with a combined population of only 95,000 in 1790, had nearly one million people in 1850. In addition, thousands of new Americans were arriving each year from Ireland, Britain, Germany, and other parts of Europe.

In a material sense the point of closest comparison between Russia and the United States at this time was their common dependence on servile labor: feudalism in most of rural Russia and the plantation economy of the American Old South. But the Old South was only an anomalous fragment of the republic, containing not more than a third of its total population (and less than a fourth of its free citizens). Eight Russians in ten were enserfed peasants; well over half the American population consisted of yeoman farmers, artisans, and bourgeois. Russia remained, in this period, a fundamentally poor, immobile society, in which—especially under Czar Nicholas I—government became increasingly authoritarian and repressive. Although stratified, American society by European standards was remarkably open, with abundant opportunity for private enrichment and for climbing the social ladder. Under Andrew Jackson—no Nicholas!—and his successors it achieved a measure of political democratization that made the young republic the most equalitarian of the world's great powers in mid-century.

In searching for a national identity, Americans understandably inclined to an optimistic, expansive, liberal image of themselves, stressing the power of the individual to control his own destiny and the goodness of nature and society. "Progress" and "democracy" became holy words. The reality of class, sectional, and racial conflict in American society was often ignored or explained away. Flaming rebellion, so characteristic of romanticists elsewhere, was rare in the American context because the circumstances of American life persuaded thinkers and writers that old orders could be reformed or evaded with relatively little difficulty. "Doubt of enlarging Good," declared William Ellery Channing in 1843, "is virtual Atheism, and Fear of Progress the unpardonable Sin."

If America, in Goethe's familiar judgment, "had it better," Russia had it worse. Economically far behind the West, plagued with accelerating peasant unrest, saddled with an unresponsive and ineffectual governmental apparatus, Russians felt no temptation to believe in automatic progress along established lines. Strong medicine alone, they argued, could save the body social from its diseases. By the middle of the nineteenth century, the Russian intelligentsia had divided into two opposing camps, those who despaired of traditional Russia and preached Westernization and those who despaired of Westernization and preached a return to the morally authentic Russia of the Orthodox Middle Ages. Both camps were initially romanticist in outlook, crying for radical changes with a passion as hot as any summoned up by their contemporaries in France and Germany. As a result Russia by midcentury had two national identities. The Westernizers saw it as a slate to be wiped clean and filled with fresh writing of Western origins; the nativists saw it as an icon resplendent with the higher truth of Holy Russia that had been defiled with false Western images which they could remove with the powerful solvents of their Slavic faith. It was a case of Rousseauian utopism pitted against Rousseauian primitivism.

Rousseau himself was the principal foreign influence on the first major Russian romanticist, the novelist and historian Nikolai Karamzin. After travels in western Europe during the year of the French Revolution, Karamzin returned home and published *Poor Liza* (1792), a sentimental novel full of poetic sighs and effusions; later he turned to history, writing a twelve-volume history of medieval Russia (1819–26). The seeds of both Westernism and Slavophilism were clearly present in Karamzin's work. On the one hand he was an enthusiast of Rousseau and the French Revolution; on the other hand he patriotically celebrated the glories of the Russian past.

Three poets brought Russia fully into the mainstream of literary romanticism during the first quarter of the new century. Vasily Zhukovsky introduced the Russian public to the writings of many Western romanticists including Rousseau, Schiller, and Chateaubriand. Significantly enough, he also wrote the words of the Russian national anthem, "God Save the Czar." During his lifetime two younger poets far surpassed him, Alexander Pushkin and Mikhail Lermontov. Pushkin and Lermontov nurtured Russian cultural nationalism by using Russian history and folklore extensively in their work. They also created vivid portraits of estranged romantic egos in the Byronist manner, such as Pushkin's character of Eugene Onegin in the long poem of the same name (1832) and Lermontov's Pechorin in his autobiographical novel *A Hero of Our Time* (1839). Much of the best prose of the period was written by their gifted contemporary Nikolai Gogol. By 1840 Russia had at last acquired a secular literary culture of European significance.

There was also a romanticist movement in early nineteenth-century Russian art and music, well represented by the canvasses of Karl Bryullov and the operas based on native Russian themes of Mikhail Glinka. But Russian romanticism did not by any means confine itself to the aesthetic dimension. Very much as in the German experience, but unlike the British and French, romanticism in Russia involved a massive intellectual awakening. As in Germany, much of the new thought maintained close spiritual affinities with earlier tendencies in religion and philosophy. But since the Russian philosophical tradition was at best embryonic at the beginning of the nineteenth century, it was natural for Russian thinkers to look westward for help.

Inevitably they looked to Germany itself. Most young Russians who studied abroad went to German universities, and most of the foreign scholars living in Russia at this time were Germans. But the crucial point is that German philosophy and theology during the romanticist period responded to the same kinds of needs that Russians felt in their own national situation. Like Germany, and much more than Germany, Russia was a country with an inferiority complex vis-à-vis the West, a country in search of a distinctive national soul. With no significant commercial tradition, with almost no citizen involvement in government, with a politically impotent state church and a growing stratum of alienated intellectuals, the same natural proclivity existed in Russia for introverted world views as in Germany. Eighteenth-century Russian thinkers had already found inspiration in the writings of the German mystics and the philosophy of Leibniz. From the 1790s onward, first Kant, then Fichte and Schelling, and finally Hegel were eagerly received by the Russian intelligentsia, not only by those who saw Russia's salvation in "Westernizing" but also by the Slavophiles. Without the German contribution, Russia's intellectual awakening might well have been delayed by several decades.

The awakening began, like certain literary movements in the West, with the organizing of a circle of enthusiastic and very young men, in this instance the Society of Wisdom-Lovers formed in 1823 in Moscow under the "presidency" of Prince V. F. Odoyevsky. When the Society dissolved in 1825 during the Decembrist revolt, its members had found time to do no more than conduct a sweeping study of Western philosophy, chiefly German. Spinoza and Schelling were their heroes. But most of them continued their philosophizing in later years, and as their thought matured, it often turned to the great question of the place of Russia in the modern world.

Odoyevsky, the former president of the Moscow Society, was one of the major voices in the Russian philosophical awakening in his own right. A disciple of Schelling and both Western and Russian mysticism, he developed the view, which became almost ritualistic in nineteenth-century Russian thought, that the West was exhausted. Its soul had become enfeebled through the decay of faith and the overspecialization of the sciences. Only Russia, with its still fresh spirit and untapped energies, could rescue the soul of Europe at this stage in world history.

The debate on Russia continued with the notorious *Philosophical Letters* of Pyotr Chaadayev. The publication of one of the "letters" in 1836 led to an official ban on Chaadayev's literary activity. The writer himself was declared insane by the czarist authorities. But even this single essay and its companion pieces, which circulated privately among the literati, had a galvanizing effect on Russian thinking at the time. Under the influence of Schelling and the conservative French romanticists (de Bonald, Chateaubriand, Ballanche), Chaadayev took the position that only Christianity, by which he meant primarily Roman Catholic Christianity, could have created the civilization of Europe. The glories of European history were the visible marks of divine providence, a providence that had mysteriously overlooked Russia. Chaadayev scathingly denounced the sterility of the Russian past; yet in his posthumously published work, he also indicated that this very emptiness would prove a blessing in disguise. Unfettered by the past, Russia could now take up the project of teaching Europe "an infinity of things which she could not understand without us. . . . A day will come when we shall place ourselves at the intellectual focus of Europe. . . . Our *universal mission* has begun."

In Odoyevsky and Chaadayev the themes of the controversy that unfolded in the middle decades of the century about Russia and the West are nearly all anticipated. The two camps that we have already mentioned, of Slavophiles and Westernizers, were influenced by both men, and the ideational content of their programs was patently romanticist.

The chief philosophers in the Slavophile camp included Ivan Kireyevsky, in his youth a member of the Moscow Society of Wisdom-Lovers, and the redoubtable Alexei Khomyakov. The novelist Gogol also contributed to the Slavophile cause in some of his later writing. Tutored in their student years by the thought of Schelling and Hegel, the Slavophiles agreed with Chaadayev in assigning to civilization a spiritual foundation. But they chose, very much in keeping with the nationalist tendencies in later romanticism in Germany and France, to give their spiritual interpretation of history a peculiarly Russian twist. The West, they contended, had even in medieval times fallen under the spell of an arid rationalism that desiccated its soul and deprived it of the organic wholeness still present in the more authentic Christian culture of Orthodox Russia. "In its inception," as Sidney Harcave writes, "Slavophilism looked toward a never-never land of Russian people united by the brotherly love of the Church, working together in spontaneous and free association under the protection of a benevolent emperor."[17] Like Rousseau, the Slavophiles advocated a primitive communitarian order of society purged of the sophisticated faithlessness of modern civilization.

But the midcentury thinkers who denounced the Slavophiles as obscurantists and urged Russia forward into the modern age, the so-called Westernizers, shared the basic weltanschauung of their opponents. On the one hand they partially accepted Chaadayev's depreciation of the Russian past, contrasting it unfavorably with Western Europe. On the other they were the products of the same intellectual ferment in the Russia of the 1820s and 1830s, learning their philosophy from Fichte, Schelling, and Hegel and articulating a fundamentally idealist world view that was not specifically Christian like the world view of the Slavophiles but bore many resemblances to it.

Despite their sympathies with the West and their anticlerical posture, the great Westernizers, men such as Nikolai Stankevich, Vissarion Belinsky, and at least in the first part of their lives, Alexander Herzen and Mikhail Bakunin, were by no means adherents of Western rationalism or positivism. What they took from the West was its romanticism, initially of the German variety, and the utopian socialism of France. Their thought, like that of the early Slavophiles, was thoroughly idealistic and in the Russian context countercultural, rejecting the institutions of modern czarist Russia in favor of a utopian vision that had little in common with Russian realities. It comes as no shock, then, to discover that after the failure of the Revolution of 1848 in France the leading Westernizer—Herzen—bitterly denounced Western civilization and proposed in place of his earlier doctrine a new Slavic socialism resting its faith in the vitality of the Russian village commune. Herzen's postrevolutionary gospel was simply Slavophilism without Christianity.

After the stormy oscillations of Russian romanticism, the American version seems gentle almost to the point of blandness. Yet in terms of the American experience, it was passionate and, at times, capable of touching depths not explored again in American cultural history until the twentieth century. For some critics the romanticist period is still the only golden age in American letters.

American romanticism got off to a late and not particularly glorious start. As in France, the Enlightenment reigned through the 1800s, a fact well symbolized by the presidency (1801–9) of its most remarkable philosopher-statesman, Thomas Jefferson. The first substantial American man of letters, Washington Irving, started his career writing in the vein of the eighteenth-century English neoclassical satirists. After living and traveling in Europe he converted, more or less, to romanticism. But his best work was his earliest, his tales and sketches of old New York, and even here romanticism of a sort prevailed, if not in the style, at least in the atmosphere of whimsy and sentimentality that Irving conjured up, so far removed from the gray reality of colonial Dutch life. A fuller-blooded romanticism emerged in the 1820s in the "Leatherstocking" novels of James Fenimore Cooper, the American Sir Walter Scott. Wordsworth's adoration of nature found echoes in the verse of William Cullen Bryant and the landscapes of Thomas Cole.

Up to this point American romanticism had rarely addressed itself to the big questions arising out of American life, nor had it seriously challenged the definition of the republic offered by its eighteenth-century statesmen, philosophers, and divines. But in the 1830s the romanticist conscience deepened and matured. The nation itself was changing fundamentally, from a chain of cozy seaboard colonies to a continental democratic republic of endlessly advancing frontiers. New men, self-made, penetrated the ruling class, and a new mass electorate demanded a new politics. The time had come for stock-taking and the setting of fresh goals.

One sign of the times was the transformation of Cooper, the novelist of the noble savage and the rugged frontiersman, into an amateur political philosopher after his return in 1833 from a seven-year stay in Europe. In *The American Democrat* (1838) and other works, he aligned himself with the rising democracy, but not with its undercurrents of capitalistic greed and ruthless exploitation of nature and labor. His democratic ideal was Rousseau's, joining the splendid natural ego with the sovereignty of the people so that no crack remained for vulgar, overcivilized opportunists to wriggle through and spoil things. But in real life, as Cooper was too shrewd not to see, this ideal democratic order might prove impossible to construct. He entertained many of the same hopes and fears as his French contemporary Alexis de Tocqueville.

Meanwhile, the most powerful intellectual movement of American romanticism arose in New England, the "Transcendentalism" of Ralph Waldo Emerson and Henry David Thoreau. Anyone who would understand the American national psyche must also understand Transcendentalism. The Transcendentalists were the Slavophiles and the Westernizers of nineteenth-century America. In them, the Enlightenment was simultaneously refuted and reaffirmed at deeper levels of consciousness.

Transcendentalism, in its origins, was a secession from the Unitarian movement in Yankee Protestantism. Its principal guru, Emerson, signaled that secession by resigning from the Unitarian ministry in 1832. Sailing to England, he met personally with the three writers who had already become his literary and moral heroes—Wordsworth, Coleridge, and Carlyle. In the mid-1830s he settled in the little town of Concord, which became for the next ten years or so the American Weimar. Around him gathered many other luminaries of the movement, including Thoreau, Bronson Alcott, and Margaret Fuller. Also in the Transcendentalist ranks were two outstanding Unitarian clergymen, Theodore Parker, one of the most popular preachers of his generation, and George Ripley, who left the ministry in 1841 to direct the Transcendentalist and later Fourierist utopian community of Brook Farm, near Boston.

The forming premise of Transcendentalism was the conviction that American religion had grown too cold and that American life as a consequence had become morally and spiritually undernourished. With much of the content of the old Enlightenment gospel the Transcendentalists had no quarrel. They proclaimed the intrinsic goodness of man and nature with greater fervor than any philsosophes. Like the founders of the republic, they were optimists, liberals, humanists, and unswerving foes of superstition and fanaticism in religion. But they found the rationalism of their Unitarian fathers powerless to inspire faith and action. It did not speak to the individual conscience, to the men and women who had the task of creating a new democratic society in nineteenth-century America. Emerson and his colleagues were particularly disturbed by the adherence of the Unitarian clergy to the Lockean theory of knowledge, with its view of the mind as a mere machine for processing sensory data. From Coleridge they adopted the romanticist position that, on the contrary, human consciousness was the seat of a divinely implanted faculty (Coleridge's capitalized Reason) through which man apprehended God's truth intuitively. Each of us possessed divinity in the depths of his own heart.

The Transcendentalists went on to develop an organismic view of the unity of man and nature, a philosophy of education not unlike Rousseau's, and a joyful theology as fluid and formless as the rest of their thought. But none of it was thought for thought's sake. The whole point of thinking, in the Transcendentalist outlook, was to shape character and inspire action. In the pragmatic spirit of American life, they were unable to summon up enthusiasm for prolonged abstract speculation.

As it evolved the Transcendentalist movement struck out in many directions. It celebrated spiritual self-reliance, as in Emerson's essay of 1841 and Thoreau's record of his monkish communion with nature, *Walden, or Life in the Woods* (1854). It pressed for reformation of the schools and churches, for women's rights, for the abolition of slavery. It inspired experiments in utopian communalism. It taught democracy, since all men and women were, by its doctrine, children of the same universally indwelling God, but it warned against the spread of an amoral capitalism that might destroy democracy by turning free workers into little more than slaves. As one Transcendentalist minister (Orestes Brownson) put the matter in 1840, the division of the community into two classes, owners and workers, was "the great evil of all modern society.... Universal suffrage is little better than a mockery where the voters are not socially equal.... To be rendered efficient, it must be coupled with something like equality of fortunes." The abolition of all inequality, social and economic as well as political, was the very "premise" of the American system, said Brownson, without which America would become only a second Europe.

The Transcendentalists were too tender-minded for the world they hoped to convert, and the movement faded out of view in the 1850s and 1860s, but they left behind a heritage of reformist idealism that has made a tangible difference in American life. Their efforts to spiritualize the young democracy were continued most forcefully in the next generation by the greatest American romantic poet, Walt Whitman. His *Leaves of Grass* (1855 and later editions), although it appeared in the twilight years of romanticism, has all the freshness of vision, all the ecstasy and anarchy of romanticism at its purest. No writer did more to define the democratic conscience, and none better personified it in the style of his own living, than the good gray bard from Brooklyn.

As in the France of Jules Michelet, historians had their share in the promulgation of romanticist politics in America. Hoping to furnish the young with inspiring heroes, America's first professional historian, Jared Sparks of Harvard, compiled patriotic lives of Washington, Franklin, and Gouverneur Morris. At the same time that Michelet was writing his many-volumed histories of France and the French Revolution, George Bancroft produced the ten volumes of the first comprehensive history of the United States (1834–76), a work of far greater scholarly integrity than those of Sparks but no less romantic and political than Michelet's. The Frenchman had represented France as the champion of liberty and the popular will in modern history; Bancroft, an ardent Jacksonian democrat, idealized the American republic in much the same terms. It was the highest form of polity in world history, and its democratic society, whose character was evident from earliest colonial times, showed all humanity the path to virtue. Democratic drama also filled the pages of J. L. Motley's *The Rise of the Dutch Republic* (1856), plotted as the glorious triumph of liberty over the despotism of imperial Spain.

The roster of great American romanticists includes many other familiar names: W. H. Prescott, the brilliant historian of the conquests of Mexico and Peru; Henry Wadsworth Longfellow, the most popular of nineteenth-century American poets; John Greenleaf Whittier, his nearest rival; Harriet Beecher Stowe, the sentimental Puritan whose *Uncle Tom's Cabin* (1852) helped prepare the mind of the nation for civil war; and even a scattering of American Byronists, writers outside the consensus who grappled obsessively with the problems of evil, estrangement, and human destiny. Edgar Allen Poe's tales of horror, Nathaniel Hawthorne's brooding studies of Puritan New England, and Herman Melville's novels of cosmic adventure on the high seas all belonged to the climactic years of American romanticism, but they lacked the exuberance of the American literary mainstream. Poe wrote with the morbid intensity of the young Coleridge or his own French contemporary Gérard de Nerval. Hawthorne and Melville were essentially psychologists, closer in spirit to Dostoyevsky than to Whitman.

Be this as it may, one cannot doubt that in the romanticist era American thought and literary culture came of age. Optimism, energy, faith in democracy and the free man, a love of nature, and repeated warnings against the perils of materialism characterize most of its best work. Occasionally its writers caught glimpses of perils still more terrible, of red deaths and white whales. But by and large they had confidence in the American mission. Like their Russian contemporaries, but without Russia's schizophrenia, they saw a great place for their land and people in the sun of the new century.

Summation

On balance, we must see romanticism as a desperately needed spiritual exercise for the mind of Western man. Romanticism forced him back to his sources: his passions, his ancestors, his religious heritage, his childhood, his dreams, his grounding in a nature directly experienced. At the same time, romanticism helped project him into the future, a future of swiftly changing social relations, new loyalties, uprooted egos, and proletarized masses.

The new weltanschauung wielded its greatest influence between the French Revolution and the middle of the nineteenth century, but it was long in coming. All through the eighteenth century, the rationalism of the Enlightenment had encountered challenges to its ascendancy, some of them originating within the Enlightenment itself. The Germans were especially reluctant to embrace rationalism, but Hanoverian England had its sentimental novelists, its aficionados of medieval poetry, and its intuitionist schools of ethics and aesthetics; and even France had to contend with the rudely dissenting voice of that extraordinary *génevois*, Jean-Jacques Rousseau.

Romanticism enjoyed a continuous history in Germany from the 1770s, with the Sturm und Drang period in literature, the philosophies of Kant and Herder, and the new appreciation of Shakespeare. The ignition point was reached in Britain in the 1790s, in France and Russia in the 1820s, and in the United States not until the 1830s. Romanticism generated a great literary and artistic culture that released the Western world from the cold enchantments of neoclassicism. It inspired the idealist movement in German philosophy, which directly or indirectly affected serious thought in every other Western country. It was the moving force in French Eclecticism

and American Transcendentalism. It provided most of the intellectual substance of the political ideologies of the time, from conservatism and nationalism to democratic radicalism and utopian socialism. Only the liberals
owed more to other world views, and even they were hardly untouched by
the romanticist flood tide.

In all of its impact, romanticism conveyed the message that reality was
mindlike (or spiritlike) and that men could best perceive it by intuition and
feeling. Because of its affinity with human consciousness, reality was also
viewed by the romanticists as a stream of events flowing in time, not the
logico-mechanical structure of rational analysis. Romanticism was thus a
world view peculiarly well suited to expression in literary and artistic form,
in works of narrative history, or in historically grounded ideologies. It
flattered the artist, the man of imagination and passion, at the expense of
the logician and the mathematician. It favored the Christian, the man of
superrational and historical faith, at the expense of the skeptic and the
materialist.

Germany, seeking a national identity different from that of its formidable
neighbor across the Rhine, found in romanticism the perfect answer to its
needs, and in Germany romanticism underwent its fullest development.
Romanticism was of special value in its power to connect modern Germany
spiritually with the Germany of happier days: of medieval wealth, of Christian mysticism and piety, of the old Teutonic folk culture. It also had deep
resonances with the trends in early modern German philosophy, from Paracelsus to Leibniz. Only in Germany, and to some extent in Russia, were
professional philosophers, theologians, and scientists able to establish organic ties with the formal thought of their own immediate past. In Great
Britain and the United States, romanticism carried little weight in the
academic world; romanticism did invade the French academy, but its
achievements there were anything but spectacular. As a result, the romanticisms of Britain, France, and the United States appear lopsidedly aesthetic
and anti-intellectual by contrast with Germany's. This is especially true of
Britain, where many of the keenest intellects of the period were not romantics at all.

Nevertheless, in each country romanticism supplied invaluable help in
achieving a definition of national character and goals in an age of ever-
growing nationalist fervor. It gave the Germans pride in their past and, since
it offered them the chance to assume the cultural leadership of Europe,
pride in their present. It gave the British new faith in the wisdom of their
constitution and the French an opportunity to work out new conceptions
of self and society in an age of revolution. For the Russians it furnished the
contrasting visions of a Holy Russia that would save Europe's soul and a
Westernizing Russia that would redeem Slavdom from centuries of despotism. For Americans it provided the ideal of a robust, expanding democracy

destined to be the light of the world. The romanticists were dreamers; but so, in their own style and vein, were the philosophes of the Enlightenment. Later generations would dismiss them both as incorrigible utopists.

Chapter Four

Positivism: The World View of the Age of Improvement, 1840–90

Overview

Some people, as Ernest Renan observed in 1848, long for the enchanted landscape of prescientific thought, finding science too severe for their tastes. But such an attitude only betrayed their ignorance, "for the true world that science discloses to us far excels the fantastic world created by the imagination." The wonders of nature "when laid bare in all their splendor will comprise a poetry one thousand times more sublime" than all the rude fictions of antiquity. To science, in the judgment of Renan's Victorian contemporary John Morley, fell the task of producing "the religion of the future."

The passion for science—objectivity, matter-of-factness, for "realism" as opposed to "idealism," for the "hard" and the "cold" truth—that overtook the Western mind in the middle of the nineteenth century did not always clothe itself in the lyrical language of Renan. The great Frenchman himself acquired his doubts over the years. Writing at the end of his life, in 1890, he confessed that "if through the constant labor of the nineteenth century the knowledge of facts has considerably increased, the destiny of mankind has on the other hand become more obscure than ever." Perhaps we needed the chimeras of faith after all, to safeguard us against moral decay. Some prophets of the new scientific world view were no less afflicted with weltschmerz than Schopenhauer or the loneliest romantic poets.

Nevertheless, a new world view did arise in the middle decades of the century, a world view that in reasonably short order overthrew romanticism and created what F. L. Baumer calls the "New Enlightenment," a continuation "in spirit if not always in doctrine" of the old Enlightenment of the age of Voltaire.[1] It had clearly become the prevailing weltanschauung of the intellectual avant-garde of Europe by the 1840s, and it did not encounter serious opposition until the 1890s. Following W. M. Simon, we could label it *scientism*, but the looser and, on the whole, more suitable term is *positiv-*

ism.[2] It was the world view of Comte and Mill, of Darwin and Spencer, of Marx and Engels, of Haeckel and Pavlov, of the realist, and even more emphatically, of the naturalist movements in literature and art. Positivism inspired the rise of the social and behavioral sciences as academic subjects, and under its auspices a revolution in physics, chemistry, and biology took place that compares favorably with the great Scientific Revolution of the seventeenth century.

In defining positivism care must be taken not to confuse it with the Positivism of Auguste Comte and his followers. Like Fascism, Positivism began as the party label of a single specific movement and then became a generic term for a variety of systems and tendencies animated by the same spirit. Comte was certainly a positivist, as well as the founder of Positivism; but not all positivists were disciples of Comte, or even aware of his work. Yet the lowest common denominators of both Comte's Positivism and generic positivism were much the same. For the positivist, the real, or at least the knowable, consisted of the data of sensory experience as verified, analyzed, and organized by the empirical sciences or by a methodology analogous to theirs. Positivism abolished metaphysics and theology or merged them with science; it denied or ignored the existence of supersensory reality, arguing that the world was not mindlike but on the contrary that mind was worldlike. In other words positivism insisted on the objectivity of truth. In this sense it was the exact opposite of romanticism, and basically nothing less than a revival of the rationalism of the Enlightenment, differing from rationalism only in its diminished reverence for reason, its more complete adherence to the empiricist tendencies in Enlightenment thought, its greater historical consciousness, and its stronger antipathy to Helleno-Christian tradition. As carried into the world of art and literature, it rejected both classicism and romanticism in favor of a realistic, unsentimental style that strove to reproduce the world as it was actually perceived by the observing eye.

Another distinction familiarly drawn between positivism and earlier world views was its alleged skepticism. The positivist made fewer formal truth-claims; he typically accepted Kant's postulation of the unknowability of the thing-in-itself; he was less reluctant than either the rationalist or the romanticist to avoid philosophy's "ultimate" questions. But the skepticism of the nineteenth-century positivist, at least by contrast with twentieth-century skepticism, seems unconvincing. Most positivists convey to us the strong impression that in their own judgment what they did not know was not worth knowing. They knew or could in time learn what humankind needed to know to conduct its affairs in accordance with the requirements of the natural order. If the law-bound matter of the sensorily observable universe were only phenomenal, and not ultimate or noumenal, it made no practical difference to humankind, which belonged integrally and indissolubly to that universe. If God did exist, which most positivists in any case denied, his existence could not alter the fundamental conditions and imperatives of human life. In spirit if not always in letter, the positivists followed in the tradition of the seventeenth- and eighteenth-century prophets of dogmatic materialism, the tradition of Hobbes and Gassendi, of La Mettrie and d'Holbach. Their self-confidence was high, their convictions firm, their pretensions messianic. In this last respect, ironically, they also borrowed something from the romanticist idea of the poet or philosopher as hero, casting themselves or some revered master as high priest of the new scientific humanity.

Why positivism succeeded in dislodging romanticism, and succeeded in such a relatively short time, is apparent from the radically altered conditions of life during the Age of Improvement. Although the positivist victory was, in part, just another example of sons repudiating their fathers in order to find an identity of their own, the choice of positivism as the banner of the new rebellion could not have been accidental. After two generations of political revolution and reaction, midcentury Europe settled herself into a new pattern (as did the United States after the tumult of the Civil War) characterized by the rapid progress of industrialism in all spheres of economic life, the transfer of power to the capitalist bourgeoisie, and a new collectivist politics of parties and pressure groups.

Most crucial of all was the advance of industrialism. Although pioneered in the manufacture of textiles in the late eighteenth century in England, the Industrial Revolution (a composite of the factory system, mechanization, and the use of high-yield power sources such as steam or electricity) did not really occur until the nineteenth century. It spread from Britain to western Europe, the United States, and finally Russia with Britain achieving a moderately industrialized economy by 1850, France by 1870, Germany and the United States by 1880, and Russia not until the twentieth century. Even as late as 1850, there were almost as many domestic servants in Great Britain as textile workers, more blacksmiths than iron workers, more carters and coachmen than railway workers. Barely half the population lived in towns and cities. Nor did basic scientific research begin to make a regular and significant contribution to industrial progress until the second half of the nineteenth century. The ascendancy of positivism was therefore simultaneous with the arrival of the industrial age and the wholesale application of modern science and technology to industrial production. Positivism was a world view well suited to a civilization freshly intoxicated by the promise of unlimited material progress.

At the same time democratic electoral politics, the struggles for national unification in central and southern Europe, and the rise of trade unions shifted attention from revolutionary heroics to the need for highly organized collective effort in the political sphere. In politics as in economics, the message of the Age of Improvement was clear: the ideal man was no longer the philosopher-patriot or the citizen-general but the factory manager, the union organizer, the faithful backbencher. In 1800 the aristocratic age had ended, but the bourgeois age had not yet begun. The individual had suffered from massive disorientation, and romanticism supplied the appropriate tonic. In 1850 the revolutions and the would-be utopias were finished, at least for the moment; everyone expected the interminable progress of science and industry; great objective forces, not great men, ruled the world. Positivism endowed the new age with a credible self-image and in so doing helped to reinforce the patterns of behavior that it was invoked to justify.

Very much like romanticism the positivist weltanschauung had its intellectual origins in a small group of seminal thinkers who belong, chronologically, to the era that preceded it; again like romanticism it ran its course as the dominant world view of Western civilization in two generations. Like the rationalism that it so much resembles, it germinated in Britain and France and achieved no more than modest victories in central Europe and Russia. Even in the United States, which by the end of the positivist period had become the world's leading industrial power, positivism was slow in taking hold. Britain and France were its natural habitats, and it thrived there best.

The fathers of positivism in Britain, who did all or most of their work during the era of romanticist ascendancy, were the political economists T. R. Malthus and David Ricardo; the founder of Utilitarianism, Jeremy Bentham, and his first disciples, especially James Mill; and the pioneers of socialism in Britain, William Godwin, Robert Owen, Thomas Hodgskin, and William Thompson. In France the fathers include some of the best minds of the last generation of the Enlightenment, such as the *idéologues* P. J. G. Cabanis and A. L. C. Destutt de Tracy and the great scientist Pierre Simon de Laplace. But the most influential founder of positivism in France was Henri de Saint-Simon, who played a role in nineteenth-century French thought analogous to Bentham's in England.

The first full generation of positivists consisted of men and women born between 1795 and 1825. In France this was the generation of Comte and his early followers, Littré and Laffitte; of such major scientists and savants as Bernard, Pasteur, Renan, and Charcot; of the realistic novelists Balzac, Flaubert, and E. de Goncourt; and of the founders of realism in art, Daumier, Millet, and Courbet. Among the British positivists of this first generation were the philosophers J. S. Mill, Lewes, Congreve, and Spencer; in the natural sciences, Lyell, Darwin, Joule, Galton, Kelvin, and Huxley; the historians Buckle and Stubbs; and in literature, Thackeray, Dickens, Trollope, and Eliot. Germany, turning with an almost savage suddenness against its idealists, romantics, and nature-philosophers in the course of the 1830s, produced the philosophers Feuerbach, Strauss, Bauer, and Büchner; the scientists Wöhler, Liebig, Du Bois-Reymond, Helmholtz, and Clausius; the scientific socialism of Marx and Engels; the scientific historiography of Ranke and Waitz; and in literature and art the realism of Ludwig, Hebbel,

Menzel, and Fontane. In Russia positivism was reflected in the philosophy of Lavrov and the qualified literary realism of Gogol, Turgenev, and Dostoyevsky.

The heyday of this first generation came in the third quarter of the century, the period to which belong such classics of positivism as Comte's *System of Positive Polity*, Spencer's *Social Statics*, Darwin's *On the Origin of Species*, and Marx's *Capital*. Another generation followed, of positivists born between 1825 and 1850, with a scattering of still younger members, especially in the United States.

The most noteworthy positivists of the second generation in France were sociologists and scientific historians such as Taine, Fustel de Coulanges, Monod, and Durkheim; the novelists Verne, Daudet, Zola, de Maupassant, and the younger Huysmans; and the artists Pissarro, Manet, Degas, Monet, Cézanne, and Seurat. In Britain, the positivist world view continued in the philosophy of Harrison, Stephen, and Pearson; in the social science of Bagehot, Tylor, and Frazer; and in the naturalist fiction of Hardy, Gissing, and the younger Moore.

The German-speaking world contributed, in the second generation, the science and scientific philosophies of Dühring, Haeckel, Weismann, Mach, Avenarius, Ostwald, and Hertz; the sociology of Schäffle, Gumplowicz, and Ratzenhofer; the Marxism of Liebknecht, Bebel, and Kautsky; and in the arts and letters, Liebermann and Hauptmann. Positivism flourished in Russia in the science and scientific philosophies of Chernyshevsky, Mendeleyev, Pisarev, Metchnikov, and Pavlov; the social thought of Lilienfeld and Kropotkin; and the literary art of Tolstoy and Chekhov. The United States, where romanticism both arrived and disintegrated somewhat later than in Europe, produced a single generation of positivists with births centered in the period 1835–60: philosophers such as Peirce, Fiske, W. James, and Dewey; social scientists and socialist thinkers such as H. Adams, Sumner, Ward, De Leon, and Veblen; novelists such as Twain, Howells, H. James, and Garland; and the artists Whistler, Homer, Eakins, Cassatt, and Sargent. In Scandinavia the second positivist generation yielded the realism and naturalism of Ibsen, Björnson, Brandes, Jacobsen, Skram, and the younger Strindberg.

In summing up the positivist achievement, what stands out above all is the close parallelism between its science-intoxicated thought and that of the age of rationalism. As in the seventeenth and eighteenth centuries, many of its greatest intellects were natural scientists. The positivist era saw astonishing progress in all the basic scientific disciplines, continuing in the tradition of Galileo and Newton. Despite the brief reign in Germany of romanticist *Naturphilosophie*, which the chemist Justus von Liebig bitterly described as "the black death of our century," the old empiricism survived to produce new theories of electricity and magnetism, the sciences of thermodynamics and organic chemistry, the periodic law of the elements, and in biology the new science of bacteriology, together with Darwinian evolutionary theory and major advances in genetics and experimental psychology.

With the possible exception of Darwin's evolutionism, the progress recorded by the sciences during the positivist era had less impact on the rest of thought than was exerted in its time by the mathematical physics of the Scientific Revolution. But it all helped immensely to strengthen the prestige and credibility of scientific method. A man whose son did not die on the operating table because of Pasteur and Lister, a farmer whose land greatly increased in value because of the agrochemical research of Liebig and Gilbert, and the general in the field who could communicate instantly by telegraph or telephone with his government because of Morse, Bell, and Edison (and the fundamental research into the nature of electricity carried out by their more learned predecessors) could not help but develop a hearty respect for the powers of science.

In philosophy as such, its positivist practitioners conformed chiefly to the model of the philosophes of the Enlightenment rather than to the model of the medieval schoolmen or the mandarins of the modern German academy. Equally inspired by scientific method, most of them were free-lancers, active in the world and more interested in religious, social, and political problems than in pure thought. The place of such remarkable "amateurs" as Bentham, Mill, Spencer, St.-Simon, Comte, Feuerbach, Büchner, and Marx in the history of philosophy is scarcely an exalted one in the eyes of most professional philosophers of our own century. W. T. Jones, for example, spares only fifteen pages in the 1,036 pages of his *History of Western Philosophy* for Bentham, Mill, Comte, and Marx, and fails even to mention the other four. But they addressed the concerns of their age, like the Voltaires and the Diderots who preceded them. Through their efforts the philosophical enterprise of Western man continued more vigorously than in the somewhat dusty world of their strictly academic contemporaries.

This was the age, then, of the Saint-Simonians and the Positivist school of Comte in France and Britain, of the Philosophical Radicals or Utilitarians in the Britain of Bentham and the Mills, of the Young Hegelians and philosophical materialists in Germany, and in Russia of the scientific nihilism of Chernyshevsky and Pisarev. In a slightly later period positivist philosophy offered to the world the synthetic philosophy of Spencer, the monism of Haeckel and Ostwald, and the pragmatism of Peirce and James. Whatever its shortcomings, its tendency to leap to logically untenable conclusions, and its frequent misunderstanding of scientific method, nineteenth-century positivist philosophy brimmed with its own form of moral idealism aimed at world betterment. If some of its more extreme representatives demoted thought to the rank of cerebral "secretions" and declared sententiously that "man is what he eats," if others subjected the whole course of world history to iron laws, nonetheless its prophets were as imaginative (in their fashion), and certainly as energetic, as any romanticist.

Near the end of the positivist era, moreover, some of its keenest minds were pointing the way to the fundamental revision of scientific philosophy that culminated somewhat later in twentieth-century "logical" positivism. Of special importance in this development was the work of two members of the second positivist generation in the German-speaking world, Mach and Avenarius. In their thought the skeptical attitude implicit in the whole family of naturalist world views since antiquity began at last to reveal itself fully. The American pragmatists, especially James, contributed to that same self-revelation. But on the whole, nineteenth-century positivist philosophy lacked the skeptical turn of mind. It gloried in its affirmations, not its negations.

The Age of Improvement was also the time when most of the social sciences were established as disciplines and, in the end, as academic disciplines. Already well started by Adam Smith and the Physiocrats in the late eighteenth century, economics advanced much further through the work of Malthus, Ricardo, Sismondi, the Mills, Marx, Jevons, and many others. Of the new sciences, sociology traces itself to Comte, who coined the term, and to such early successors of Comte as Spencer, Schäffle, Gumplowicz, Ratzenhofer, Ward, and Durkheim. Anthropology originated as a positive science with the labors of Morgan and Tylor. History shifted from art to science under the guiding genius of Ranke in Germany, Guizot in France, and such younger scholars as Taine, Fustel de Coulanges, Buckle, Stubbs, and Gardiner. Jurisprudence and human geography also became standard academic disciplines on empirical foundations during the positivist era, and a beginning was made toward a positive science of politics in the writings of de Tocqueville, Bagehot, and others. At the same time, positivism entered deeply into the ideological thought of the nineteenth century. It captured some of the best minds in liberalism and socialism and, chiefly through the medium of Spencerian and Darwinian ideas of evolution, strongly affected the development of racist, nationalist, and imperialist doctrine toward the end of the century. Nothing in any of the ideologies required them to be positivist, but none escaped its influence entirely.

In nearly all the social theory and ideological programs attuned with positivism, we should note, there lurked an ingredient seldom to be found in the thought of the Enlightenment, which belonged in fact to the romanticist world view and survived its disintegration to carry on a new life in positivism. The common ingredient is a concern with temporal processes, an insistence upon viewing reality in genetic or developmental terms in addition to, or instead of, viewing it mechanically. Often the positivist social thinker sought to combine mechanistic and genetic analysis, and in most instances—an obvious exception is the scientific historiography of the Ranke school—he did not adopt anything like pure historicism. Nevertheless, it became difficult after the romanticist period for Western thinkers to ignore the genetic dimension for all the same reasons that drove the romanticists themselves to incorporate it into their thought in the first place. In any case, as the natural sciences, led by geology and biology, turned more and more of their attention to the evolutionary process in nature, the static Newtonian model of the universe inevitably lost its cogency for the most implacable partisan of empirical method.

Another lingering effect of the romanticist rebellion could be found in the literary, artistic, and musical life of the Age of Improvement. So powerfully did romanticism persist in its aesthetic culture that the positivist world view was unable to gain more than a superficial influence in several media or provide more than serious competition in several others. Throughout the whole range of aesthetic culture, moreover, the romanticist image of the artist or poet as the embattled hero struggling against a conventional society that failed to understand his mission was popular with creative people of all persuasions in the Age of Improvement. The positivist artist succumbed to such self-images as readily as the positivist social prophet.

In poetry, the oldest literary form and the one that romanticism had most completely conquered, positivism scarcely won a toehold. A poetry of science and industry, of social realism, of photographic description did not arise, just as Locke and Newton had failed to inspire a poetry of scientific rationalism in the eighteenth century. There were occasional reversions to classical style, as in the Italian poet Carducci or the Parnassians in France. The major Victorian poets, such as Tennyson and Arnold, wrestled on occasion with issues raised by positivist thought. Arnold's "Dover Beach" is a striking example of romantic melancholy brought on by the poet's perception of the spiritual impact of modernization. What was once "a land of dreams," a magical world of imagination, had become "a darkling plain." Or, as Tennyson lamented, we cannot know God, even if we trust blindly in him, "for knowledge is of things we see," and the poet was only "an infant crying in the night." All the same, romanticism remained the dominant world view of Victorian poetry, even if sometimes it was a disillusioned romanticism verging on decadence. Poetry in midcentury France followed a similar course.

In music, where romanticism did not overthrow classicism until at least the 1820s, composers worked almost exclusively in the romanticist idiom through the end of the century. Even then, a respect for classical forms continued, especially in the music of Brahms, but positivism had no opportunity to affect musical development except to some small degree on the operatic stage. Realistic stories (treated romantically as in *Carmen* or *Cavalleria Rusticana*) tended to replace the stock themes of classical and romantic opera. There was also a touch of positivism in the music dramas of Wagner, which—in their hidden ironies, their weltschmerz, their undercurrent of skepticism—expose a certain spiritual kinship with the thought-world of "Dover Beach."

The best examples of positivism in the aesthetic culture of the middle and later nineteenth century can be found in prose literature and in painting. France led the way with the realists of the 1850s and 1860s, in novels such as Flaubert's *Madame Bovary* (1857) or *Germinie Lacerteux* (1864) by the Goncourt brothers, and in the canvasses of Courbet. Even before the self-conscious realism of midcentury, Stendhal and Balzac had veered away from romanticism to present their meticulous, dry-eyed analyses of modern society. In Great Britain the comedic genius of Thackeray, Dickens, and Trollope had turned in the same direction, in the case of Dickens not without a massive admixture of romanticist sentimentality. Realism was also arriving at about the same time in Germany and Russia and a bit later in the United States. Everywhere it strove for an objective view of life marked by spectatorial detachment, and the life it examined was most often that of the middle and working classes, or even the peasantry, the life of everyday folk in the modern world, the more sordid and grimy the better.

In the 1870s and 1880s, realism was supplemented, although not supplanted, by other closely related movements in which the methods of science played a more direct role, the naturalism of Zola and Hardy, and in painting the Impressionism of Manet and his gifted *bande*. Naturalism took from the sciences a rigorously deterministic theory of human destiny, stressing the force of heredity, environment, and circumstance as opposed to subjective factors; and the Impressionists applied scientific knowledge of light and color to achieve the heightened visual realism of their canvasses.

Architecture, as John Ruskin complained and as most critics still agree, had meanwhile sunk to unprecedented depths. The Gothic revival lingered on through most of the second half of the century but ran out of fresh ideas, despite the occasional striking effect of a Disneyesque castle like Neuschwanstein perched on its Bavarian mountain top or the grandeur of the new parliament house that sprawled along the Danube in fin-de-siècle Budapest. Classicism also had its inevitable revivals. For the most part, architects failed to develop a style appropriate to the new age until the twentieth century. Factories were grim, most new homes and shops ugly, most public buildings bombastic. It took an engineer, Gustave Eiffel, to design the most stunning public monument of positivism, the tower that still bears his name, erected for the Paris Exposition of 1889. It horrified fastidious Parisians, but the Eiffel Tower was a unique marriage of science and art, a gigantic sculpture in iron by a builder of bridges, heralding the age of steel-boned skyscrapers that was yet to come.

By the time of the Paris Exposition, the positivist era was already falling apart at its spiritual and intellectual seams. Its mechanistic-materialistic picture of the universe was not destined to survive the revolution in physics already initiated by James Clerk Maxwell's purely mathematical representation of electromagnetic phenomena and the Michelson-Morley experiment of 1887 that opened the way to relativity theory. Neo-Hegelianism, neo-Kantianism, vitalism, and the more stringent empiricism of Mach and Avenarius were rising up to do battle with the fading positivism of Comte and Spencer. Young Dr. Freud was studying hysteria with Breuer in Vienna. Symbolism, dandyism, and *la Décadence* were threatening the reign of naturalism in literature. The avant-garde was starting to read the feverish pronouncements of an obscure and—after 1889—insane German philologist named Nietzsche. For anyone with benefit of hindsight, a new world view had already crystallized by the last decade of the nineteenth century, a world view that still prevails in many areas of the Western psyche in the eighth decade of the twentieth century. The new weltanschauung was irrationalism. With its emergence positivism acquired a much more dangerous rival than anything it had hitherto confronted. The Age of Improvement inexorably gave way to the Age of Anxiety.

The Authority of Science: France

Like the rationalism from which it descended, the positivist world view had two homelands: Britain and France. In both countries the Enlightenment had struck deep roots, and the position of the empirical sciences was well established. In both countries, despite the upsurge of romanticism, the Enlightenment continued its career in at least certain departments of thought through the early decades of the nineteenth century. Industrializing Britain provided an ideal milieu for the further development of the rationalist science of political economy, founded there by Adam Smith in 1776 with the publication of his classic treatise, *The Wealth of Nations*. British liberalism in the age of Grey was in many respects only an extension of the Whiggery of the age of Fox. The chief philosopher of the early nineteenth century in Britain was not a romanticist but a skeptical, pragmatic old man of the Enlightenment (born in 1748), Jeremy Bentham.

In France, as we have seen earlier, the Enlightenment flourished vigorously all throughout the years of the Revolution and the First Empire, fending off the arrival of romanticism until the 1820s. The most important philosophical movement in France between the Revolution and the triumph of romanticism, the *idéologie* of Cabanis and Destutt de Tracy, followed very much in the well-worn tracks of Locke, La Mettrie, and Condillac. France, too, had its liberal political economists and statesmen who carried on the work of the generation of Turgot, men such as Jean-Baptiste Say and the doughty Orleanist premier François Guizot.

But whereas for the mind of early nineteenth-century Britain the overwhelming fact of life was the progress of commerce and industry, for early nineteenth-century French intellectuals the most notable fact of life, next to the avalanche of political change, was the progress of mathematics and the natural sciences. It was in these fields, rather than in philosophy, literature, or even social thought, that the Enlightenment most distinguished itself in its final decades. From the 1770s to the 1820s French savants dominated almost every branch of active scientific inquiry in the world. Lagrange, Monge, Laplace, Haüy, Fourier, Ampère, and Fresnel in mathematics and physics; Lavoisier, Berthollet, and Gay-Lussac in chemistry; and Lamarck, Bichat, Cuvier, and Geoffroy Saint-Hilaire in biology were among the leading lights. From their success sprang the strong emphasis in virtually all the French positivist thinkers of later years on the authority of science and the central place of science in the reconstruction of society. Respect for science was a tenet of positivism in all countries, but it had a special salience in positivism *à la française.*

The reasons for the prominent place of France in the history of science at this time are complex. In part it was a matter of momentum. Starting off relatively later than the British in the seventeenth century, the French had acquired a redoubtable national establishment of bureaucrats, scientific academies, and colleges since the days of Colbert and Louis XIV. Into them flowed much ampler funds than their related institutions abroad were accustomed to receive. The Revolutionary Convention added the Ecole Normale Supérieure and the Ecole Polytechnique, great colleges where the sciences thrived very well indeed. Nearly all the masters of French science were closely tied to one or more of the scientific institutions with which Paris was so generously endowed.

The practical needs of the embattled regimes of the Revolution and Napoleon also stimulated French scientific progress, not only because scientists could and did aid the national war effort, but also because the regimes themselves were ideologically committed to the values of the Enlightenment. Later, as the costs of scientific research continued to soar and as industry and the universities came to play a larger role in sponsoring scientific work, France slowly fell behind. But at this particular point in time, the years 1775 to 1825, it unquestionably had more wealth and energy invested in science than any other country. "The home of the scientific spirit," J. T. Merz recognized many years ago, "was France: for though not born there, it was nevertheless there nursed into full growth and vigor."[3]

The mental climate was further prepared for positivism by the burgeoning of industry in the middle decades of the nineteenth century. France lagged well behind Great Britain, but it was ahead of every other European nation except little Belgium. The early 1840s were the period of industrial "takeoff," followed by the great boom of the Second Empire, when industrial production doubled in eighteen years. It tripled again between 1870 and 1914 despite a sharp decline in population growth and various deficiencies in resources and enterprise that never permitted France to spurt forward with the same élan as Britain before it or Germany and America after it.

Long before the French industrial takeoff, the place of science and industry in the society of the future was foreseen by a remarkable seer and world-betterer, Henri de Saint-Simon. His career recalls that of his crankish fellow spirit of the early eighteenth century, the abbé de Saint-Pierre. Like Saint-Pierre he was full of "projects" for improving the human condition through the application of science and reason to urgent social problems. Like Saint-Pierre he was a philosopher of history and progress. But Saint-Simon was born more than a full century later, in 1760, and he figures in intellectual history as one of the principal human links between the thought-world of Saint-Pierre's Enlightenment and the new world of nineteenth-century positivism. He may also have been—although this is debatable—the first socialist.

The man himself, descended from a famous old aristocratic family, followed many careers. A young officer who fought with Washington at Yorktown, a land speculator who nearly lost his head during the Terror, a paid spokesman for the rising industrialists of the Restoration era, Saint-Simon gathered little glory during his lifetime for his prophetic ideas. Human progress, he argued, resulted not from the doings of priests and kings but from the productive genius of scientists—the brains of humanity—and their allies in the body social who organized the world's physical work. Step by step, with advancing enlightenment, men were losing their illusions about the usefulness of the old ruling classes.

In the new society a-dawning, states and churches would be replaced by public administration, and the administrators would be scientists, engineers, and businessmen. In place of war, peace. In place of general poverty, abundance for all. In place of superstition and whim, the positive facts of science. Decision making would be "the result of scientific demonstrations, absolutely independent of any human will."

Shortly before his death Saint-Simon amended his vision to include vital functions for a new class of secular clergymen, the moralists of a humanized Christianity who would mobilize the hearts of men, complementing the brainwork of the scientists and engineers and the body work organized by the businessmen. But as Frank E. Manuel remarks, neither Saint-Simon's quasi-romanticist "New Christianity" nor the bizarre cult invented by his posthumous disciple Enfantin became anything more than social doctrines "with a religious aura." They were never religions.[4]

All the same, Saint-Simon had by the time of his death in 1825 endowed France and the Western world with a program for the future firmly grounded in the realities of the new age. Its guiding principle was not so much reason as expertise. It shied away from metaphysical questions, concerning itself strictly with the most efficient way to manage human society. The heat of warfare and politics would give way to a world of productive labor, presided over by men of knowledge, not by men of power. In one sense, Saint-Simon was only carrying to a new summit the bureaucratizing, centralizing, rationalizing tendencies so characteristic of the whole history of France since the seventeenth century. But he did so in a thoroughly stripped-down, secular, positive spirit, with no more frills than were necessary to ensure the enchainment of human passion.

Among Saint-Simon's followers, and for a brief time his personal secretary, was Auguste Comte, a young graduate of the Polytechnique who broke with his master in 1824. Comte had more than one motive for abandoning his ties with Saint-Simon, but his most rational consideration was Saint-Simon's inability to be a full-fledged Saint-Simonian. The old prophet, largely self-taught, was almost a scientific ignoramus and far from a doctor of philosophy. Comte conceived his own life's work as the anchoring of Saint-Simon's social vision in the solid seabed of a thoroughly systematic and comprehensive scientific philosophy. He never gave Saint-Simon the credit that ordinary filial piety would prescribe, but in essence Comte executed the plan that he had set for himself. In the end he too nurtured delusions of messianic grandeur and tried to found his own religion before his death, on the edge of insanity, in 1857.

The grotesqueries of Comte's personal life do not diminish the magnitude of his accomplishment as a thinker. His positive philosophy, argued in ten laborious volumes published between 1830 and 1854, was the most significant exposition of positivist thought to appear in any country, excluding the works of Marx, which did not come into their own until the twentieth century. It presented a far-ranging system for classifying the sciences, a definition of positive method, a thorough renunciation of theology and metaphysics, a philosophy of history, a program for the establishment of sociology as a science, and a blueprint for worldwide technocracy that in many ways describes the structure of twentieth-century society. W. M. Simon has shown that few of Comte's so-called followers took more than a small fraction of their thought from him, but even Simon concedes that his total influence was considerable.[5] Over the bona fide disciples, such as Emile Littré and Pierre Laffitte in France or Richard Congreve and Frederic Harrison in England, Comte cast a powerful spell. The various organized Positivist movements in Europe and the Americas helped to keep his doctrine alive throughout the Age of Improvement.

Social thought was the strongest suit of both Saint-Simon and Comte, and it is not surprising that many of the other great positivists of nineteenth-century France were sociologists and historians. Ernest Renan, a passionate skeptic and gifted historian, trusted that science would somehow become the religion of the future but rejected the specific teachings of Comte. His own best efforts were devoted to a multivolume critical history of early Christianity, including his once scandalous *Life of Jesus* (1863), the most popular attempt in nineteenth-century biblical scholarship to understand the man Jesus in the context of his times. Equally powerful history was written by Hippolyte Taine, who sought out the ultimate causes of human behavior in the effects on consciousness of racial characteristics, geography, and the historical "moment." Taine arrived, on positivist premises, at a technique for analyzing both national "souls" and dominant world views. France also produced an impressive crop of historical scholars who combined the historicism of the romanticist world view with exhaustive and rigorously critical treatment of the available primary sources. Such historiography, well represented by the works of N. D. Fustel de Coulanges, was scientific without relying on the positivist conception of sociological laws; it paralleled the school established by Leopold von Ranke in Germany.

In sociology proper, French scholars followed Comte, but the appearance of sociological schools and theorists of Comte's own stature takes us beyond 1890. One of the first Comtean sociologists was the Gallicized Russian Eugène de Roberty, a member of the short-lived Sociological Society founded by Littré in 1872. At about the same time, another Gallicized Russian, Jacques Novicow, developed a sociological system based on evolutionary theory. Sociology was then elevated to an academic profession after 1890 by two more significant scholars, both strongly indebted to Comte, Emile Durkheim and René Worms. Marxist thought found a faithful French exponent toward the end of the positivist era in Jules Guesde.

In France more than in any other country positivism also deeply penetrated literature and the arts. The "realism" of the 1850s and 1860s and the "naturalism" of later decades were preached, as well as practiced, with extraordinary vigor in both fiction and painting. Literary realism had already arrived in fact if not in theory in the middle of the romanticist period in two novels that at first received little notice, *The Red and the Black* (1830) and *The Charterhouse of Parma* (1839), by Marie-Henri Beyle, better known by his nom de plume of Stendhal. In real life a lonely, disdainful misfit in the best romantic tradition, Stendhal nevertheless viewed his characters with the objective eye of the clinician; there is no trace of the mystical in the world view of Stendhal. On the contrary, he was a conscious follower of the psychology of Destutt de Tracy. His novels candidly accept man as a being motivated only by self-interest, by the search for happiness through sensual enjoyment.

Another pioneer of realism in French letters was Honoré de Balzac, whose elaborate cycle of tales and novels, *The Human Comedy* (1829–47), supplies a psychosocial anatomy of the early nineteenth-century French bourgeoisie that rivals the best efforts of modern scientific history. Intrigued by the work of Cuvier and other biologists of his time, Balzac saw his characters as inevitable products of their milieu and background and described the social universe from which they emerged with photographic precision.

Yet it was not until the 1850s that a new generation of writers consciously rejected the romanticist world view and installed in its place the gospel of literary realism. Gustave Flaubert created in *Madame Bovary* (1857) the one obvious masterpiece of the new wave, a work of chilling skepticism and detachment, but it was Edmond and Jules de Goncourt in the preface to their *Germinie Lacerteux* (1864) who gave it the most incisive programmatic defense. The novel, they proclaimed, had today become a form of "social inquiry" or "contemporary moral history." It had "assumed the methods and the duties of science," and it would leave no one, not even the poor and the humble, outside its ken. Their fellow realist in the world of painting, Gustave Courbet, was meanwhile shocking and even disgusting Parisian art lovers with his stark, ferociously honest canvasses of peasant life.

The turn to a still more explicitly positivistic and scientistic literature later in the century was led by Emile Zola in his twenty *Rougon-Macquart* novels, subtitled "The Natural and Social History of a Family under the Second Empire" (1871–93). Seldom has a literary man submitted himself so fervently to the authority of science, although it seems unlikely that Zola's reading of scientific works had much tangible effect on his style or methods. He himself named as his chief mentor the physiologist Claude Bernard. He was also attracted to Taine's theories of the influence of heredity and environment on history. But the positivism in Zola was more a matter of informing spirit than of specific doctrine. Like Balzac before him, he was determined to produce in the *Rougon-Macquart* cycle a sociological analysis of France, exploring a still greater variety of social strata and leaving no crime, passion, or disease undetected. Even more than Balzac, Zola was the master of the minutely researched detail. His best passages are inventories, sheer accumulations of impersonal physical fact more overwhelming than all but the most prodigious heroes of literary history.

Among Zola's contemporaries the positivist world view was also delineated in Jules Verne's romances of invention and exploration, the novels and plays of Alphonse Daudet, the stories and novels of Guy de Maupassant, and the early fiction of Joris-Karl Huysmans. The revolt against romanticism in art launched by Courbet continued in the 1870s and 1880s in the Impressionism of Edouard Manet, Camille Pissarro, Claude Monet, Edgar Degas, and Pissarro's brilliant pupil, Paul Cézanne. Impressionism at times resurrected romantic values, as in the canvasses of Auguste Renoir, but its main function was to facilitate a new objectivity in art with the help of modern optical theory. The point was to see reality, unadorned and undistorted by academic clichés, and in particular the reality of out-of-doors, with all its changing aspects, painted from life. If in the process the Impressionist eventually became more concerned with his own craft than with nature, and thus helped to usher in the radical subjectivity of twentieth-century art, such was not his original program.

In the natural sciences themselves, despite the exploits of the incomparable Louis Pasteur and the important studies of radioactivity of Henri Becquerel and the Curies, the second half of the nineteenth century was not a golden age in France. By the 1880s new movements in philosophy, poetry, art, and even social thought had begun to shake the grip of positivism on the French conscience. A straw in the wind of change was the desertion of the naturalist camp by Huysmans, leading in 1882 to his pessimistic novel *Down Stream* and in 1884 to *Against the Grain*, a catalogue of neoromantic excesses in which nothing remained of naturalism except its penchant for cataloguing. Zola himself stood firm, but for Huysmans and many other younger men, it was time to try new paths.

Utility and Progress: Great Britain

Jeremy Bentham, as the romanticist critic William Hazlitt once complained, "turns wooden utensils in a lathe for exercise, and fancies he can turn men in the same manner." Preferring the artificial to the natural, he had "a great contempt for out-of-door prospects, for green fields and trees." Nearly a century later, H. G. Wells accused those latter-day Benthamites, Sidney and Beatrice Webb, of harboring similar sentiments. "If they had the universe in hand," he wrote, "I know they would take down all the trees and put up stamped tin green shades and sunlight accumulators. [Beatrice] thought trees hopelessly irregular and sea cliffs a great mistake."

The sarcasms of Hazlitt and Wells do not miss their marks by much. During the course of the nineteenth century the positivist world view took firm hold of British intellectual life in a form superficially antithetical to French positivism, but in substance not very different. As in France, the crux of the matter was the veneration of scientific method, the project of a new social order grounded in reason and experience, overthrowing the tyranny of tradition. British positivism was several shades more pragmatic and less systematic than the French variety and attached far more importance to the individual and his struggle for worldly happiness, but it all worked out to much the same thing in the end: mankind would be saved by the scientific management of its affairs, and by nothing else.

Britain also provided a hospitable climate for the progress of the natural sciences from the latter part of the eighteenth century onward. Men such as Black, Cavendish, Priestley, Dalton, Davy, Young, Faraday, Lyell, Darwin, Joule, and Kelvin compare favorably with the great figures of the Scientific Revolution and with their own contemporaries in France. The only important difference was that the British scientist tended to work independently of universities and academies. After the good start supplied by the Royal Academy in the age of Newton, British science lost much of its effective institutional support. As in commerce and industry, so in science and philosophy: most outstanding achievement in early modern Britain was the work of the free-lancer, the provincial entrepreneur, or the local eccentric. In the case of science, private enterprise did not succeed in creating a body of scientific work as great as that creditable to the scientific community in France, but many individual accomplishments were impressive. The prestige of science remained high.

Yet it is quite obvious that the business of nineteenth-century Britain, as Calvin Coolidge once said of the United States, was business. All through the revolutionary age on the continent and what we have called the Age of Improvement, from the 1790s to the 1880s, Britain was the leading economic power in the world. Relatively less successful in promoting scientific research, free enterprise achieved incredible victories in the realm of production for profit. Despite substantial emigration, the kingdom's population tripled during the nineteenth century and still at the end of the century enjoyed by far the highest per capita income of any major European country. By all the conventional measures of industrialization—iron, coal, and steel production; railroad lines and steamship tonnage; investments and sales of manufactured goods abroad; industrial horsepower—Great Britain surpassed every nation in the world until the last decade of the Age of Improvement. Only then, in the "hungry" 1880s, did it begin to fall behind. Germany and the United States, each with much larger populations than Britain by the year 1890 (49 and 63 million, respectively, compared to 33 million in Britain), finally forged ahead in the industrial race.

Since the long ascendancy of Britain's industry had been due in good measure to the ruthless ingenuity of its entrepreneurial class, most of whom had sprung from the lower and middle bourgeoisie and had started out with relatively modest capital stakes, the "lesson" that economic life impressed on the British mind was clear and simple: nature favored the individual acting rationally in his own rationally conceived self-interest. By a combination of efficient management, applied science and technology, minimal public interference, and hard work and unrelenting struggle, the individual could simultaneously procure happiness for himself and for his nation. The agent of progress was the individual, fettered only by the dictates of his own reason, and the test of his worth was its value in the modern holy of holies, the marketplace.

The foundations of this stalwart Victorianism, cartooned so effectively in the angry comedies of Charles Dickens, were all laid before Victoria was born. More even than in France, positivism in Britain welled out of the thought-world of the Enlightenment. One of its mainstays, the science of political economy, was based directly on eighteenth-century models, above all on the thought of Adam Smith. As it evolved, political economy remained essentially a British discipline and remained imprisoned in the conceptual framework invented in the preceding century. Even the thinkers who at least partially succeeded in escaping that framework—from Sismondi to Marx and Engels—took the political economists of liberal Britain as their points of departure, reacting against them and using the development of industry in Britain as their principal index to the woes and evils of modern capitalism. Meanwhile, the "classical" school in British economic thought, descending from Smith through T. R. Malthus, David Ricardo, and James Mill to Nassau Senior, W. S. Jevons, and Alfred Marshall, established a case for capitalism rooted in the rationalistic, mechanistic world view of the Enlightenment. Despite many valuable amendments and elaborations, the heirs of Adam Smith were clearly heirs, differing only in their typically positivist tendency to avoid the larger philosophical issues that Smith (a sometime lecturer at the University of Glasgow on subjects ranging from natural theology to ethics) had not dodged.

Utilitarianism, the other great mainstay of British positivism, had equally venerable origins in the fertile intellect of Jeremy Bentham. Since Bentham did not become a celebrity of the first rank until the nineteenth century, it is easy to forget that he published his first book, *A Fragment on Government*, in 1776, and the major text of Benthamism, *Principles of Morals and Legislation*, in 1789. Although he lived to write much more, Bentham belongs to the Enlightenment as surely as Tom Paine or the Marquis de Condorcet. As a philosopher he offered few ideas not already fully expounded in the writings of such Enlightenment worthies as Hume, Hartley, and Helvétius.

But Bentham did, in effect, turn those ideas in a somewhat new direction. Beginning with a grossly simplified Hobbesian psychology that represented all human behavior as the attempt to maximize pleasure and minimize pain and a standard eighteenth-century empiricist theory of knowledge, he deduced that society should be reorganized from top to bottom on strictly utilitarian principles. Only those laws and institutions that produced the greatest quantity of pleasure for the greatest number of individuals, scientifically observed and measured, could survive the test of utility. Appeals to such theological or metaphysical abstractions as the word of God, natural rights, and the social contract were invalid. In short, a radical empiricism demanded that human beings be regarded as simple machines, born free of all ideas or prejudices, seeking only happiness; further, in view of the infinite malleability of the natural man, such happiness could be engineered, as Helvétius had always maintained, by sound education and good laws. The task before the philosopher was to found "a scientific morality on a scientific psychology," to build the good society on positive knowledge of the actual needs of actual men.[6] Except in the sphere of economics and in a few other limited undertakings such as Beccaria's work in penology, eighteenth-century thinkers had preferred rhetorical flourishes to the brass tacks of scientific reform. Getting down to the tacks was Bentham's view of his own function.

After making his own rhetorical flourishes, Bentham did involve himself in the grimy details of social reconstruction, and it was by example even more than by precept that he inspired a whole generation of Victorian reformers. The list of his projects over the long span from the French Revolution to the Reform Bill of 1832, the year of his death, is truly formidable. He proposed a new kind of penitentiary (and poorhouse), a scheme for reorganizing the French judicial system, a plan for speeding up procedures in British equity courts, a project for Parliamentary reform, a suggested constitutional code "for the use of all nations professing liberal opinions," a plan for tax reform, and much more. There was even an unpublished essay found among his manuscripts on the "farther uses of the dead to the living," which envisaged the planting of ancestral mummies on the grounds of estates. By his instructions, Bentham's own skeleton, dressed in his usual clothes and fitted with a wax head, was installed in a glass case for the edification of the students and faculty of University College, London. In the efficient society, nothing goes to waste.

In all of this and in the work of Bentham's several disciples, it is clear that the goal was not, as is sometimes claimed, the establishment of a liberal society. In their economic ideas the Benthamites did echo—with a certain logical inconsistency—the laissez-faire philosophy of Smith and Ricardo, and the immediate practical effect of the reforms inspired by Benthamism was to enhance the power of the new liberal bourgeoisie. But although Bentham valued the happiness of individuals above all other social desiderata, he made no essential distinction among individuals. The "greatest good of the greatest number" is a formula without liberal content and without commitment to any political system whatsoever. Although the Benthamites could not fail to respect the practical achievements of capitalism in the British context, their goal was not freedom for individuals or for any rising class, but scientific management. "In most of Bentham's reformatory projects," as George H. Sabine wryly notes, "it appears that he was more moved by a love of order and efficiency than by humanitarian motives."[7]

Bentham's followers included some of the most vigorous minds in early Victorian Britain. James Mill, his closest disciple, died in 1836, but many good Benthamites of the younger generation survived to carry on their work. Of the professional reformers the outstanding young Benthamite was no doubt Edwin Chadwick, remembered for his contributions to poor law reform and public health administration. In matters of the intellect the first half of the Age of Improvement was dominated by the austere figure of John Stuart Mill, prodigious son of James.

The younger Mill, systematically indoctrinated in childhood by his father, staged a romantic rebellion of his own in his twenties, discovering the poetry of Wordsworth and the philosophy of Coleridge. The socialism of the Saint-Simonians and the historical sociology of Comte further stretched his mind. He was soon puzzling the Benthamite faithful with essays on such unlikely topics as "Poetry and Its Varieties," "Writings of Alfred de Vigny," and "Coleridge." But although Mill supplemented and modified Benthamism at several critical points, he remained throughout his life a Utilitarian. His *System of Logic* (1843 and later editions), *Principles of Political Economy* (1848 and later editions), and *Utilitarianism* (1861) mirror the eclecticism of his mature years without fundamentally altering the premises of Bentham's thought. Mill's system was empiricist to the core. It took its epistemology from Newton, Locke, Hartley, Hume, Bentham, and his own father, and it continued to put all values and institutions to the supreme test of utility. Even the civil and political liberties that Mill celebrated with such eloquence in his short treatise *On Liberty* (1859) he viewed not as ends in themselves or as sacred or natural rights, but as means to the higher end of promoting the greatest happiness of the greatest number. "I regard utility as the ultimate appeal," he insisted, "on all ethical questions; but it must be utility in the largest sense, grounded on the permanent interests of man as a progressive being."

When Mill died in 1873, Utilitarianism was long past its prime, in good measure because John Stuart Mill for all his sedulously cultivated "many-sidedness" could not bring it more fully into the mainstream of nineteenth-century thought. In its scientism, its love of efficiency, its rejection of theology and metaphysics, and its pragmatic bent, it ministered quite well to the spirit of the age, above all in business-minded Britain. Mill's success in advancing beyond doctrinaire economic liberalism to a consideration of the merits of the socialist case prefigured that peculiarly British version of scientific socialism, the Fabian movement. But for all its virtues, Utilitarianism never quite managed to incorporate into the basic structure of its thought the vital nineteenth-century ideas of historical development, progress, and evolution. As the positivist world view continued to unfold in Britain through the 1860s, 1870s, and 1880s, these became the central themes in scientific and sociological thought.

One line of development was pursued by scholars who sought to apply positivist methods in the interpretation of the processes of human history. The places of Taine, Renan, and Fustel de Coulanges were filled in Britain by H. T. Buckle—author of *The History of Civilization in England* (1857-61), a vigorous effort in the spirit of Comte to ascertain the "laws" of history with special attention to the effects of the natural environment on the character of nations—and a rising school of scientific historians headed by William Stubbs, S. R. Gardiner, and Lord Acton. Comte's idea of progress together with his project for a positivist religion attracted two major British prophets, a former Anglican clergyman, Richard Congreve, and a lawyer, Frederic Harrison. The two men went separate ways after a schism that disrupted the international Positivist movement in 1878, but each did what he could to promote Comte's teachings, including his philosophy of history.

Another and much more significant trend in later British positivism centered on the idea of evolution. Nowhere in the Age of Improvement did evolutionism wield such a potent influence in science, philosophy, and social thought as in Britain. Two British scientists, Charles Darwin and Alfred Russel Wallace, arrived independently in midcentury at the biological theory of evolution by the natural selection of random genetic variations; even before their work the philosopher and sociologist Herbert Spencer had published the outlines of a system of evolutionary philosophy more ambitious even than Comte's, linking cosmic and human history. Darwin's *On the Origin of Species* (1859) and *The Descent of Man* (1871), along with the nine volumes of Spe   er's *Synthetic Philosophy* (1855-96), supplied to a whole generation of thinkers in Britain and abroad a body of theory, well fortified with empirical evidence, that seemed to establish beyond reasonable doubt the immensely deep roots of all human behavior in the prehuman cosmos.

At one level the new evolutionism was nothing more than a further application of positivist methodology to the problems of natural history along lines more fruitful than those previously followed. It was also heavily indebted to the emphasis in British political economy on the importance of competitive struggle in the marketplace. Darwin's famous tribute to Malthus and Spencer's lifelong attachment to laissez-faire economics suggest the intimacy of the rapport between evolutionism and capitalism. If in modern capitalism progress resulted from free enterprise, so in nature progress represented "the survival of the fittest," a phrase coined by Spencer, in 1864.

At another level the turn to evolutionism in later British positivist thought reflected some of the same neoromanticist tendencies that prompted Saint-Simon and Comte to try to elevate positivism to a religion. The collapse of orthodox faith and the separation of rational man from nature, history, and culture achieved in the Utilitarian philosophy left large gaps in the emotional life of Victorian man that needed bridging. The earnest but somewhat arid Positivist religion of Congreve and Harrison was too much like a parody of Christianity to appeal to most British intellectals, just as its French original failed to seduce more than a handful of late nineteenth-century Frenchmen. But evolutionism was something else, grounded in the latest scientific revelations and able, as Comte's doctrine was not, to integrate humankind into all of cosmic being. Darwin addressed himself to the whole of organic creation, Spencer even to the inorganic realm. It was all very heady stuff while the freshness of it lasted.

In any case evolution became the watchword of late Victorian social thought. In addition to Spencer himself, there were the founders of British anthropology, Edward Tylor and James Frazer; the famous editor and political scientist Walter Bagehot, author of *Physics and Politics* (1872); and those long forgotten messiahs of "social Darwinism," Benjamin Kidd and Karl Pearson, who used Darwinian arguments to demonstrate the inevitability of competition among individuals and competition among races, respectively. It was Pearson, most ominous of the lot, who—in a lecture on the embarrassments of the Boer War—advised an audience in Newcastle in 1900 that "the scientific view of a nation" demanded the recruitment of its citizens "from the better stocks" and its maintenance at "a high pitch of external efficiency by contest, chiefly by way of war with inferior races, and with equal races by the struggle for trade-routes and for the sources of raw material and of food supply." The path of progress was "strewn with the wreck of nations." Darwin's staunchest ally among biologists, Thomas Henry Huxley, made no secret of his objection on ethical grounds to the modeling of individual human behavior after the laws of the jungle, but even he left unclear whether those laws could be repealed at the international level.

Most of the great Victorian intellectuals, as we have seen, were committed in one way or another to the positivist world view, but for the literary gentry and the artists it had fewer charms. A somewhat stolid romanticism lived on in poetry and architecture. The liveliest movement in the graphic arts, the pre-Raphaelite sect, affected a neomedieval style. The theater continued moribund as in romanticist times. The leading Victorian critics of culture, John Ruskin, Walter Pater, and Matthew Arnold, scarcely qualify as positivists.

But in the novel, British counterparts of French realism and naturalism did make their appearance, although their work displayed none of the programmatic purity of the Goncourts or Zola. The British Balzac was obviously Charles Dickens, who started out his literary life as a master of comic satire and sentimentality and gradually darkened into the creator of such realist masterpieces as *Bleak House* (1853) and *Hard Times* (1854). His gifted contemporaries, William Makepeace Thackeray, Anthony Trollope, and George Eliot, studied the realities of English life with a drier eye. Of their number the most complete positivist was Eliot, not only for her painstaking fictional scenes of everyday life, but also for her activities as an intellectual middleman, the translator of Strauss and Feuerbach, the associate of the Comtean philosopher G. H. Lewes, and a brilliant journalist. Near the century's end naturalism found its British followers in Thomas Hardy, George Gissing, and—during the middle period of his career—George Moore.

All in all "those earnest Victorians" were a large and able company, satisfied with themselves if not always with their times and more at ease with the positivist world view than any other. "Life is good," sang William Ernest Henley, who might be called the positivist's poet, "and joy runs high between English earth and sky: Death is death; but we shall die to the Song on your bugles blown, England—to the stars on your bugles blown!" Not even "the fell clutch of circumstance," not even "the bludgeonings of chance" could bow Victorian heads. They were the masters of their fate, the captains of their soul. If one happened to be English, male, and middle-class or above, the poet's formula breathed common sense.

Matter and Energy: Germany

Positivism came to France and Britain in a way that, retrospectively, seems almost effortless. The positivists offended conventional opinion by their hostility to orthodox religious belief and by their tendency to political leftishness, but their world view harmonized with the rationalist-empiricist thrust of modern French and British thought. It also suited the practical needs of fast-rising elements in modern French and British society. Romanticism had secured no central place in French and British philosophy, nor had it become inextricably associated with the "national" cause in either country. For Germany, positivism was a far more seditious doctrine, and its arrival an occasion for deep national anxiety.

The characteristic German form of positivism, almost unknown in the West in the nineteenth century, was "materialism," which I have put in quotation marks because it so seldom appeared in anything like a chemically pure state. Many of the greatest postromantics in German thought have been dubbed materialists, often by their enemies rather than by their friends. David Friedrich Strauss, Ludwig Feuerbach, Karl Marx, Ludwig Büchner, Ernst Haeckel, and Eugen Dühring are prominent examples. Against them historians of thought usually identify men such as Richard Avenarius and Ernst Mach as true "positivists," thinkers who decried the metaphysical implications of materialism and adhered in a stricter or more "critical" way to the epistemology of the natural sciences.

This controversy, still important today if only because of the attacks mounted by Marx, Engels, and Lenin on their contemporaries in both camps, was more than a petty dispute among haggling philosophers. Great issues were involved. Nevertheless, at the still higher level of the strife between contending weltanschauungen, we can be forgiven if we elect to de-emphasize the intramural warfare between the "materialists" and the "positivists" and concentrate, instead, on their similarities. In the greater struggle against the powerful Christian and romanticist-idealist tendencies in German thought, they were almost as one. By the close of the romanticist era in German cultural history, about 1830 or 1835, the German intelligentsia had succeeded in imposing on Germany a thoroughly romanticist self-image. The West was the world of Descartes and Bacon, a cold universe of shopkeepers and technicians, scoffers and skeptics; Germany alone knew and nourished the spirit of man. Yet in a few years the avant-garde was in open rebellion against this "old-German" thought and returning, as its most daring members had done a century before, to Western influences, including the materialism of Hobbes and La Mettrie and the empiricism of Locke and Hume.

In good part the new temper of German thought can be seen as a reflection of political disillusionment. After the excitement of the French Revolution and the national rising against Napoleon, the German lands subsided once more into political impotence, division, and repression. Once the banner of German reawakening, romanticism petrified into an official credo, an instrument of reaction, the tool of church and state. Industrial and commercial progress, justice for workers, freedom of thought and belief, and

even the idea of a unified nation-state came to be identified in many minds
with the West, and especially with France. Such things were not "German"
—and if not, said many young thinkers, to the devil with our *Deutschheit!*
Let us be French, if being French means being free! Men like Heinrich
Heine, Arnold Ruge, and Karl Marx, all exiles in Paris at one time or
another for political reasons, sent the word back to Germany that Western
air was more bracing than their own. It was also obvious that Germany still
lagged behind the West commercially and industrially. The France of Louis
Philippe and, still more, the Britain of William IV and the young Victoria
preserved the economic leadership of the Atlantic powers despite all the
progress made by the German-speaking countries since the eighteenth century.

In the realm of ideas, the reigning orthodoxies in the 1830s were Hegelian
idealism and a Christian faith lately reinvigorated by its liaisons with romanticism and idealism but also tainted by the close identification of the ecclesiastical establishment with the German states. So complete was the
triumph of idealism in the academic world that philosophy itself seemed
suspect in some younger eyes. "Philosophy had lost its charm," writes F.
A. Lange, "since it had entered into the service of Absolutism." It had
performed "the meanest beadle-offices long enough to excite a universal
distrust."[8] The only recourse in a restless and disgruntled age was to turn
the respectable values upside down with the help of the most radical ideas
available from Western thinkers. The West might even be beaten at its own
game. A three-pronged attack ensued, of a somewhat vague and hot-tem-
pered materialism against idealism, of strident humanist atheism against the
official religions, and of liberalism and socialism against the conservative
political credos of Prince Metternich and his various allies throughout the
German lands.

Among the first radical voices were the writers and intellectuals of the
Young Germany movement, a loose fraternity of leftish patriots hopeful of
continuing the process of national regeneration in a new vein. They preferred prose to poetry and roundly criticized the romantics for their obscu-
rantist tendencies. Their leaders, Karl Gutzkow and Theodor Mundt, are
now forgotten, but on the periphery of Young Germany stood more formidable figures, including Heine.

At about the same time another "young" movement emerged, the Young
Hegelians—university-trained scholars, philosophers, and social thinkers
attracted to Hegel's dialectical logic but hostile to the conservatism of
official German philosophy. To this group belonged the radical theologians
Bruno Bauer and David Friedrich Strauss, the political journalist Arnold
Ruge, the philosopher Ludwig Feuerbach, and, of course, Marx and Engels.
They were difficult young men, relentlessly ostracized and persecuted, but
with benefit of hindsight clearly the best minds of midcentury Germany.
They brought together elements of both the romanticist and the positivist

world views, but in the main they were positivists, protesting against the orthodoxies of the established order in the cause of reason, science, realism, and humanity. Their materialism, if any, was less a formal metaphysical position than a determination to rid themselves of the old official idealism, in the Marxian phrase, by standing it on its head. Instead of world-spirit making man, they proclaimed, it was man—flesh and blood man, feet planted on solid earth—who made world-spirit, who invented his gods and his ideologies, and could therefore change them.

As the Young Hegelians matured through the 1840s and 1850s, the distance between them steadily grew, and they were drawn more fully into the main currents of European positivist thought, including the social and natural sciences. Feuerbach developed an interest in the implications of physiology and food chemistry for human progress. "Man is," in his celebrated slogan, "what he eats." Strauss wound up a Darwinist, preaching a secular religion of science and humanity in the post-Christian pages of his last book, *The Old Faith and the New* (1872). Marx and Engels delved into the murky depths of the science of political economy, expounding a "dialectical" materialism which held, with Hegel, that history unfolded through the contest of opposing forces, but also held, pursuing the philosophical implications of economics, that human life and thought were determined at every step by material circumstances, notably by the means and relations of production.

In the 1850s, although the Young Hegelians were far from old, with half their adult lives still ahead of them, a younger crop of thinkers had made its appearance for whom Hegel meant nothing. The new generation doted on science and tended (except for the Marxist Left) to see Germany's salvation in terms of industrial, technical, and scientific progress.

The 1850s marked an important turning point in modern German life as well as thought. The country's course was fixed for the next hundred years. After the disappointments of the age of Metternich, the failure of the Young German movement, the waning of romanticism, and the catastrophe of the Revolution of 1848, the energies of the German elites were channeled increasingly in new directions. Bismarck's diplomatic and military drive to unify Germany under Prussian leadership, which ended with the establishment of the German Reich in 1871, was one of these new directions, so dazzlingly successful that it virtually destroyed liberalism and social democracy as commanding forces in German politics. Henceforth a militaristic authoritarianism, allied with heavy industry, was to dominate German public life.

At the same time, the German bourgeoisie finally found its feet and began the march to industrial maturity. The march was more like a hundred-yard dash. During the first twenty years of the great industrial boom that began about 1850, Germany had caught up with and already passed well beyond France when war broke out between France and Prussia in 1870. The next major goal, the overtaking of Britain, took longer, but the job was done in due course. By 1900 Germany was producing more steel than Britain; by 1910 almost twice as much. Even the volume of Germany's international trade had nearly equaled Britain's by 1910. Only in per capita income did Germany fail to match the wealth of Britain, in part because it retained a larger rural population.

In addition to the convincing progress of German arms and German industry, intellectuals could not fail to be impressed by the veritable explosion that occurred in science and scholarship in the German-speaking world between about 1830 and 1870. From being a very minor scientific power, Germany advanced to uncontested world leadership in most of the sciences by the last quarter of the nineteenth century. The roster of great names is long, but it speaks for itself. If we mention only those scientists born between 1800 and 1850, who were responsible for nearly all the scientific triumphs of the Age of Improvement, the mathematicians include Jacobi, Riemann, Pasch, Cantor, and Klein; the physicists Helmholtz, Clausius, Mach, and Röntgen; the chemists Wöhler, Liebig, Bunsen, and Meyer; the biologists Müller, Schleiden, Schwann, Du Bois-Reymond, Virchow, Mendel, Haeckel, Weismann, and Koch; and the experimental psychologists Fechner and Wundt. Although a few of these scientists imported romanticist or idealist assumptions into their thought, they all utilized the orthodox mathematical-empiricist methods perfected in the West, and their work was readily accepted by the international scientific community. Nor did German science lose its momentum after 1890; despite the decline of positivism as a world view, German and Austrian scientists continued to lead the world until the Nazi debacle.

The same may be said of many of the other *Wissenschaften*. In historiography, in biblical and classical studies, in archaeology, in linguistics, in legal studies, in geography, in sociology and anthropology, German scholars came quickly to the forefront between the mid-nineteenth and early twentieth centuries. The fathers of modern scientific historiography, Barthold Niebuhr and Leopold von Ranke, were Germans. Ranke's numerous students fanned out to all corners of the country, taking with them his insistence on meticulous archival research and exhaustive critical analysis of sources. The Rankeans, in whose number stood such dedicated scholars as Georg Waitz, Wilhelm von Giesebrecht, and Heinrich von Sybel, along with an occasional outsider like Theodor Mommsen (a self-described disciple of Ranke's own master, Niebuhr), avoided the conversion of history into a social science directly analogous to physics, but their methods were fundamentally positivistic. The data of carefully sifted primary sources replaced the data of scientific experiment or observation; as in the hard sciences, the goal of Rankean historiography was scrupulous objectivity, the reconstruction of the past "as it actually happened," without the intrusion of present-day values. The German-speaking countries also gave the world the anthropology of Adolf Bastian, and J. J. Bachofen, the sociology of Albert Schäffle and Gustav Ratzenhofer, the geography of Friedrich Ratzel, and much more. The German professor was soon known worldwide as the paragon of the technically advanced, thorough, and intellectually sophisticated scholar or research scientist.

German excellence in all these fields reflected the pervasive influence of positivism, but what really made it possible was the German university system, which we explored briefly in an earlier chapter. Although it had been the creation, ironically, of the princely particularism and churchly conservatism of a bygone era, the fact remains that in the nineteenth century, as in the eighteenth, Germany had many more, and many better universities than any other Western country, some thirty-four throughout the German-speaking world as of 1890. The intensive specialization of knowledge in the nineteenth century as all fields of research expanded rapidly, along with the growing costs of library and research facilities, made the university an ideal center for higher learning. The German universities were small enough to encourage close ties between colleagues, large enough to support research along many different lines, and numerous enough to permit the development of a plethora of rival schools of thought, which in turn interacted vigorously thanks to the frequent transfers of students from university to university, the high mobility of their teachers, and the countless scholarly journals and associations that flourished throughout the century. The teaching function of the university, taken with the utmost seriousness by many professors, was also of crucial importance in an age when the headlong growth of complex methodologies required careful training of neophytes. In time, other nations caught up with Germany academically, following its example, but during the Age of Improvement none could touch it.

For the production of works of general philosophy and avant-garde social thought, however, the university was still not necessarily the most propitious place, even in Germany. It continued to frown on anything that smacked of atheism. Radical political and economic views were unwelcome. As the Young Hegelians had encountered heavy-handed official opposition to their views in the 1830s and 1840s, so in the next few decades they themselves and their counterparts in the younger generation thrived for the most part outside academic walls, even though the progress of science and industry in official Germany (and elsewhere) inspired much of their thought.

The role of Mill, Comte, and Spencer in German intellectual life in the second half of the century was played by a variety of thinkers, none up to the level of their genius except Marx and Engels, who carried on their work in the safety of Victorian England. *Capital*, Marx's masterpiece, was published in three volumes in 1867, 1885, and 1895. Better known in their own time in Germany were that now almost comic triumvirate of scientific materialists, Carl Vogt, Jacob Moleschott, and Ludwig Büchner, whose chief manifestoes appeared in the 1850s: Vogt's *Blind Faith and Science* (1854), Moleschott's *Cycle of Life* (1852), and, most popular of all, Büchner's *Force and Matter* (1855).

Büchner is a fair sample of nineteenth-century German materialism. Born in 1824, he was a physician and lecturer in medicine at the University of Tübingen until the notoriety of *Force and Matter* compelled him to resign. His pen remained active in spite of academic disapproval, but none of his later books enjoyed the success of the first. What most shocked its readers was the young Büchner's uncompromising rejection of God and religion. Claiming to base his thought on the best wisdom of modern science, he declared that matter was immortal; the universe had always existed, without benefit of creation by a supernatural being. Even the activity of the human mind could be reduced by analysis to the motion of cerebral matter, an explanation only one step removed from the biologist Vogt's scandalous dictum that the brain secretes thought as the liver secretes bile. Yet even Büchner was nothing like a doctrinaire materialist. In *Force and Matter* he regularly confused materialism with empiricism and in a later book conceded that science would probably never be able to solve the deepest mysteries of the cosmos, including the problem of the ultimate nature of matter. Like the Western positivists of his time, he had to make room for the "unknowable."

The same world view returned to *épater le bourgeois* all over again at the close of the century in the philosophical books of two well-known scientists, the biologist Ernst Haeckel and the physical chemist Wilhelm Ostwald. The principal text here was Haeckel's vastly popular book *The Riddle of the Universe* (1899), which preached a monistic "religion" centered on the concepts of matter, energy, and Darwinian evolution. Like Büchner before him, Haeckel dismissed Christian faith and the notion of a personal God as obsolete. The clergy protested, and many of his own scientific colleagues rebuked Haeckel, but he did not lose his professorship at Jena, where he had already taught for nearly forty years when *The Riddle of the Universe* first appeared. In 1906 Haeckel joined Ostwald in establishing a "League of Monists" to propagate the new materialist credo.

The latter part of the nineteenth century also witnessed the transition in German academic philosophy to a more severely critical form of positivism that stressed the limits of scientific knowledge. Some of the scientists themselves had taken public notice of its limits, including the great Helmholtz and, in a remarkable lecture delivered in Leipzig in 1872, the physiologist Emil Du Bois-Reymond. But in academic philosophy, which had made little progress throughout most of the Age of Improvement, the step to a revival of Humean scepticism came in the 1880s with the first major works of the Austrian physicist and philosopher Ernst Mach, and his German contemporary Richard Avenarius. In league with their British intellectual forebears,

Mach and Advenarius maintained that outside sensation there is no knowledge. The objective of science was, accordingly, the systematic description of human sensory experience, beyond which neither science nor philosophy could hope to advance. Even the Kantian idea of the unknowable "thing-in-itself" went too far in their view, since no one could know the existence of the unknowable. At least for human beings, the world consisted only of sensation. We could know nothing else. The theories of physics and metaphysics, the ideas of matter and energy, the notion of laws of nature were all just so many words, convenient or inconvenient as the case might be, and readily expendable if at any time they ceased to be useful in scientific rhetoric.

Mach and Avenarius were forerunners of the still more stringent logical positivism yet to come in the twentieth century, which they influenced. But in the context of the nineteenth century, the theoretical differences between Feuerbach, Büchner, Marx, Haeckel, and even Mach should not be exaggerated. For all of them, mankind was capable of knowing its world through the empirical methods of science, and the mysteries of Christian theology and idealist metaphysics had lost their relevance. How much was unknown or unknowable, the question of the reality of matter, the mechanisms of historical and cosmic evolution, the ethical implications of Darwinism, all this and more remained to be fought over. But the German positivists, like their colleagues elsewhere, were true believers in scientific method, ebullient humanists, and devotees of progress. Their muscular faith reflected Germany's growing confidence in herself during the second half of the nineteenth century.

Bismarckian Germany was far less richly blessed in its aesthetic culture than in science, scholarship, and positivist propaganda. Historians of art and literature regard the Bismarck era as a wasteland. Not one German or Austrian painter or poet of the barren years between the death of Heine in 1856 and the symbolist verse of Stefan George in the 1890s equaled the giants of romanticism.

But Germany adhered to the same fashions in art and literature as the Western countries. Romanticism fell under severe attack, despite the continuing demands of the sweet-toothed German public for works in a sentimental vein. A generation of realist novelists and playwrights surfaced in the 1840s, led by Otto Ludwig, Friedrich Hebbel, and Theodor Fontane; in the fine arts, their most interesting contemporary was Adolf von Menzel, famous in his own time for florid historical paintings and book illustrations, but gifted also as a genre painter who was not even afraid of industrial subjects. In the 1880s and 1890s, Germany had its naturalists in the manner of Zola, of whom the most successful were the playwrights Gerhart Hauptmann and Hermann Sudermann. Hauptmann's *The Weavers* (1892) was a fierce indictment of the exploitation of workers comparable to Zola's *Germinal.* Max Liebermann produced outstanding canvasses of working life much like Millet's and in the 1890s turned to impressionism, also under French influence.

It was not, therefore, a literal wasteland. Yet for anyone familiar with the earlier history of German culture, the age of Bismarck seems like a replay of the German Enlightenment. Imported French classicism had blended uneasily with the Teutonic volksgeist. Positivism served a wider range of authentic German needs, yet in such vital fields as philosophy, art, and poetry, it accomplished far less than romanticism before it or the irrationalism that followed after 1890. Another great epoch in Austro-German aesthetic culture was about to open, just as the positivists had reaped their last meager harvest.

Gilded Ages: Russia and the United States

Having discovered national missions during the romantic era, Russia and the United States continued on their separate and increasingly divergent paths in the second half of the nineteenth century. Russia failed to complete the transition to a mature industrial economy, despite vigorous prodding by the czarist regime; the United States became the world's greatest economic power in little more than a generation. The Russian body politic was more and more painfully racked by irreconcilable differences of interest and ideology; American society, after the crushing of the rebellion of the Southern states, underwent an accelerating process of both real and imaginary embourgeoisement that had a dampening effect on class struggle. Reactions to positivism in Russia were mixed; Americans welcomed it with enthusiasm.

Not every basis of comparison disappeared. As happened before, with romanticism, Russia and the United States lagged behind western Europe in assimilating the new world view, Russia by at least ten years, the United States by at least twenty. Yet both countries by this time were culturally autonomous, able to make original contributions of internationally recognized value. The same was true of Scandinavia, which embraced positivism relatively late but, having done so, gave to the world thought and literature of high distinction. Russia and the United States also continued their phenomenal growth in both population and territory. By 1897 Russia was a sprawling Eurasian empire of 129 million people. By 1900, after the conquests of the Mexican and Spanish-American wars and an influx during the preceding half-century of 17 million immigrants (chiefly from Ireland and from eastern and southern Europe), the United States had become a polyglot empire in its own right of 76 million people, with possessions from the Bering Strait to the West Indies, and from Maine to the South China Sea. It is a further curiosity that both Russia and the United States had chiefs of state who in the early 1860s formally emancipated their servile agricultural workers (serfs in Russia, slaves in America), suppressed civil insurrections (the Polish uprising of 1863–64, the Civil War of 1861–65), and were later assassinated by outraged fanatics (Alexander II in 1881, Abraham Lincoln in 1865).

But, next to the contrasts, the comparisons are almost trivial. At the close of the nineteenth century czarist Russia was a terminally sick society, with only a few years to live before the great revolution that would put it out of its misery forever. The flush on its cheeks was the fever of a wasting disease, not the ruddy glow of health. America, meanwhile, had reached the prime of life, the richest and most fully developed capitalist society in history, with many possibilities for good and evil still untested, "from sea to shining sea." Europe had never seen its like, not even the lusty Reich of Wilhelm II.

All the same, Russia in the reigns of Alexander II and III was not without its glories. Scientists appeared who still enjoy worldwide fame. Russian social philosophers, especially advocates of the new gospel of anarchism, became European celebrities. In literature, Russian writers of the period produced some of the greatest novels in the history of belles lettres, and Russian composers wrote music that equaled the work of their best European contemporaries. It was a different sort of Gilded Age from the one portrayed in Mark Twain's novel of American life, but a Gilded Age no less.

The role of the positivist world view in shaping Russian culture during these years is something else again. That positivism did reach and influence Russian minds can hardly be questioned. But it clashed with the fundamental tendencies in the Russian tradition, and too little had changed in Russian life since the days of Napoleon and Alexander I to give it the kind of support it was winning, at least temporarily, in Germany. The Germans, too, were ill-prepared by the facts of their own cultural history to find positivism convincing. But the transformation of Germany from a society of princes and peasants into a society of businessmen and workers during the course of the nineteenth century created a climate of opinion in which the veneration of science, technology, and the methods of both could thrive very well indeed.

Russia, by contrast, remained essentially what it had been ever since the time of Peter the Great: a nation of peasants, with a ruling class of bureaucrats and landowners at the top, and little in between. Only 8 percent of the population lived in towns and cities in 1851, and by 1897 the percentage had risen to only 13. Although some industrialization occurred, especially between 1890 and 1905, Russia lagged behind all the other great powers in industrial output. In the last year before the First World War, even France (with one-fourth as many people) still mined more coal and produced more pig iron than Russia. In the absence of large middle and working classes, the natural constituencies of positivist thought, positivism could not hope to drum up the broad support that it attracted in the West.

Wherever positivism did flourish in Russian thought in the second half of the nineteenth century, it was typically associated with radical political causes, carrying on the labors of the Westernizers of the romantic era. The old Westernizers had been earnest Hegelians; the new Westernizers not unnaturally turned to the post-Hegelian generation in Western philosophy for their inspiration. Feuerbach, Comte, Marx, and Spencer were among their principal mentors. Their Slavophile enemies retained a basically romanticist world view, but became more and more closely identified with the ideological defense of tsarism. In the middle, a small party of liberals representing commercial and professional interests pressed for moderate reform. But the keenest minds veered either to the extreme Right or the extreme Left.

The turn to positivism occurred in the mid-1850s, at a time when the Crimean War had dramatized Russia's weakness vis-à-vis the Western powers and the death of the despotic Nicholas I had rekindled hopes for fundamental changes in the whole structure of Russian life. The loudest voices on the Left were at first the so-called nihilists, a band of thinkers expounding materialism in the German manner. Their most effective spokesman was Nikolai Chernyshevsky, a devotee of Feuerbach, whose arrest and exile to Siberia in 1862 electrified the radicals and in the long run aided their cause. Still more militant was Dmitry Pisarev. A religious mystic in his university days, Pisarev converted to the materialism of Moleschott and Büchner soon thereafter, but his death in 1868 at the age of twenty-seven cut short what promised to be a brilliant career. Later in the century came the humanistic positivism of Pyotr Lavrov and Nikolai Mikhailovsky, intellectual leaders of Russian agrarian socialism. Critical positivism was represented by Vladimir Lesevich, an early disciple of Comte and Littré who fell toward the end of his life under the influence of Avenarius.

None of these thinkers can be ranked as a philosophical giant. Nor was their positivism entirely pure. Although they upheld an empiricist theory of knowledge, reveled in the possibilities of science for human enlightenment and betterment, and scorned theology and metaphysics as proudly as Auguste Comte himself, it is tempting to argue that the Russian positivist philosophers of the nineteenth century were simply idealists in disguise. What seems to have gripped them, above all, was the hope for sociopolitical reform or revolution in Russia. In their ethical thought, they nearly all ignored the deterministic implications of science to maintain a passionately libertarian doctrine that asserted the fundamental goodness of each man's moral instincts. The generous spirit of Jean-Jacques lingered on, together with a goodly measure of German ethical idealism. Unshackle the natural man from the chains of despotism and reaction, and—so they believed—he would save the world. As Zenkovsky comments, Russian positivism arose from "a need to satisfy religious demands." Even its atheism was a "stormy and passionate atheism" that concealed a deep longing for faith.[9]

It goes without saying that many Western positivists harbored similar motives for rallying to the cause of science and enlightenment, not the least of them Comte himself. But in their view of human nature they were further removed from the romanticist outlook than their Russian colleagues and more inclined to put their trust in cosmic processes. Face to face with the crushing might of czarist state power, Russian radicals could not afford a moment's complacency; progress was for them scarcely guaranteed by "cosmic processes." In the absence of cosmic or divine aid, they had to assume that man himself was instinctively good and only prevented from leading a righteous life (shades of Rousseau!) by the evils of the sociopolitical order. Overthrow that order, and all would be well.

The utopian and ethical idealism of Russian social thought was nowhere more evident than in its most notorious radical credo, the anarchism of Mikhail Bakunin. Starting out in life a Hegelian, Bakunin formally renounced his Hegelianism in the 1860s, when it was no longer fashionable, to become a self-professed atheistic materialist. Whatever party label he adopted, however, he remained the same passionate foe of laws and governments and the same passionate believer in the instinctive virtue of the natural man. His place in the anarchist movement was taken later in the century by another Russian, Prince Pyotr Kropotkin, who discovered a scientific basis for anarchism in his reading of the function of "mutual aid" in both animal and human evolution.

In the natural sciences themselves, Russians made outstanding contributions throughout the second half of the nineteenth century, which had some effect, as elsewhere, in making positivism more acceptable to the intelligentsia. The great names included Ivan Sechenov and Ivan Pavlov, the founders of modern behaviorist psychology; Dmitry Mendeleyev, the chief proponent of the periodic law of the elements; the comparative embryologist Alexander Kovalevsky; and the bacteriologist Ilya Metchnikov. Several notable Russians also turned to positivist sociology during the Age of Improvement, but they did most of their work abroad and published in French or German.

Of course the most notable Russians of all were the novelists and the composers, an incomparable array of virtuosos. We may leave out the composers—Moussorgsky, Rimsky-Korsakov, Tchaikovsky, and the rest—since their music was unambiguously romantic, like most of the music of nineteenth-century Europe. But the realist movement did penetrate Russian letters in some of the last work of Gogol and in the novels of three midcentury masters who easily rank with Balzac, Flaubert, and Dickens.

The oldest and the most straightforwardly realistic of the trio was Ivan Turgenev, author of *Fathers and Sons* (1862), whose hero Bazarov was modeled on the young "nihilists" of the period (Turgenev coined the term himself). A great and sensitive craftsman, he was soon eclipsed by two younger men, Fyodor Dostoyevsky and Leo Tolstoy. In Dostoyevsky most of the tendencies of European literary realism are clearly in evidence: the tragic episodes from contemporary life, the obsession with crime and poverty, and the gift for careful observation of detail. His early work *Poor Folk* (1846) was also perhaps the first Russian "social" novel, a vivid rendering of life among the poor. But as Dostoyevsky's career unfolded, and especially after the religious experiences of his prison years in the early 1860s, he turned to a heterodox Christian mysticism that reached its artistic apotheosis in the pages of his greatest novel, *The Brothers Karamazov* (1879–80). Realistic techniques, and a psychological method all his own, were enlisted by Dostoyevsky in the service of a world view far removed from positivism. In retrospect his work seems more like a prolegomenon to twentieth-century irrationalism than anything else; it was also a powerful literary expression of the Slavophile doctrine of the sacred mission of Holy Russia.

The youngest of the three, Tolstoy, followed a still different course. After writing his colossal realistic masterwork, *War and Peace* (1865–69), which he himself explained as an illustration of the strict determinism of historical processes, he underwent a personal crisis that transformed him into a tender-minded Christian anarchist. All his writing after 1880, and some of it is artistically comparable to his realistic fiction, breathes the gentle spirit of Tolstoy's conversion, but as with the bulk of Dostoyevsky's work, it leaves the positivist world view well behind.

Positivism, clearly, did not answer all the needs of Russian artists and intellectuals during the Age of Improvement. Much of it was an imported product, imperfectly digested, and used for purposes not consistent with its own inner value structure. In any event, few Russians swallowed it raw. More than elsewhere, it was heavily adulterated with romanticist, Christian, and utopian ideas. Positivism helped drive Russian society toward the apocalypse of 1917, but only in league with other tendencies in thought for which it can bear no responsibility and which had no doubt a firmer grip on the Russian national soul.

In the United States, the great divide between romanticism and positivism came significantly later than in the Old World. When Darwin was writing his *On the Origin of Species* and Büchner his *Force and Matter*, Emerson, Thoreau, and Whitman were still in the prime of life. Not until the Civil War and the industrial boom that followed it did Americans begin to shift their allegiance to positivism. The period from 1865 to 1900 or even 1910 was the American Age of Improvement, the Gilded Age, a long and virtually uninterrupted time of spectacular economic and demographic growth, of imperial expansion, of social reform, of adventure and exuberance surpassing the enlightened optimism of Jeffersonian America and the democratic ardors of the Jacksonians. In midcentury the republic, as Tocqueville understood only too well, was up and coming. But by the end of the century, the United States had almost suddenly outstripped every great power in the world. Per capita income was twice that of any continental European country. Total industrial output increased tenfold between 1860 and 1910.

Rapid growth had always been a prominent feature of American life, but the vast population, world economic leadership, and high-heaped wealth of the Gilded Age were something new. So too was the influx of immigrants of chiefly peasant stock from the poorest countries of Europe and Asia, the conquest of the deserts and mountains of the Far West, the invasion of the Pacific, and the shift from an overwhelmingly rural to a preponderantly urban society that took place during the second half of the century. In no country at any time had material change occurred more rapidly or more fully absorbed the energies of a people. In its Gilded Age, America was a study in growth and transformation.

So much change was not necessarily conducive to the progress of thought and art. It is interesting to note that even in science the heroes of Gilded America were not giants of pure research but men of invention and technology. One is hard-pressed to think of any American scientist equal to Darwin or Pasteur or Helmholtz during this period, but who is likely to forget Bell and his telephone, Edison and his electric light, the Wrights and their airplane, Ford and his assembly-line automobiles? Americans of the half-century invented the typewriter, the phonograph, the submarine, the machine gun, and a variety of other technological curiosities from air conditioning to zippers.

Fortuitously, by the time romanticism had run its course in American culture, the most widely discussed variety of positivist thought accessible to readers in the English-speaking world was Darwinian biology. With its timely emphasis on change, progress, struggle, and material forces, Darwinism became an instant success in the American thought-world, more so than anywhere else in Western civilization, not excluding Britain itself. The evolutionist gospel also reached America in the variant form of the synthetic philosophy of Herbert Spencer, and Spencer, too, was received with more enthusiasm in the New World than in his own.

In the result, the idea of evolution became the common denominator of practically all the philosophical, theological, and social thought of the late nineteenth and early twentieth centuries, although very little of that thought has survived the scrutiny of later generations. A typical evolutionist and fervent admirer of Spencer was John Fiske, whose *Outlines of Cosmic Philosophy* (1874) and later writings earned him a reputation as a deep thinker that he probably did not deserve. The Berkeley geologist Joseph Le Conte was another prophet, hailing evolution as "glad tidings of great joy which shall be to all peoples. Woe is me, if I preach not the Gospel." Both men extracted from their faith in evolution a confirmation at higher levels of the core truths of Christian theism, as did the numerous evolutionary theologians of the day, such as Francis Howe Johnson and Minot J. Savage.

The quasi-idealist belief that evolution was God's true mode of creation, now at last revealed by the Book of Nature, enjoyed wide currency in the Gilded Age. It reveals a thick residue of romanticism in the late nineteenth-century American psyche, but it also reminds us once again of the fundamental difference between the European and American ecclesiastical establishments. In Europe the churches remained for the most part hopelessly entangled in reactionary politics; in America the many denominations were like rival corporations or trade unions, well integrated into the structure of modern life. The defiant atheism and anticlericalism of European radicals and even many liberals had few echoes in the United States. The American God was as smart and up-to-date as a Model T.

The social thinkers of the positivist age in the United States offered rather more substantial fare than the philosophers of evolutionary naturalism, but Darwin and Spencer inspired them to much the same degree. American anthropology was founded by Lewis Henry Morgan, whose *Ancient Society* (1877) deeply impressed Marx and Engels and was the first serious effort to explain the origins of civilization from an evolutionary perspective. Morgan's counterparts in economics and sociology were William Graham Sumner and Lester Ward, shortly followed by Albion Small, F. H. Giddings, and Thorstein Veblen, a constellation of intellects comparable to the social scientists of any European country during the Age of Improvement.

At the same time positivism made deep inroads into American historiography. The turn from romanticism began with German-trained scholars such as Herbert Baxter Adams, who brought the methods of German scientific history to the New World. The outstanding historians of the positivist era were Adams's student Frederick Jackson Turner, well remembered for his geographical explanation of the regional differences in American history, and another Adams, the formidable Henry Adams, who attempted to derive laws of historical development from physics. Positivism was further represented in American social thought by the Marxism of Daniel De Leon, the legal naturalism of Oliver Wendell Holmes, Jr., and the racism of Josiah Strong and Nathaniel Shaler.

One more strand in the thought of the positivist era in America requires special mention: the emergence of pragmatism. Although science and evolution counted for as much in the development of pragmatism as of any other school of thought during the period, pragmatism moved along lines that were uniquely its own, anticipating both the logical empiricism and the existentialism of twentieth-century philosophy. In the context of the late nineteenth century, pragmatism was an American cousin of the critical positivism of Mach and Avenarius.

Founded by the mathematician and logician Charles Sanders Peirce, and continued by William James and John Dewey, the pragmatist school dismissed as fallacious the assumption of the more naïve varieties of positivism that the natural sciences could give human beings a finished portrait, as it were, of the material universe. Evolutionary theory itself disputed such a view of the cosmos. The cosmos—like Gilded America!—was not a frozen chunk of matter, but a fluid process of unending change, a complex of phenomena in action and movement with no predetermined goal. In James's phrase, both materialism and idealism had posited a "block universe." But the pragmatists preferred the image of an evolving universe, open to the play of chance and will, in which almost anything could happen. At the bottom of their thought rested the familiar dictum of Anglo-Saxon empiricism that all knowledge consisted of experience. If so, why not say that reality itself consisted of experience, defined not as consciousness in the manner of subjective idealism, but as something objectively real?

But if we can agree that the world can be reduced to experience, then we must be able to submit all theories of it, including ethical theories, to the test of practicality, and herein lay the philosophical scandal of pragmatism. The pragmatists proposed that the proof of human knowledge was in the doing rather than in the thinking. In Peirce's original formula, which James and Dewey expanded, the meaning of a concept was our idea of its consequences. If no practical difference could be discovered between two concepts, if they made no difference in the real world of experience, then there was no difference between the concepts at all. As Dewey later phrased it, the true is the successful.

At one level, pragmatism was only a more radical form of empiricism, and fully in accord—as its protagonists always claimed—with scientific method, which requires that every theory "work," that its predictions be correct when tested in the world of measurable experience. At another level, one cannot overlook the European criticism of pragmatism that it was only a clever way of gaining the endorsement of philosophy for the American worship of profit and progress, and in particular for the anti-intellectualism of the Gilded Age, which cared little how a thing was done so long as it made money. Pragmatism was the philosophy of a society of inventors rather than a society of scientists. It also, in the Jamesian version, bordered perilously on idealism in its emphasis on the power of the will and in its doctrine of the "finite God," the deity who struggles alongside man to make a better world. At James's end of pragmatism, it merged with Bergsonian vitalism and became part of the irrationalist rebellion against positivism, although Dewey did much to give it a more credibly scientific basis.

As for literature and art, few critics have made extravagant claims for the aesthetic culture of positivist America, but its showing was at least as good as Germany's during the same period, and perhaps better. Realism arrived in American letters in the 1860s with the first published works of Mark Twain, William Dean Howells, and Henry James. Howells and James excelled in fastidious analyses of middle-class life; Twain was almost an American Dickens. America's "naturalist" generation came much later, in the 1890s, with the measurably lesser work of Hamlin Garland, Frank

Norris, Stephen Crane, and Theodore Dreiser. Most surprising was the plethora of first-rate American painters. Although several of them lived and worked chiefly in Europe, they were a brilliant group. Thomas Eakins and Winslow Homer painted American life with uncompromising objectivity. Among the expatriates, James Whistler and John Singer Sargent worked chiefly in London, on the outer fringes of realism, and Mary Cassatt joined the French Impressionists, painting in a style not unlike that of her friend Degas.

All things considered, the minor figures together with the major, freelancers and journalists as well as academicians, both émigrés and those who clung to the native sod, positivism enjoyed a deep and broad success in American life. Despite both French and German influence, the closest comparison was still with British thought. Evolution came to America from Britain; pragmatism recalled British Utilitarianism and was even successfully exported to Britain, where F. C. S. Schiller taught his own version of it for many years at Oxford. Both countries were rich, powerful, and heavily industrialized during the Age of Improvement, reflecting their affluence in schools of social thought that identified capitalism with the natural order of things. It cannot be a coincidence that when irrationalism began to challenge positivism for the mastery of the Western mind, it was the two English-speaking countries that provided the stoniest soil for its growth.

Summation

Even during the palmiest days of the romanticist rebellion, forces were at work in Western civilization that made the replacement of romanticism as its dominant world view inevitable. On the heels of political revolution and reaction came the culminating event in centuries of capitalist enterprise: the Industrial Revolution. Beginning in Great Britain and spreading throughout the continents of Europe and North America in the middle decades of the nineteenth century, the industrialization process completed the destruction of the feudal-aristocratic system. But in so doing, it rehabilitated the values of the avant-garde of the preceding century: the modernizing values of reason, science, objectivity, secularism, and utility. At the same time, a second Scientific Revolution occurred in France and Britain, reaching academic Germany in midcentury, yielding fundamentally new knowledge of the material universe, and especially the organic universe, which further undermined the authority of the romanticist world view.

We have defined the successor of romanticism as "positivism," the world view that limits human knowledge to the data of experience as organized by the empirical sciences, thereby ruling theology and metaphysics invalid, or subsuming their problems into physics, biology, and sociology. Positivism is the rationalism of the Enlightenment in a somewhat less ambitious but also more radically "modern" form: more consistently humanistic, secularist, utilitarian, and keyed to the methods of natural science. An alternative label for it, perhaps equally appropriate, is "scientism."

Positivism originated in France and Britain during the romanticist period as an organic continuation of the thought of the late Enlightenment. Its founders were natural scientists, political economists, and social philosophers, of whom the most seminal figures were Saint-Simon in France and Bentham in Britain. The first full generation of positivists emerged in midcentury; their intellectual leaders were Comte and Mill. In Germany positivism began as a radical offshoot of the Hegelian movement of the 1830s headed by Strauss and Feuerbach. German positivism soon hardened into the "materialism" of the 1850s. Positivism invaded Russia in the mid-1850s and the United States after the Civil War. In the arts and letters, positivism expressed itself as a "realist" rebellion against romanticism. Flaubert and Courbet were the Hugo and the Delacroix, respectively, of the new realist sensibility in France. They had counterparts in every country.

As the positivist world view unfolded, it became involved in a variety of causes. Its left wing took up the advancement of an ideology born under romanticist stars, socialism, and gave it harder-headed formulations, especially in the so-called scientific socialism of Marx and Engels. Theological radicals used positivism as a weapon against Christian faith, seeking to ground the Western psyche in the atheistic humanism implicit, so they believed, in the findings of modern science. Positivism also served the needs of the rising bourgeoisie. It was enlisted in allegedly scientific defenses of capitalism, civil liberties, racism, and imperialism. The biological theory of evolution, which dominated social thought in the second half of the positivist era, especially in the English-speaking and German-speaking worlds, similarly cut leftward and rightward. Both camps found aid and comfort in its putative ethical consequences. Aesthetic culture moved in the 1870s and 1880s from the earlier realism to a "naturalism" that emphasized the determination of man's fate by environment, heredity, and chance.

Of the five great national cultures, the French and British were best suited by their histories and situations to warm to the positivist message. They assimilated it with little struggle, the French showing a greater interest in its applications in government and social reconstruction, the British rejoicing in its support of capitalism, liberalism, and—later—the British imperial mission. American positivism closely resembled the British variety. It diffused widely through American life, although it seldom generated creative work of a caliber comparable to the culture of romanticism.

In Germany, positivism originated in bitter liberal-radical disillusionment during the repressive era of Metternich. The first Russian positivists were mostly opponents of the czarist establishment who fought for fundamental changes in the sociopolitical order, taking up the cause of the Westernizing party of earlier times. In both Germany and Russia, the new world view had to exert itself against a powerful Christian and romanticist undertow. But everywhere, elements of the romanticist world view persisted, even in the most fiercely positivist minds. The mark of romanticism is clearly visible in the thought of such otherwise archetypical positivists as Comte, Mill, Marx, Spencer, Lavrov, and Peirce. The historicism of Herder and Hegel illustrates an essentially romanticist insight that lived on, in various modes, in positivist thought.

Toward the end of the positivist era, as near the end of the Enlightenment, internal criticism of the premises of the reigning world view diminished its self-confidence. As Hume and Kant had subverted rationalism from within, so the critical empiricism of Mach and Avenarius and the pragmatism of Peirce and James helped to undermine positivism. But in its time, it met the requirements of the new classes of industrial Europe and America, both capitalists and workers. In Marxism it also gave rise to a philosophy and social science whose value to civilization extends far beyond the Age of Improvement, a system of thought that is rapidly becoming the dominant ideology of postmodern humanity.

Chapter Five

Irrationalism: The World View of the Age of Anxiety, 1890–1970

Overview

"To begin with," says Jean-Paul Sartre, "man is nothing. He will not be anything until later, and then he will be what he makes of himself. Thus, there is no human nature, because there is no God to have a conception of it. Man simply is." If Sartre's critics protest against the "subjectivity" of such a teaching, he replies: you are right! "Man is, indeed, a project which possesses a subjective life, instead of being a kind of moss, or a fungus or a cauliflower." Before he wills himself to be, "nothing exists; not even in the heaven of intelligence."

Note that for Sartre intelligence is a mere "heaven." The rational order resembles a dream, a fantasy shimmering in the clouds. Nothing ultimately matters for an earth-bound mortal but his own consciousness as it wills and acts in the world of time. Outside consciousness lies only in what Albert Camus chose to call "the absurd." Such absurdity confronts us unblinkingly, like the rock that Sisyphus rolls up his hill in hell. But not to worry. "There is no fate that cannot be surmounted by scorn."

Sartre and Camus speak for the world view that began to grow from the decaying remains of romanticism in the middle of the nineteenth century. It had captured the intellectual and artistic avant-garde of Europe by the 1890s, and although it has never enjoyed the universal allegiance won by its predecessors, its position as the most characteristic world view of the twentieth century is incontestable—at least for the countries of the European mainland. In the English-speaking world and in Russia since 1917, positivism has continued to muster impressive forces. The outcome of the ideological warfare in these outlying districts of Western civilization remains uncertain.

Finding a name for the world view of the Age of Anxiety shrinks all our previous terminological embarrassments to insignificance. H. Stuart Hughes has furnished a useful inventory of the possibilities in his *Conscious-*

ness and Society. We may call it "neoromanticism," "neomysticism," "anti-intellectualism," "antipositivism," or "irrationalism."[1] These are not different labels for the same jar of pickles, but alternative ways of understanding the nature of twentieth-century Western culture. Each points to a somewhat different assortment of thinkers, writers, and artists.

Hughes opts for "antipositivism," a good choice for him, since his project was an analysis of the work of only one generation, the thinkers who reached maturity in the 1890s and led the intellectual and artistic rebellion that overthrew the reign of positivism in France, Germany, and Italy between 1890 and 1930. For Western civilization as a whole and for the twentieth century as a whole, I prefer "irrationalism." The struggle against positivism has continued, but it is no longer a rebellion so much as an interminable civil war, and in any event a world view should consist of more than opposition to another world view. Irrationalism is the proclamation and, in many instances, the celebration of unreason. It is the world view that returns to the romanticist definition of consciousness as will and feeling and goes further to argue the radical irrationality of all being. It has generated a bewildering array of conflicting ethical, political, metaphysical, and religious positions. Its common denominators are few, but the most original and distinctive movements in contemporary culture descend from it or unintendingly confirm its deepest insights.

Irrationalism, in short, holds that man and the world so far as it can be known are not fundamentally governed by reason. Whatever meaning or reality anything possesses can best be revealed by faculties that transcend or bypass discursive reason and empirical science. Irrationalism has helped produce existentialism and phenomenology, the neo-orthodox theologies, modern vitalism and mysticism, and the neo-idealist movement in philosophy of history. It has influenced most twentieth-century schools of psychology and psychoanalysis and undergirds some of the most powerful currents of thought in the social sciences. It is the world view of fascism, but also of certain deviant varieties of modern socialism and the radical counterculture of the 1950s and 1960s. It has inspired fin-de-siècle aesthetic decadence, symbolism, surrealism, expressionism, the modern psychological novel, the theater of the absurd, and the numerous neoromantic and nihilist new waves in art, literature, and music since World War II.

Even positivism, whether it wishes to do so or not, comes to the support of irrationalism in the Age of Anxiety. Through the ingenious labors of experimental and theoretical physicists, twentieth-century science has uncovered a universe that does not conform to humanly meaningful models of order and rationality. Logical positivism and linguistic analysis, the heirs of nineteenth-century positivist philosophy, have abandoned with thudding finality the search for public truth, meaning, and value, consigning almost all the traditional problems of philosophy to the domain of individual preference or passion. The lesson to be learned from the greater part of twentieth-century positivist science and philosophy is that science and philosophy have no lessons to teach. If you would know how to live, or what to believe, look within yourselves. Nature is not a new Christ, whether Newtonian or Darwinian, that man should bend to imitate, but only nature: arbitrary, opaque, silent as the tomb. In one of his most forlorn passages, Camus asks (and in asking states the modern predicament almost in its entirety), "Of whom and of what indeed can I say: 'I know that!' " Because we know nothing, because all our gods are dead, everything is permitted. Or so we might conclude.

In good measure, irrationalism can even be described as a response to the ultimate implications and logical consequences of positivism. Positivist man, as Nietzsche declared in *The Joyful Wisdom* (1882), murdered his Almighty God without even knowing the mischief he had done or its inevitable effects upon his culture. In the place of God he had installed only the theories of science, which reason itself would sooner or later identify as modern myths, no more binding on conscience than the myths of religion and at their best not always flattering to the racial ego. Historical science disclosed the relativity of all customs and beliefs to their historical milieu. Psychological research unveiled the animal and the infant lurking in every adult human being. Biology traced humankind back through the hairy ape to the scaly fish to the slimy amoeba. If the nineteenth-century positivist harbored few doubts about the essential rightness of things and imagined that he knew all he needed to know, nevertheless there lay at the heart of his thought disquieting implications about human power and man's place in the universe. Whatever such implications the irrationalist rebels against positivism did not perceive, their own neopositivist contemporaries were not slow to draw.

But irrationalism was more than a move in the historic chess game in Western thought between the idealist and the naturalist families of world views. In a sense deeper than most fin-de-siècle decadents could have realized, irrationalism bears witness to the organic degeneration of Western civilization in our time. It is a brilliant, hectic, fever-ridden phenomenon, at one and the same time a final useless effort by the mandarins and blue-bloods of old Europe to resist their engulfment in bourgeois democracy and a symptom of the decay of bourgeois democracy itself as capitalism, hurrying through its life cycle, enters late middle age. Irrationalism has been one long painful howl of dismay. More neurotic than the romanticism it often recalls, it has attacked both the modernization process within capitalism and the Marxist socialism that promises a modernity beyond capitalism. Far more than romanticism, which seldom stepped back except for the purpose of making better forward leaps, irrationalism has been the world view of reaction in its most sinister forms.

Ironically, irrationalism has also nourished movements of radical protest against some of its own most vicious offspring. During World War II it oriented the thinking of fascists, but also of segments of the antifascist underground. It sustained both anti-Semitism and Zionism, and in the postwar era it has contributed more to the shaping of the antibourgeois counter-culture than to the despised liberal establishment. A world view ideally designed for an Age of Anxiety, it must also take responsibility for some of the anxiety of the age.

The correlation between irrationalism and the discontents of modern civilization is apparent from the geography and chronology of its diffusion. Irrationalism originated independently in Germany, France, and Russia in the second half of the nineteenth century. In all three countries, the transition to industrialism and democracy aroused hostility and fear on the part of the older strata of the ruling class and also on the part of many intellectuals who saw modernization as a threat to their privileges and values or to the national "soul."

The problem of the national soul was particularly acute in Germany and Russia, which had keyed their spiritual identities to the romanticist world view and continued in some quarters to wage their old war of ideas against the allegedly materialistic West. Irrationalism also appealed strongly to the avant-garde intellectuals of two countries, Italy and Spain, undergoing national cultural revivals at the end of the century. The fact that both had been strongholds of rationalism during the Renaissance carried little weight in the drastically altered circumstances that now prevailed. Italy and Spain were now weak and backward societies, their old glory gone, suffering from massive national inferiority complexes vis-à-vis their neighbors to the north. France could not enlist in wars against the West, but it too found itself in difficult straits. The humiliation of the defeat by Prussia in 1870, the relative decline of its wealth and population, and the nagging pains of its unstable political life all took their toll of French morale.

But the main point is that in every country of continental Europe, France included, the last decades of the nineteenth century and the first decades of the twentieth were a time when many powerful forces were strenuously resisting the modernization process, or deploring its effects, or both. The first wave of enthusiasm for modernity had receded, leaving behind an assortment of beleaguered landowners, ferociously conservative peasants, hard-pressed petty bourgeois tradesmen and craftsmen, desperately exploited proletarians, and fastidious aesthetes and professors, all of whom felt a sense of loss or impending doom as they beheld the continuing advance of the industrial age. Habits of mind could not adjust rapidly enough to the new order. It demanded an outpouring of egalitarianism and individualism that class-conscious continental Europe, locked into its relatively rigid social structure, could not generate in sufficient quantities at the speed required.

Then came World War I with its attendant horrors, felt more acutely in continental Europe than elsewhere; the rise of the totalitarian superstates of the interwar period; and World War II, also a much greater disaster for continental Europeans than for its other Western combatants. Almost every continental country during the first half of the twentieth century experienced the bitterness of military devastation and defeat, occupation by foreign armies, the abrogation of established civil liberties by totalitarian regimes, and repeated changes of law and government for which the only close parallel in modern history is the revolutionary cycle of 1789-1848.

The contrast between the disorienting facts of continental European history and the course of life in Britain and America during the same period is easy to measure. Both countries, in their separate ways, completed the transition to industrialism with relatively little psychic damage or social resistance or political upheaval. Ruling elites collaborated to make that transition as swift as possible. Industrialism in turn created vast wealth, which the elites—to a degree unprecedented in world history—shrewdly shared with their working classes. Exploitation persisted, but the workers' share (especially in North America) was so high and social mobility so great that many workers had, and often still have, little awareness of their true situation. The Anglo-Saxon countries were also spared the worst effects of total war and the worst brutalities of fascism. Only in recent decades, with Britain's affluence dissipated and America's domestic morale weakened by the Great Depression, racial conflict, and imperialist misadventures, have the English-speaking countries begun to touch the spiritual depths long ago plumbed by continental Europe.

As one might expect, irrationalism has commanded its smallest followings in these same English-speaking countries. Germans, Frenchmen, Russians, and other continentals were its earliest exponents. In irrationalist philosophy and social thought, they have always led the way, with only meager contributions from Anglo-Saxondom. In aesthetic culture, Great Britain followed continental trends fairly closely, especially after 1920. But America's writers and artists trailed far behind, and even when the gap did begin to close, it was at first only through the work of its more distinguished (and scandalous) émigrés.

In its long history, spanning at least three-quarters of a century, irrationalism has passed through three generations. Its great forerunners and founding spirits, analogous to Bentham and Saint-Simon in the history of positivism, were Wilhelm Dilthey and Friedrich Nietzsche in Germany, Sören Kierkegaard in Denmark, Charles Baudelaire in France, and Fyodor Dostoyevsky in Russia. Composed of men and women born between 1850 and 1875, its first complete generation in the German-speaking countries included the philosophers Husserl, Driesch, Klages, Scheler, and Cassirer; the social and psychological thought of Tönnies, Freud, Meinecke, Rickert, Sombart, Weber, Adler, and Jung; the writers George, von Hofmannsthal, Rilke, and Mann; and such artists and composers as Böcklin (born 1827), Klimt, Mahler, R. Strauss, Barlach, and Schönberg. In the French-speaking world, where irrationalism arrived quite early in aesthetic culture, the first generation was on the average slightly older, with birthdates from 1840 to 1875. Among the philosophers under its influence were Fouillée (born 1838), Boutroux, Guyau, Bergson, Blondel, and Le Roy. Its social thinkers included Le Bon, Tarde, Sorel, Lévy-Bruhl, Durkheim, Jaurès, Barrès, and Maurras. The literary advance guard of irrationalism ranged from Villiers de l'Isle Adam (born 1838), Mallarmé, Verlaine, Huysmans, and Rimbaud to Maeterlinck, Rolland, Claudel, Gide, Louÿs, Valéry, Proust, Jarry, and Péguy. In the arts and music, irrationalism found its early champions in Moreau (born 1826), Redon, Rousseau, Gauguin, Debussy, Satie, Matisse, and Rouault.

Russia, guided toward irrationalism by its greatest literary figures, Dostoyevsky and Tolstoy, and by its world-renowned Theosophist Mme. Blavatsky (born 1831), contributed two generations of outstanding irrationalists before the wholesale national conversion to Marxism in the 1920s. The first of the two, with birthdates from 1850 to 1875, included the philosophers Soloviev, Y. Trubetskoy, Shestov, Bulgakov, and Berdyaev; and the writers, artists, and composers Merezhkovsky, Kandinsky, Hippius, Scriabin, Rachmaninov, and Roerich. For Italy, this was the generation of Pareto, D'Annunzio, Croce, Pirandello, and Gentile; for Spain, of Unamuno; for Norway, of Hamsun and Munch; for Holland, of van Gogh.

British thinkers and writers participated in the development of the irrationalist world view from its earliest decades, but they have seldom committed themselves to it as deeply or radically as their continental *confrères*. In the first generation, born between 1850 and 1875, irrationalism figured to some degree in the work of the neo-idealist philosophers, especially Bradley (born 1846), and in the metaphysics of Alexander and Whitehead. It had some impact, as well, on the social psychology of Wallas and McDougall. The Decadents of the 1890s—Wilde, Beardsley, Johnson, and Dowson—were irrationalists. The new world view also gave direction to the vitalism of Shaw, the symbolism of Yeats, and the musical impressionism of Delius. In the United States, William James leaned toward irrationalism, and his former student Gertrude Stein plunged into it headlong: otherwise few Americans born before 1875 figured significantly in its origins.

For Western civilization as a whole, nearly all the members of this first generation had made their mark by the beginning of World War I, and some were long dead when the war came. Their places were filled by a second generation of irrationalists born between 1875 and 1900, no less and perhaps more gifted than the first. The German countries continued to produce the greatest number of philosophers, scientists, and religious thinkers. This was the generation of the new theoretical physics of Einstein, Born, Bohr, Schrödinger, Pauli, and Heisenberg (born 1901), which had irrationalist implications for many laymen. Among its philosophers were N. Hartmann, Jaspers, and Heidegger, together with the neopositivism of Schlick, Wittgenstein, and Carnap, and the Marxists Bloch, Korsch, and Marcuse. Theology in the German-speaking world was carried forward by Schweitzer, Buber, Bultmann, Barth, Tillich, and Brunner. This was the generation of the ideologists of German fascism, Moeller van den Bruck, Hitler, and Rosenberg, and in psychological thought of Rank and the founders of Gestalt psychology, Wertheimer, Koffka, and Köhler. Its sociologists included Michels, Spengler, and Mannheim. Irrationalism permeated the literary art of Hesse, Kafka, Benn, and Jünger and the painting and music of Klee, von Webern, Beckmann, Berg, Kokoschka, Ernst, and Grosz. It was a generation that changed the world.

In the French-speaking countries, the notables in philosophy and theology included Teilhard de Chardin, Maritain, Lecomte du Noüy, and Marcel —all, as it happens, good Catholics. But the chief ornaments of the second irrationalist generation were its writers and artists. Apollinaire, Bernanos, Cocteau, Artaud, Breton, and St.-Exupéry headed the literary contingent; among the artists were Braque, Arp, Duchamp, and Magritte. Russia contributed the art, literature, and music of Blok, Stravinsky, Chagall, Pasternak, Prokofiev, Mayakovsky, Chelishev, and Nabokov. Spain's greatest modern philosopher, Ortega y Gasset, belonged to the second irrationalist generation, as did its incomparable artists Picasso, Gris, and Miró.

British philosophy continued to resist the siren call of irrationalism, but in letters Joyce, Woolf, Hulme, Lawrence, Eliot, and A. Huxley brought the British Isles fully into the modern age. Dunsany, Tolkien, and C. S. Lewis were brilliant fantasists. Collingwood and Toynbee continued the work of Croce and Spengler, respectively, in historical thought. Finally, there were the first American irrationalists: in literature, Pound, e. e. cummings, and Faulkner; and in social and religious thought, irrationalism influenced the political psychology of Lippmann, the theology of Niebuhr, and the eclectic humanism of Krutch and Mumford.

As the work of the first generation was already entering its later stages by the outbreak of World War I, so much of the work of the second was complete by the outbreak of World War II. Following the chronologies of romanticism and positivism, we might have expected the emergence of a new weltanschauung during the 1930s and 1940s, and by 1950, at the latest, the start of a new generation adhering to its values. Instead, all that is clearly visible from our limited perspective is a third, but distinctly inferior, generation of irrationalists, with birthdates ranging from 1900 into the 1930s. Through this assortment of epigones and echoes of the great irrationalist masters, only a few men and women of comparable genius are scattered. Meanwhile, neopositivism and Marxism have continued their sway in much of Anglo-American and Soviet thought.

Of the third-generation irrationalists, the most interesting and coherent group are the French existentialists and dramatists of the absurd, from Sartre, de Beauvoir, and Merleau-Ponty to Genet, Ionesco, and Camus. The

Irish playwright and novelist Beckett also belongs in their company, and perhaps the "new wave" novelists and film makers of the 1950s and 1960s, such as Robbe-Grillet, Butor, Godard, Truffaut, and—in Sweden and Italy —Bergman, Antonioni, and Fellini. Other French irrationalists of the third generation include the novelist Malraux, the artist Dubuffet, the philosopher Mounier, the composer Messiaen, and the social anthropologist Lévi-Strauss.

Elsewhere on the European mainland, the third generation has accomplished very little. Fascism and Stalinism drove the cultures of most of the continental countries into a state of shock from which they have still not recovered. The novels of Böll and Grass in Germany and of Solzhenitsyn in Russia may portend better things to come, but more likely they are late-blooming representatives of a species soon to be extinct.

In the Anglo-Saxon world, somewhat more has happened in the third irrationalist generation. Britain has contributed such writers as Auden, Golding, Durrel, Thomas, Burgess, Pinter, and Stoppard, and in the United States irrationalism has flourished in the work of Burroughs, Bradbury, Vonnegut, Ginsberg, Albee, and Barth. Both countries have also (along with France) fathered several adventurous movements in irrationalist art and music. Such artists as Bacon, Pollock, Motherwell, Lichtenstein, and Warhol have at least kept our eyes open. In sheer variety and audacity of technique, the artists of the third irrationalist generation compare well with their forerunners, although to anyone who remembers Dada and surrealism, the sense of déjà vu is inescapable.

In all this great mass of art and thought, taking the three generations together, I think what stands out most clearly—apart from the underlying theme of irrationalism itself—is the absence of public moorings. Some irrationalists limit themselves to the discovery of unreason in the affairs of humankind or in the cosmos. Others celebrate what they have discovered, reveling in their self-identification with the tidal forces of will, passion, life, history, the *Volk*, or whatever. Much of the conspicuous religiosity of the Age of Anxiety takes the form of a compulsive "leap" into faith, accompanied by scorn for human power and human values. Other irrationalists are embittered atheists, grumbling like the Marquis de Sade at the gods who have deserted them. As Franklin L. Baumer writes, the twentieth century is less an age of faith than an age of longing for faith.[2]

Not that certain favored individuals have failed to find something holy. Many irrationalists of the period since 1890 have made their peace with reality. For every Kafka or Beckett there must be two or three Shaws, Jungs, and Teilhards who offer us their patented formulas for salvation. Each has his disciples. But these are essentially private formulas, too idiosyncratic, except perhaps for those firmly rooted in Christianity, to serve whole populations over long periods of time. Every man has become, as the French vitalist J. M. Guyau once proclaimed, "his own providence." Unreason leads in too many directions to provide the anchorage that the central values of rationalism, romanticism, and positivism, each in its time, did somehow once provide.

The radical uncenteredness of irrationalism is apparent above all in its aesthetic culture. Every previous world view inspired more than one kind of art, literature, and music, as it inspired more than one kind of metaphysics, ethics, and political philosophy. But the varieties of irrationalist aesthetic culture are beyond counting. They disclose a fragmentation of perception, a disjunction from reality, and a chaos of values that in their pooled effect have been catastrophically disorientative for the modern psyche. At its deep end, irrationalist aesthetic culture has even disoriented its public deliberately: the artist, writer, or composer fully comprehend the value confusion of their age and communicate what they perceive in the symbols of their various crafts. A painting, novel, or musical composition that consists only of random bits of paint, language, or sound plainly tells its consumer that the artist no longer has a value system to transmit. The furthest flung experiments of the irrationalists comprise a kind of anti-art. The implications of irrationalism are so nihilistic that it has evolved, by its own internal "logic," into an anti–world view.

But its time is nearly over. Just like the advanced bourgeois society from which it evolved in the late nineteenth century, irrationalism has exhausted its creative potential and will eventually wither and die. Its vitality was, for more than half a century, incontestable. It gave humankind deep glimpses into its own psychic space. It inspired a riotous complexity of images that revolutionized aesthetic culture. It carried segments of the romanticist world view to their ultimate limits. But its main thrust has been reactionary, a hopeless effort to turn back the clock of history, and its passing should not be mourned.

The Revolt of the Mandarins: Germany

The sudden flowering of German industrialism and the equally sudden eruption of German social democracy in the second half of the nineteenth century contributed to what Fritz Ringer has described as a reaction of the mandarinate, a movement of protest against the modern world led chiefly by Germany's academic intellectuals. The "mandarins," he notes, feared the imminent extinction of the social order that sustained the privileges of their class. Professors led the way, supported by bureaucrats, school-masters, clergymen, and the like, all terrified by the dramatic rise to power of industrial magnates at one end of the social scale and unionized, politicized workers at the other.[3] I am reminded of A. J. P. Taylor's quip, in a roughly comparable British context, that all the fashionable talk in academic circles nowadays of the decline of civilization "means only that university professors used to have domestic servants and now do their own washing-up."[4]

In the German-speaking countries, this academic counterrevolution produced the most important and characteristic segment of the intellectual culture of irrationalism. The mandarins, all their respect for scholarship notwithstanding, were profoundly irrationalist. Together with a relatively smaller number of artists, writers, and composers, they made German-speaking Europe the principal arena of irrationalism for some fifty years, from the 1890s to the tragic denouement of 1945. In the irrationalist circus, France and Russia were the side rings, Germany (with Austria) the center ring.

The connection between fear of modernity and irrationalism is one that we have already drawn. From the perspective of anyone alive in the late nineteenth century, modernity meant the world view of physical science, a secular society, the methods of industry and technology, the rationalizing of business and public administration, a realistic art and literature grounded in contemporary themes, and the ideologies of liberalism and socialism. Positivism was the weltanschauung of modernity; irrationalism became the weltanschauung of all those who feared and opposed modernity.

The very suddenness of Germany's entry into the modern era made the experience more traumatic than elsewhere. The mandarins were allowed little time to accommodate their thinking to the new order of things. They feared it for the sake of their social privileges and also because it did not chime with the German national spirit. To the mystics, the Reformers, the Kantians, the idealists, the romanticists, the old Germany of Eckhart and Böhme, Herder and Goethe, positivism was thoroughly alien. Although the natural sciences had been converted, more or less, to the positivist world view in the course of the nineteenth century, academic philosophy never made its peace with positivism; history and the social studies preserved links with earlier values, as did law and theology. Music remained a citadel of romanticist feeling, and the art and literature of the positivist era in Germany was a poor thing compared to the great aesthetic culture of German romanticism. What could the steel barons of Essen or the teeming proletariat of Berlin know about the sources of German greatness? Were they German at all? What had heavy industry and social democracy to do with the German soul?

By the same token, what had they to do with the structure of German society? Of all the economically advanced countries of Europe, Germany was the most rigidly stratified, with the lowest degree of social mobility and the least experience of popular self-government. The German leap into industrialism, and all its attendant social changes, inevitably frightened and perplexed everyone in German society, not only the mandarins of the bureaucracy and the academic world, but also the military elite, the landowners, the farmers and peasants, the petty bourgeoisie, and even the capitalists and workers themselves, who scarcely knew what to do with their immense new power. In point of fact the old classes lost relatively little of their control over German life until the 1920s. They felt threatened, but the institutions and habits of mind necessary to give the new classes their full share of power did not exist until at least the time of the Weimar Republic.

The German experience after 1914, needless to say, also contributed to the unusually powerful grip of irrationalism on the German psyche in the first half of our century. Germany and Austria lost the Great War, after sustaining horrendous casualties. Abortive socialist revolutions in 1918–19 badly scared the ruling classes, and the ruinous inflation of 1923 and the still more ruinous business depression of the early 1930s did nothing to restore confidence. Germany and Austria were stripped of much of their prewar territory and forced to accept a humiliating peace that denied them the means of self-defense. Under the circumstances, which seemed to return Germany to the bleak situation that prevailed in the aftermath of the Thirty Years War, a renewal of the old romanticist "war against the West" was virtually unavoidable. Many Germans, led by their professors, had conducted such a war of ideas in the decades of bitter international tension and rivalry just before 1914, demanding a replacement of Western positivism and materialism by "true" German values. But after 1919 the claims of the German national spirit became even more pressing. The Nazi counterrevolution of 1933 was no more than the voluntary submission of at least half the nation to the subrational logic of those claims. One can imagine regimes equally true to "Germanhood" that would have conducted themselves far less brutally then Hitler's, but he was the most effective politician on the scene in 1933, and despite his madness, authentically German.

In the result, however, Hitler unintendingly stifled and perhaps laid to final rest the German national spirit. By the very violence of his irrationalism, he brought upon Germany a ruin incomparably greater than anything endured in the period between 1914 and 1933. The power of the feudal sector of old German society and also of the mandarinate was broken at last. Part of the country experienced a socialist revolution and emerged as the German Democratic Republic. The rest of it successfully adopted Western capitalism and Western bourgeois democracy, as Weimar for all its efforts never could. The Germany of the post–1945 era bears little comparison, politically or intellectually, with the Germany of old. Irrationalism as a force in the German thought world has faded with astonishing swiftness. National souls die hard, and perhaps this one is far from dead, but for the time being it does not dictate the course of national life.

The chronology of irrationalism in the German-speaking world since 1890 matches its political chronology. Two generations of irrationalists with birthdates from 1850 to 1900 produced an extraordinary volume of high-value work, above all in philosophy and scholarship, the first generation reaching the summit of its powers just before the Great War, the second generation in the interwar years. The first included Freud and Jung, Husserl and Scheler, Meinecke and Weber, Rilke and Mann; in the second were Jaspers and Heidegger, Buber and Barth, Spengler and Hitler, Hesse and Kafka. But for all practical purposes there is no third. The best German minds born after 1900 either stand outside the irrationalist camp, emigrated to other countries during the Nazi years, or were never able to piece their lives together and failed to realize their potential. A few masterworks, such as Günter Grass's novel *The Tin Drum* (1959), do not make a generation.

But while it lasted, the irrationalist movement in German culture was awesome in its creative thrust, drawing not only on the traditional resources of the Hohenzollern Reich, but also on the newly liberated millions of German-speaking Jews, on the prosperous urban centers of German-speaking Switzerland, and on the German lands of the Austrian empire. About one-half of the leading figures in German thought and culture between 1890 and 1945 were actually Jewish, Austrian, or Swiss. The Nazi führer himself was Austrian, and his chief ideologist, Alfred Rosenberg, was born and raised in Russia. Never before had German *Kultur* owed so much of its brilliance to "outsiders."

In any event, German irrationalism is clearly distinguishable from the irrationalist movements in other countries, in good part because of its affinities with German romanticism. Like much of the thought of the romanticist era, but unlike that of the positivist, its intellectual culture was firmly grounded in the universities, which remained the liveliest in Europe until the Nazi debacle. In common with German romanticism, the central concerns of its thought were ontological and historical, neatly bracketed in the title of Heidegger's *Being and Time* (1927). German irrationalism also followed the problems of theology and psychology to their furthest reaches, but typically from the perspectives of metaphysical and historical inquiry. The shades of Herder, Kant, Fichte, Schelling, and Hegel haunted nearly all German academic thought during the irrationalist era.

German aesthetic culture in the same period was very much a mixed bag. Although its composers, such as Mahler and Schönberg, continued the evolution of German musical romanticism, in literature and art there was a tendency, after the lean years of positivist ascendancy, to follow French models. Nonetheless, artists and writers in the German-speaking countries were centrally involved in all the major innovative movements in Western irrationalist culture.

But the heart and soul of the mandarin reaction in Germany was its academic philosophy, where irrationalism inspired an efflorescence comparable in genius to the movement that extended from Kant to Schopenhauer in the romanticist era. The advance guard of German irrationalist philosophy, and German irrationalism generally, was furnished by several thinkers born well before 1850 who swam against the prevailing currents of Bismarckian thought. Some had no direct progeny and need hardly be mentioned, such as the lugubrious Eduard von Hartmann, a follower of Schopenhauer, and the neo-idealist religious philosopher Rudolf Eucken, nowadays forgotten in spite of his Nobel prize for literature (awarded in 1908). But two others, less well known in their own lifetimes, are today generally recognized as the chief mentors of German irrationalism: Wilhelm Dilthey and Friedrich Nietzsche.

Born in 1833, Dilthey was a contemporary of such doughty positivists as Ernst Haeckel and Eugen Dühring and felt drawn to positivism himself in his youth. Kant also influenced him, but in his mature thought he criticized Kant for reducing man to a machine for reasoning. The search for knowledge, Dilthey insisted, involved not the brain alone, but the whole person as it strives to grasp the world in its fullness. Although reason may suffice for physics or biology, in the "spiritual" sciences (*Geisteswissenschaften*), the sciences concerned with man and his history, the way to knowledge is empathy and intuition. From his theory of knowledge, Dilthey went on to a definition of man as indefinable save through his actions and thoughts in their total sociohistorical context. "What man is, only his history tells." Yet history itself was not a fixed body of rational knowledge, but a historical process in its own right, as historically conditioned scholars attempted to relive past life in their own consciousness.

Dilthey emerged from his charting of the spiritual sciences a confirmed relativist, amazed and delighted by the fecundity of life. Infinitely meaningful, life had no single, rationally demonstrable meaning. In the same way, the three varieties of world view that he identified (see my discussion of them in Chapter 1) were all of equal validity. In his optimistic nineteenth-century consciousness, Dilthey could not have known it, but his thought helped lead to the flattening out and even annihilation of value characteristic of twentieth-century irrationalism. If all life expressions are equally valid and meaningful, one can just as easily argue that all life expressions are equally invalid and meaningless. From Dilthey to Dada was not, after all, such a big step.

But Dilthey was largely neglected during his own quiet lifetime as a university professor at Breslau and later Berlin. As with Kant, his revolutionary ideas were expressed in the baffling jargon of a German mandarin, and only after his death in 1911 did he begin to wield a major influence. The parallels with his younger compatriot Nietzsche are striking. Both men were little known during their lives, and both were academics. Although Nietzsche taught philology rather than philosophy and retired from academic service after only ten years at Basel, he was an exceptionally brilliant scholar, described by his own mentor, Friedrich Ritschl, as the best student he had seen in forty years of teaching. Like Dilthey, Nietzsche was essentially a philosopher of life, an irrationalist who interpreted the systems of philosophers as so many verbal monuments to their own egos. Life was the "will to power," a passion to grow, thrive, and acquire mastery over oneself. Philosophers, he contended, should be creators of value, not mirrors of the values of their age.

Nietzsche carried the ethical implications of his thought much further than Dilthey, avoiding the technical language of the older man, but exceeding him in boldness of vision. His central idea was the *Übermensch*, the "superman," a distant echo of the world-historical hero in Hegel's philosophy, possessed of a will so powerful that it transcended every circumstance, defied tradition, and legislated for itself alone. At the heart of Nietzsche's thought was an intuition of the final collapse of all the truth-claims of Western philosophy and religion. Reason had failed, revelation had failed, and only the will of higher men could carve paths through the chaos that remained. There had been such supermen before, most recently during the Renaissance celebrated by Nietzsche's one-time colleague at Basel, Jacob Burckhardt. They might be numerous again, and soar higher then ever, in the next century, if the West did not fall into the dehumanizing dead end that had already trapped China. Nietzsche, the mandarin *malgré lui*, the champion of elitist reaction against modernity, entertained a typically Western contempt for his own Asian prototype.

But from Dilthey and Nietzsche descended nearly all the master themes of later German irrationalism. Their influence on psychology, phenomenology, existentialism, historical thought, theology, and irrationalist literature is incalculable. Dilthey in his tortuous abstractions and Nietzsche in the enigmatic passions of his inimitable prose-poetry recalled two full generations of Germans to the old haunts of their national spirit.

The impetus given to German thought at the beginning of the irrationalist period by Dilthey and Nietzsche did not, however, ensure a uniformity of approach even in the lofty realms of academic philosophy. There turned out to be much less unity than in the golden age of German idealism, and few of the systems proposed were unambiguously antirationalist or even antipositivist. In the first full generation of the irrationalist period, the best examples of philosophical irrationalism in the strictest sense were Ludwig Klages, who saw the rational mind as a dangerous intruder into the harmonious, vibrant life of the soul, and Hans Driesch, the embryologist and vitalist philosopher, who identified an indwelling life force as the motor of all processes above the level of inorganic matter.

Other much discussed systems occupied a middle ground between the extremes of irrationalism and the philosophies of science. One popular approach adopted the slogan "back to Kant," an approach in which Dilthey himself had, in some ways, enthusiastically shared. Neo-Kantian thought rejected the skeptical thrust of positivism and tried, in the spirit of Kant, to find ways of making philosophy possible again, independent of science, but equally objective. Among the most powerful neo-Kantians were the

Marburg school, headed by Hermann Cohen and Paul Natorp, and their still more brilliant disciple Ernst Cassirer, best remembered for his scrupulous analysis of the function of symbolizing in human culture; and the Baden school of Wilhelm Windelband and Heinrich Rickert. Windelband and Rickert did much to revive historicism in German thought, with their quasi-Diltheyan distinction between the generalizing form of scientific discourse and the individualizing form of historical discourse.

No less momentous, and more influential today, was the phenomenological school founded at the turn of the century by Edmund Husserl. Phenomenology cut across the irrationalist-positivist conflict to suggest a new way of linking subjectivity and objectivity: Husserl's self-proclaimed goal was to develop a "scientific" method of describing the essences of all the objects present in human consciousness. His method, somewhat like that of Descartes, required the rejection of all presuppositions and the use of a rigorous process of intellectual intuition through which reality in effect revealed itself. Husserl continued his work well into the twentieth century (he died in 1938), and he also attracted many important followers, including Max Scheler and Ludwig Landgrebe.

Despite the claims of neo-Kantian and phenomenological thought to rationality and objectivity, in the final analysis they both stand nearer to irrationalism than to positivism. Their ultimate master (and Kant's, too) was Plato. In both cases we are given to understand that reality consists of ideas, forms, or essences accessible within consciousness by direct introspection. They both, in I. M. Bocheński's observation, finally "come round to a transcendental idealism."[5] Opposing empiricism, naturalism, and scientific rationalism, they do not say—with pure irrationalism—that the world is subrational or absurd, but they cut loose from the whole scientific enterprise of modern man to return to ancient and primitive man's magical identification of reality and consciousness. It comes as no shock to find that Husserl's last years were devoted in part to the establishment of a liaison between phenomenology and Western religious values, or that Scheler was during his most productive years an Augustinian Christian as well as a follower of Husserl. Ernst Troeltsch even described Scheler as "the Catholic Nietzsche."

In the second generation, born after 1875, came a procession of philosophers just as long as in the first. Irrationalism dominated the "wisdom philosophy" of Count Hermann Keyserling, although his work has not been taken seriously by most academic philosophers. A weighty contribution to ontology and ethics from a mixed Platonist-Aristotelian and Kantian-Hegelian perspective was made by Nicolai Hartmann. But the most original philosophical thought in the second generation, and at all odds the most consistently irrationalist and Nietzschean, was that of the existentialist movement, founded in Germany by Martin Heidegger and Karl Jaspers. From the 1930s to the 1950s, existentialism made a deeper impact on the

European public mind and on literature than any other philosophy since the idealism of the romantic era.

In contrast to the French thinkers who followed them, the German existentialists were above all else metaphysicians. Using a modified version of Husserl's phenomenological method, they discovered the kernel of man's humanity and of being itself in the irreducible and absolute fact of existence. Before a human being, or being itself, could be said to have "qualities," it existed, and its existence was unique, concrete, and subjective, not unlike the events of history in the thought of Dilthey. The mistake of most philosophy was that it converted being and human being into objects with fixed natures or essences. It sought to classify, and not to let being be.

Abstract as Heidegger and Jaspers may appear to the uninitiated, their thought centered on that which is absolutely not abstract and at the same time prior to the categories or rules of reason. Applied to the problems of the outside world, German existentialism urged a life of engagement, of freedom and struggle against all the tendencies in modern civilization that worked to pigeonhole, manipulate, and robotize the human agent. Their most eloquent attack on the dehumanizing forces in modernity was Jaspers's *The Spiritual Situation of the Age* (1931, translated as *Man in the Modern Age*), an indictment of industrial society and the "mass order" worthy of a Thomas Carlyle.

Ironically the same philosophy that inspired Jaspers to adopt an antifascist, anticommunist conservative liberalism led, in Heidegger's case, to overt Nazi sympathies for a short period in the mid-1930s. But nothing in existentialism compels a given political allegiance: the only absolute in existential ethics is the demand, in Heidegger's phrase, "to bear witness to being," which means to act from concrete personal decisions. Conformity to the so-called laws of science or any other prefabricated code of conduct is inauthentic. When bloodless reason, rather than the full man, rules, life is degraded to the level of insecthood.

The other principal new school of philosophy in the second irrationalist generation was irrationalist only in its implications. Descended directly from the nineteenth-century positivism of Comte, Mill, Mach, and Avenarius, it has been variously known as neopositivism, logical positivism, or logical empiricism. In the German countries, it originated in Vienna in the 1920s through the efforts of Moritz Schlick, Rudolf Carnap, and Hans Reichenbach; it also benefited from the incisive thought of Ludwig Wittgenstein, an Austrian philosopher who spent most of his academic years at Cambridge University. Intimately connected as well with the philosophy of Wittgenstein's Cambridge mentor, Bertrand Russell, the new positivism pushed to extremes the antimetaphysical tendencies in nineteenth-century positivism, culminating in the view that only the statements of mathematics and empirical science could be dealt with by the philosopher, whose empire was reduced to the single province of logic.

It followed that since the problems of metaphysics, ethics, aesthetics, theology, political theory, and even epistemology were pseudo-problems, and since all statements in these areas were empty of cognitive content, one's values became a matter of purely personal preference or feeling. Evicted from the mansions of philosophy, judgments about the good, the true, and the beautiful had to find lodging on Mt. Parnassus. The thinkers of the Vienna Circle were not irrationalists themselves, but by limiting philosophy to strictly logical tasks, they gave aid and comfort to the irrationalist cause.

Even the hard sciences have helped promote irrationalist thought in the twentieth century. By a curious reversal, biology has become more and more mechanistic, whereas physics—in the nineteenth century a citadel of mechanistic materialism—has moved steadily closer to organismic or open-ended conceptions in which the old model of the rigid, predetermined cosmic machine no longer seems to work. Most of the best theoretical effort has come from savants in the German-speaking countries, including Max Planck, Albert Einstein, and Werner Heisenberg. Relativity, quantum and field theory, indeterminacy theory, and cosmological speculation have constructed (chiefly in mathematical form) a disjointed universe that lacks the straightforward reasonableness we had come to expect from our natural scientists. The universe, in a word, is no longer picturable; the theories we have, in keeping with neopositivist philosophy of science, are fallible and contingent, and they do not even fit together to provide a unified scientific cosmology.

In the social and behavioral sciences, where again the German-speaking countries led the world in the first two generations of the modern era, the fundamental discovery has been the irrationality of the human animal. The momentous work of the Austrian founder of psychoanalysis Sigmund Freud —his interpretation of dreams, his exploration of the origins of madness and neurosis, his cartography of the unconscious, his theory of human sexuality, his inquiries into precivilized thought—has done more to change Western man's understanding of himself than any other modern thinker. His various followers, such as Alfred Adler, Carl Gustav Jung, and Otto Rank, stressed elements of irrationalism in human psychology that Freud had neglected or ignored.

Of special importance was Jung's investigation of myth and symbol and the roots of religious experience in what he termed the "objective psychic," or, alternately, the "collective unconscious." For Freud unreason was an awesome fact of life which man had to struggle perpetually to bring under rational control, but for Jung spiritual health required submission to the forces of the psychic underworld. Of all irrationalist thinkers, he was one of the most articulately anti-rational, with the true mandarin's deep-seated hatred of modern civilization. By contrast, Freud could almost be described as a latter-day (but somewhat disillusioned) positivist.

At the same time, the exploration of the irrational was pursued in German sociology by Ferdinand Tönnies, Max Weber, Robert Michels, and Karl Mannheim, with varying degrees of personal commitment or antagonism to modernity, and in German historiography by the founders of *Geistesgeschichte*, Dilthey, Friedrich Meinecke, and Ernst Troeltsch. The comprehensive comparative study of world cultures and their historical life cycles by Oswald Spengler in *The Decline of the West* (1918–22) was a transparently irrationalist manifesto inspired by Nietzsche. It idealized the prerational early ages of culture growth and condemned the modern world to a life of increasing artistic and spiritual sterility, ending in the total exhaustion of its genius and, finally, historical death. Spengler's study of cultural configurations was paralleled in psychology by the neoromanticist Gestalt school of Max Wertheimer, Wolfgang Köhler, and Kurt Koffka.

Although many irrationalists in the German countries felt nothing but horror and disgust for Hitlerism, it also sprang organically from the irrationalist movement in German thought, and it also constituted—among other things—a scream of protest against the modern world. Hitler and his more devoted followers dreamed of a new pagan Reich, guided by the dark, subrational forces of the German folkish soul, by instinct, will, and warrior virtues, in which the artificiality of modern urban civilization would be counterbalanced by the more organic life of a sturdy peasantry planted in Greater Germany's expanded living space. Hitler's political psychology, his reading of history, his policies as führer, and his whole world view were the epitome of German irrationalism.

Scraps of Herder, Fichte, Hegel, Schopenhauer, Nietzsche, Dilthey, and Spengler may be detected, usually in second-hand or third-hand versions, in the meager literature of Nazism, but its more direct sources were such folkish philosophers of the late nineteenth and early twentieth centuries as the cultural historian H. S. Chamberlain and the swarm of minor ideologues inventoried in George L. Mosse's illuminating volume, *The Crisis of German Ideology*.[6] Well into the 1920s many German social prophets were still developing political credos parallel to Hitler's from the same raw materials that he used—for example, Arthur Moeller van den Bruck in his irrationalist tract *The Third Reich* (1923). The Hitler phenomenon reflected some of the deepest tendencies in German thought, and it was no coincidence that many of Germany's highly educated mandarins embraced or at least tolerated it during the twelve years of its enshrinement as the nation's official faith.

The same fear of the disorienting, fragmenting, and uprooting effects of modern industrial society that herded millions of Germans into the outstretched arms of Adolf Hitler sent others stumbling back to Christianity. The 1920s and 1930s in particular were a period of reawakening of the German religious conscience and German theology that few students of intellectual history would have predicted in the years of growing infidelity before World War I. Even Nietzsche's awful proclamation of the death of

God was enlisted in the service of the revival. The old God, said the preachers, was indeed dead. God-consciousness had been obliterated by a century of cowardly compromise on the part of the churches with the secularizing forces in modern history. Instead of fighting back, Christianity had become liberal and worldly, identifying the progress of science and industry and the national state with the coming of God's kingdom on earth, as in the "positive" or "social" theology of Albrecht Ritschl and Adolf von Harnack. It was time now to abandon the ersatz God of progress and return to the transcendental Almighty Father of Augustine and Luther. It was time, especially after the catastrophe of 1914, to listen to the word of God.

The chief prophet of this neo-orthodox movement in Christianity during the interwar years was the Swiss Calvinist preacher and theologian Karl Barth. His message was implacably irrationalist. Not only did Christians have to stop worshiping the false God of modern civilization: Barth demanded that theology break off its post-Kantian alliance with philosophic idealism and rationalism and return post haste to its primitive function of interpreting the Bible. Man's word, whether street talk or the clever jargon of philosophy, could never be more than the word of a proud, sinful, fallen, clay-footed creature who had no power to save itself and had no worth apart from its creator.

But Barth and his associates in postwar neo-orthodoxy were not so unworldly that they could resist the temptation to invade academe. University-trained themselves, Teutonic mandarins in fiber and soul, they spared no effort to capture the theology faculties of the German universities. Barth left his working-class congregation in Switzerland in 1921 to accept a chair at Göttingen, later teaching at Münster, Bonn, and Basel. His able compatriot Emil Brunner joined the professoriate in 1924 at Zürich, after a similar early career in the ministry. Between them, Barth and Brunner produced scores of volumes of academic theology that tended to mellow over the years, although it never lost its mooring in the radical irrationalism of the Reformed gospel.

Their most brilliant German colleague, Rudolf Bultmann, was a professor all his life, primarily of New Testament studies. At Marburg, however, where he taught from 1921 to 1951, he fell under the enchantment of Heidegger's existentialism. Defying Barth's warnings against philosophy, he developed in later years an influential quasi-existentialist theology that preserved many of the insights of neo-orthodox faith in a "demythologized" form that took full account of modern historical scholarship. Since Heidegger's thought was itself irrationalist, Bultmann could well argue its eligibility for marriage to Christian theology.

Many other names could be mentioned, including that of Paul Tillich, who executed a still more difficult fusion of existentialism with neo-orthodoxy and the romanticist philosophy of Schelling. But all the ferment in German theology after 1914 had the same ultimate goal. With or without aid from philosophy, its hope was to appease the spiritual hunger of a generation that had become massively disillusioned with the modern world. It was irrationalist, nostalgic, and at least in an intellectual sense reactionary, harking back to a God-consciousness that was truly dead and all but impossible to resurrect.

Our lengthy journey through the groves of German academe in the irrationalist era leaves us little space for the prodigious achievement of German aesthetic culture in the same period. The somewhat numbing effect of Bismarckian-Wilhelmine imperialism and materialism on artistic life did not wear off in time for the German countries to establish themselves in the vanguard of irrationalist aesthetic culture in the 1880s and 1890s, but they lagged only a decade or so behind their French neighbors.

On one front, they did not lag at all. Profiting from more than a century of leadership in European music, they continued to blaze trails during the first two generations of the irrationalist ascendancy. From the midcentury masters Wagner, Bruckner, and Brahms, the initiative passed to three brilliant Wagnerians, Gustav Mahler, Richard Strauss, and Arnold Schönberg. All three were models of irrationalism. Their uneasy synthesis of Nietzschean titanism, decadent world-weariness, neoromantic religiosity, nature-worship, and folkish themes ran the gamut of irrationalist moods in such masterpieces as Mahler's *The Song of the Earth* (1908), Strauss's *Thus Spake Zarathustra* (1896), and Schönberg's *Gurrelieder* (1900–1911). Aided by his disciples Anton von Webern and Alban Berg, Schönberg also turned in mid-career to the development of the twentieth century's most important musical innovation, atonalism, the counterpart in music to abstract expressionism in art. The atonal scores of Schönberg and his followers, although devoid of the old Wagnerian lushness, are not less irrationalist than his early romantic works. They testify in chilling explicitness to the fragmentation, value relativity, and anxiety of the modern conscience.

German literature, after the drabness of the positivist era, returned to new glory at the turn of the century. The German countries imported symbolism, the first great movement in irrationalist literature, from France, and they also had a share in the "decadent" sensibility of fin-de-siècle art and literature. Symbolism came to Germany through the quasi-priestly offices of Stefan George, who was exposed to the symbolist vision of poetry through association with Mallarmé and others in Paris during his formative years. In the 1890s George emerged as the head of a "circle" (*der George-Kreis*) that aimed at the spiritual regeneration of Germany through an elitist cult of beauty and austerity. George and his followers displayed a mandarin horror of modern science and industry; his ideals were mystical, medieval, and Greek in a combination reminiscent of Nietzsche; he composed the finest poetry in the German language since Heine. The poetic revival was continued by two Austrians, Hugo von Hofmannsthal and Rainer Maria Rilke, and a little later by "the German Eliot," Gottfried Benn.

The German-speaking world also produced three novelists of universal stature in Thomas Mann, Hermann Hesse, and Franz Kafka. Mann was a

Goethe of the Freudian age, Hesse a Jungian mystic, Kafka a tormented prophet of the absurd. All three conveyed in at least part of their work the spiritual vacuum in which twentieth-century man gasps for life's breath. Hesse, with his religious sensibility, indicated mystical escape routes. Kafka's characters remain suspended in a nightmarish void of futile expectation, and Mann offered a bewildering variety of perspectives, both for and against irrationalism. Only in exile from Nazi Germany after 1933 did Mann manage to fight his way to a defense of reason and humane values, somewhat in the spirit of the German Enlightenment. Mann's *Joseph* novels of 1933–43 represent a hard-won but very late triumph of the German artistic conscience over the irrationalism that shackled it through two fateful generations.

The period from 1890 to 1933 was also a time of renascence in German art. Its most characteristic school was "expressionism," a movement that saw the arts as a medium for revealing the inner psychic and emotive life. German expressionist art, as in the work of Ernst Barlach, Max Beckmann, and Oskar Kokoschka, produced images of extraordinary visual force. The Austrian painter Gustav Klimt was a major exponent of decadent sensualism at the turn of the century, and the deliberately nonsensical art of the Dadaists was well represented in Germany by Max Ernst and Kurt Schwitters. The three "junk cathedrals" (*Merzbauten*) of Schwitters, although only the third has survived the vicissitudes of time, are bold monuments to twentieth-century irrationalist nihilism.

All in all, the irrationalist epoch in German academic and aesthetic culture was an incredible time, not only in German history but in the history of humanity. Perhaps never before have so many redoubtable talents flourished in a single culture in so few years. Never has there been such a determined flight from reality, never a deeper exploration of the underworld of the mind, never a broader-ranging effort to encompass the whole of cosmic being, never more violence and madness and reaction and despair. The peculiar nexus of circumstances that made German irrationalism possible will, one hopes, never occur again in human affairs, but it is difficult not to feel a certain awe in contemplating what did occur, for two brief generations, in the heart of twentieth-century Europe.

The Vital Thrust: France

History is retrospective prophecy, but a scholar forecasting the progress of French thought and art in the year 1880 would quite likely have anticipated several more decades of positivist ascendancy. The romanticist movement had faded only thirty years before. Zola and Taine were at the zenith of their powers. The latest major movement in art, Impressionism, demanded objectivity and gloried in everyday scenes. The Third Republic, after an inauspicious start, was about to enter its second decade, fortified with a new constitution breathing the spirit of 1789, relieved by the timely resignation of its royalist president MacMahon, and safely on its way to becoming a business-minded, progress-minded, modern-minded liberal democracy. Although no longer the wealthiest or the biggest country in Europe, France remained fundamentally prosperous and solid. No less a man than Prince Bismarck kept alive a healthy fear of French arms, in spite of the victories he had fashioned ten years before. In light of the French national spirit, with its long established respect for reason, order, and science, we should have expected the irrationalist world view to arrive late, fare poorly, and exit promptly. The very term *irrationalism* seems to be a contradiction of the best and highest traditions in *la civilisation française.* In a country where every restaurant is ablaze with light and even romantic verse is often composed according to the strict rules of classical prosody, what market can there be for "irrationalism"?

Yet irrationalism did come to France. It arrived early, fared well, and still persists. The France of Descartes, Voltaire, and Comte became the France of Bergson, Proust, and Sartre. All the characteristic features of irrationalist thought and sensibility found expression in French culture after 1880: radical subjectivity, dependence on intuition and mystical illumination, stress on the rule of unreason in human and cosmic affairs, religious revivals, fragmentation of the artistic consciousness, renewed high valuation of romanticist culture, fierce hostility to positivism and modernity. In the arts and letters, French irrationalism surpassed that of any other country, and during the third irrationalist generation, the generation that came to maturity in the 1940s, France replaced Germany as the principal center of Western irrationalist culture in all departments.

In trying to account for the success of French irrationalism, several qualifying remarks need to be made at the start. By no means all of late nineteenth- and twentieth-century French thought and art succumbed to irrationalism. Especially in history and the social sciences, the irrationalist impulse has been kept under control, and France is the leading country in the postwar wave of neopositivist scholarship in these fields. Wherever irrationalism has prevailed in France, it has usually done so with more restraint, clarity of expression, and urbanity than elsewhere. The German preoccupation with ontological problems and also with speculative philosophy of history finds only an occasional echo in French irrationalism. For the French, as during the romanticist era, the primary issues have been the possibilities of the self in relation to the larger life of society. The powerful radical thrust in French thought has also affected the quality of its irrationalism. The Right has often exploited irrationalist themes, but the Center and the Left have used them as well, so that in the French context irrationalism is not necessarily or even primarily a handmaiden of political reaction.

All the same, there can be no question that the vogue of irrationalism correlates with the failures of nerve in the national experience since 1880 or 1890. Even at its most optimistic and virile, French irrationalism has tended to serve as a vehicle for expressing disillusionment with typically French values. Consciously or unconsciously, it has been a reflection of national anxiety. Intellectuals and artists have favored irrationalism precisely because it offers more cogent explanations of, and more drastic remedies for, the procession of national disasters that have made Frenchmen so unhappy with France, not to mention modern civilization, in the past hundred years.

Modern civilization has been disappointing enough, but to its discontents has been added, in France, the piecemeal decline of ancient glory that began with the overwhelming defeat of the armies of Napoleon III in the summer war of 1870 against Prussia. The war heralded a fundamental change in power relationships in modern Europe. France's population growth came almost to a halt in the second half of the nineteenth century, while the other great powers were still expanding; in industrial development the Third Republic dropped far behind Germany, America, and its old rival Britain. The relatively stronger position in France of the small independent peasant, the artisan, and the small businessman not only created a poor economic climate for industrial growth. It produced a society unreceptive alike to proletarian socialism and aggressive capitalism, a society too much dominated by its great capital city to take on a clearly agrarian character and too agrarian to adopt the institutions and mind-set of twentieth-century urbanism, a society too individualistic to resort to dictators but too class-conscious and politically inexperienced to make democracy in any of its forms work well. The outcome was economic, political, and military weakness vis-à-vis the other great powers, and chronic political instability at home. While the rest of industrial Europe marched, for better or worse, into the twentieth century, France was a case of arrested development, great of mind and heart, but small of body.

After 1890, the calamities came thick and fast. The Panama scandal of 1892–93 shook public confidence in the political system. The Dreyfus affair illuminated with a piercing light the deep divisions within French society, as did the later battles over the disestablishment of the Church. In World War I, France suffered horrendous losses; it emerged victorious, but thanks only to massive Anglo-American and Russian involvement, without which no one doubted that it would have gone under in short order. The twenty interwar years were a time of steadily decaying national morale, climaxed by the German victory of 1940, the shame of Vichy, and the long night of German occupation. Algeria and Indochina completed the tale of national humiliation. When the nation "revived" in 1958, it was under the leadership of a retired army general with a mentality somewhere between that of Louis XIV and that of Napoleon III. Only in France could such an absurdity as Gaullism have materialized. But Gaullism changed nothing, and France remains a divided society, ruled by bureaucrats and capitalists, its potentiality for maturation as a modern social democracy still thwarted by the unresolved class struggle.

The impact of all these developments on art and thought has been, more than anything else, disorientative. Old meanings have dissolved, old missions have been abandoned, old hopes have been dashed. The France of *la Révolution*, the grand armies of *l'Empereur*, the utopias of *les philosophes* seem gray and remote. During the irrationalist era, French artists and thinkers have been searching for new religions to give them, by convenient flashes of intuition, the moral guidance that history and reason may no longer offer. Sometimes the search ends at the foot of blank walls. Almost always it has been blessed by Gallic intelligence and vitality.

In contrast to romanticism, which stirred little serious philosophical thought in France, irrationalism encouraged a reawakening in French philosophy that has continued through all three of its generations. As in Germany, the philosophers were central to the irrationalist endeavor, although there were not so many of them or so many contending schools. Their work is the best place to begin a review of the fortunes of the irrationalist world conception in French culture.

In some respects the founder of French irrationalist philosophy was the now distant figure (1766–1824) of Maine de Biran, the *idéologue* discussed in Chapter 3 who had converted the sensationalist psychology of Cabanis into a romanticist psychology of will and spirit. Today he is hailed as a forerunner of French existentialism. In the context of the nineteenth century, Maine de Biran was also a forerunner of vitalism, the first important movement in irrationalist thought. His explorations of the inner world of mind emphasized not only the spiritual nature of man, but also the dynamics of the will, through which human beings advanced from a crude *vie animale* to the *vie humaine* of psychic freedom. Such freedom realized itself through an immanent "active force," a power of striving in the psyche that linked the romanticist world view (including Lamarck's theory of the "progressive force" in all organisms) with the later élan vital of French vitalism.

Another link was supplied by the neo-Kantian idealist Charles Renouvier, much of whose best work appeared in the 1880s and 1890s, near the end of his long life. Despite his idealism, Renouvier opposed the "block universe" of many of his colleagues. In a world composed of ideas, each human being, and indeed all beings, were unique and undetermined. For Renouvier, the so-called laws of nature were only generalizations of rough utility serving human convenience, not the straitjackets of being. Renouvier decisively influenced William James, when the American philosopher was ill and despondent in early life, with his doctrine of the freedom of human will: from it James drew his resolve to abandon all determinisms and build a philosophy of action. Renouvier was also one of the guiding spirits of the first full generation of irrationalist philosophers in France.

Three of these philosophers are little known outside their own country—Alfred Fouillée, important for his concept of *idées-forces;* Fouillée's stepson Jean-Marie Guyau; and the idealist academician Emile Boutroux, professor at the Sorbonne from 1888 to 1921. Boutroux taught Henri Bergson, the one philosopher of his generation who has most emphatically escaped neglect. In all these thinkers, again, the leading ideas were action, will, indeterminacy, freedom, the life force that originates in the lower universe and reaches its most impetuous form in man himself, lord of an evolving creation. By the time Bergson wrote his best-selling philosophical masterpiece, *Creative Evolution* (1907), his doctrine of the élan vital, the vital thrust impelling creatures to ever higher states of consciousness and freedom, was already a commonplace of French philosophy.

Bergson coupled his vitalism with a frontal attack on materialism and rationalism. Matter, he proposed, did exist, but it represented the lowest form of action, a kind of negative action perpetually running down and wearing out. Life alone, growing and changing by its own inner thrust, possessed creative power. Bergson had no doubt that conscious life could transcend matter altogether, confirming the ancient idea of immortality. Moreover, only the force of intuition could grasp such things; to reason and physical science belonged the lesser faculty of analyzing lifeless matter. If reason perceived the universe as a mechanically determined stasis, intuition taught freedom and transcendence. Bergson and his predecessors were advising the nation, in effect, to renounce its dependence on material resources, of which it no longer had competitive quantities, and to seek instead psychic solutions for its problems. French military strategists may have had the same idea in 1914 when they imagined that red-trousered French troops could overwhelm numerically superior *Boches* by sheer offensive courage.

Gerhard Masur reminds us, however, that Bergsonism cannot properly be interpreted as an endorsement of "the titanic drive which impelled Western civilization toward shores yet unexplored."[7] Some of his readers may have so understood it, but Bergson was a deeply religious man, appalled by the materialism and hedonism of modern society. Whatever ambiguities may have flawed *Creative Evolution* he removed in his later work, *The Two Sources of Morality and Religion* (1932), a call for a new asceticism grounded in religious faith in which Bergson equated his élan vital with the divine will.

Nor was Bergson alone in arranging an alliance between idealistic vitalism and religious tradition. The Christian philosopher Maurice Blondel urged a similar doctrine in his *Action* (1893), omitting only Bergson's interest in biological evolution. In the second generation of French irrationalists, Bergsonism found new modes of expression in the popular writings of two Christian biologist-philosophers, Pierre Lecomte du Noüy and Pierre Teilhard de Chardin. Teilhard's nebulously ecstatic work *The Phenomenon of Man*, published posthumously in 1955, was the philosophical sensation of the next several years among lay readers, who responded warmly to its blend of optimism and mysticism.

Escape into new or reformed religious visions became the distinguishing mark of much of the thought of the second irrationalist generation in France. In addition to the vogue of Bergsonism and the work of Lecomte and Teilhard there was the saintly figure of Albert Schweitzer, half-French, half-German, remembered more for his medical mission in Africa than for his books; the Christian existentialism of Gabriel Marcel; and the neo-Thomism of Jacques Maritain and Etienne Gilson. The most substantial thinker of the group was perhaps Maritain. Significantly, the turning point in Maritain's spiritual life came when he began attending Bergson's lectures at the Collège de France. Although as a Thomist Maritain could hardly assail the faculty of reason with the same passion as Bergson, he was a lifelong critic of modern civilization and its positivist thought. The same religious impulse directed many of the celebrities of French letters during the second generation, including François Mauriac and Georges Bernanos. The painter Georges Rouault, born late in the first generation, and the composer Olivier Messiaen, born early in the third, also contributed to the Catholic revival.

In the third generation, however, irrationalism advanced to a new and radically antireligious phase. The atheistic existentialism of Jean-Paul Sartre, Simone de Beauvoir, and Albert Camus maintained its solidarity with Bergsonism on the question of human freedom but turned away from Bergsonism, Christian faith, and German existentialism alike in its view of the world outside consciousness. With a skeptical clarity that bears the unmistakable odor of Cartesianism, Sartre and his colleagues built their thought on the triumphant and yet illusionless affirmation of existence, to which they added, "but nothing else follows." The free acting, feeling, and thinking of the self demonstrated its existence, prior to all the "essences" that human reason might invent. But of that great external reality from which human beings borrowed their perishable flesh and to which all flesh inevitably returned after the annihilation of existence by death, nothing could be known except that it ran silently on its rails toward inscrutable destinies. The world outside humankind was a machine world, confined to its rails. Whereas the being of man existed "for itself" (*le pour-soi*), external reality existed merely "in itself" (*l'en-soi*). Yet even the for-itself eluded rational understanding. It was given, and nothing more, distinguished from the in-itself by its power to choose courses of action.

The ethics of atheistic existentialism are summed up in the phrase "desperate freedom." Men were free, but their freedom was for nothing. Freedom could not be alienated by submission to any determinate code of morality since any such code would constitute a definition of man, who was self-defined through action and choice and therefore not enclosable within the formulas of science or abstract reason. Bergson's élan vital, in short, had lost its cosmic ties and become the pure for-itself of the human condition. Existentialism demanded only commitment, action in the world, with no hope of cheating death or winning permanent victories. It assumed concrete form in Camus's idea of perpetual rebellion and Sartre's cyclical concept of revolution. The anarchism of Camus and the neo-Marxism of Sartre are, in fact, two different forms of the same moral sensibility, crystallized during the seemingly hopeless years of the German occupation of France.

In other recent philosophies, such as the existential phenomenology of Sartre's former associate Maurice Merleau-Ponty and the Christian personalism of Emmanuel Mounier, ethical and political questions received equally serious attention without recourse to the radical dualism of Sartre and Camus. More faithful to the French habit of making razor-sharp distinctions, Sartre and Camus had fallen into irreconcilable opposition on the role of the individual in the struggle for social justice, whereas Merleau-Ponty and Mounier, despite differences of their own, came to occupy a middle position emphasizing the concrete interdependence and intersubjectivity of humankind. Both died young, in mid-career, before they had chance to work out the full implications of their thought, a fate that also overtook Camus.

Meanwhile, in this same third generation, many French social scientists have begun to find their way back to positivism. The new historians have followed the example set by Lucien Febvre and Marc Bloch (of the second generation) in their focus on social and economic studies, with a strong commitment to quantitative method. In anthropology the outstanding scholar is Claude Lévi-Strauss, whose "structuralist" approach endeavors to identify through an analysis of the life and language of primitive man the basic forms of human mentality. But despite his self-proclaimed devotion to objectivity and his frank acceptance of determinism, Lévi-Strauss has kept at least one foot in the irrationalist camp. As Willson Coates and Hayden White remark, his sympathies lie with the savage mind against its civilized counterpart. "He enlists the aid of science in destroying a civilized man's claims to a mastery over nature superior to that of the savage." The savage for Lévi-Strauss "has foregone mastery of nature in order to retain mastery over himself; modern man, by contrast, has, in the process of gaining the world, lost his uniquely human soul."[8] It is the old complaint, familiar in intellectual history since Rousseau, that the woes of modernity are intrinsic to modernity and that only the "natural" man, unburdened by modern cleverness and sophistication, can be happy. Lévi-Strauss has used reason to exalt unreason.

Whether the new quantitative history and the new structuralism portend a revival of positivism or not, the social thought of the first two irrationalist generations in France pursued much the same course as philosophical thought. The folkish movement in Germany was paralleled by the "integral" nationalism of Maurice Barrès and Charles Maurras, who invoked national souls, sacred soils, mysteries of blood and race, and the need for authority as fervently as any German thinkers of their time. The royalist political movement founded at the turn of the century by Maurras bore the significant name of Action Française. In the well-known analysis of Ernst Nolte, French Action was the first of the "three faces" of modern European fascism.[9] It was also another face of the cult of vitality of the Bergsonian era in French thought. In the social sciences, the best French scholars of the first two generations specialized (like Lévi-Strauss) in the analysis of irrational and primitive behavior: Gabriel Tarde and Gustave Le Bon in studies of mass psychology, Lucien Lévy-Bruhl in work on primitive thought, Emile Durkheim in his explorations of such psychosocial phenomena as anomie, suicide, and totemism. Prefiguring Sartre, even French radicalism was touched by irrationalism, as in the passionate myth-making of Georges Sorel and the neo-idealist revision of Marx attempted by Jean Jaurès.

But even the riches of French philosophy and social thought were outshone by the achievements of French aesthetic culture during the three generations of irrationalism. Both in literature and in the fine arts, Frenchmen led Western civilization into the new sensibility. Almost the last romantics, they were the first poets and painters of irrationalism. In the use of symbols, the evocation of the exotic and the decadent, and the exploration of the absurd, they have had few equals. As with the case of the United States since 1933, a significant percentage of their most creative personalities were imported from other countries, but Gallicization was usually swift and thorough. The foreign-born even display that residuum of classical discipline that gives French irrationalist culture, like French romanticism, its distinctive snap and gloss.

The chief ancestor of French irrationalism in the positivist era was Charles Baudelaire. Born in 1821, and dead of venereal disease at the age of forty-six, Baudelaire attracted notice during his lifetime mostly as a figure of scandal and debauchery, the eccentric author of "obscene" poems. Yet soon after his death he had become the prime force in symbolism, the first great movement in irrationalist literature, and in our own century he has been the subject of countless analyses from every imaginable perspective, including a provocative volume by Sartre.

The symbolists, who dominated the avant-garde in French letters and to some degree French art from the 1870s to the end of the century, owed much to Baudelaire, not only the example set by his verse, but also his theories of art and literature. For Baudelaire and the symbolists who succeeded him, for men such as Arthur Rimbaud, Paul Verlaine, and Stéphane Mallarmé, the task of the poet was to plunge beneath the surface of ordinary waking consciousness into the mysterious underworld of dream and fantasy, where life's real meanings were locked. Repudiating the vulgarity of modern industrial society, they sought an existence without labels or regulations, an existence expressible only in symbols—and not the symbols of everyday currency, but the privately coined symbols of the artist himself. Symbolism was a poetry, a fiction, an art of nuance, quarried from the deepest levels of consciousness. For one great creative personage after another, it opened routes of escape from the matter-of-fact bourgeois universe that science and industry had fashioned in late nineteenth-century France. Temperamentally at opposite poles from the vital thrust of Bergsonism, inclining rather to morbidity and melancholy, symbolism was actually the perfect complement of vitalist philosophy. The two movements fit together like the archaism and futurism delineated by Arnold J. Toynbee as modes of escape from an intolerable present chosen by disintegrating societies.[10]

In the broadest interpretation, symbolism encompassed almost all the aesthetic culture of fin-de-siècle France, including the sensibility that knew itself by the delicious sobriquet of *la Décadence*. The practitioners of symbolism, beyond those already named, included the Comte de Villiers de l'Isle-Adam, J.-K. Huysmans, Jean Moréas, Maurice Maeterlinck, Pierre Louÿs, and, at least in their younger years, Paul Claudel, André Gide, and Paul Valéry. Some of the artists associated with symbolism, the "aesthetes and magicians" of Philippe Jullian's recent study,[11] were Pierre Puvis de Chavannes, Gustave Moreau, Odilon Redon, Paul Gauguin, and Maurice Denis, followed at the turn of the century by the "fauvist" movement of Henri Matisse and Maurice de Vlaminck, and the enchanted primitivism of Henri Rousseau. Composers also picked up the new vibrations, as in the opera that Claude Debussy created from Maeterlinck's drama *Pelléas et Mélisande* or the sumptuous decadence of his "Prelude to the Afternoon of a Faun" (inspired by Mallarmé) and "Sirens," his tone-poem for orchestra and female choir.

As some of the younger members of the first generation developed their art, they evolved beyond the rarefied aestheticism and weltschmerz of pure symbolism. Romain Rolland, author of *Jean Christophe* (1904–12), for which he received the Nobel Prize in 1915, became a romantic idealist of heroic proportions. Gide's early symbolism ripened into a powerful concern for moral issues that links him to the neoclassical writers of the seventeenth century. Valéry's *The Young Fate* (1917), written after a long self-imposed retirement, converted him into a poet of international standing, but in this work and the many essays he composed in middle and later life, a severity of intellect prevailed that also recalls the seventeenth century. Perhaps the most substantial literary production of any member of this first irrationalist generation was *Remembrance of Things Past* (1914–27), the voluminous life work of Marcel Proust. Influenced more by Bergson than by the symbolists, Proust conceived of literature as an effort to unearth from the depths of memory the early experiences that shape our lives. He toiled like an archeologist, using his own childhood as his source material, and the results are unique in all of literature.

Proust, born in 1871, rounded out the first generation of French irrationalist writers and artists. He was also the last irrationalist *littérateur* in the grand tradition. Despite revivals of realism by such would-be Balzacs as Roger Martin du Gard and Jules Romains, and the Nietzschean heroism of Antoine de St.-Exupéry and André Malraux, the tendency of literature and art in France since Proust has been to carry irrationalism to its "logical" conclusions, to the anti-literature and anti-art of a fully liberated absurdism for which boundaries no longer exist. Other countries have made their contribution, including Germany, but the focal point through most of the twentieth century has been France.

Absurdism is an elastic concept. As in the thought of Camus, it can denote a philosophy that the universe has no meaning for humankind. Or it may go further, to denote the view that humankind itself is irrational, meaningless, and valueless and that all rational attempts to order or assign meaning to human life, individually or collectively, are pointless. In absurdism there is no place for reason, hierarchy, purpose, law; even discussion becomes *de trop*, too much. The true terminus of absurdism, which only the arts can reach, is the play without words, the empty canvass, the silent concert. But there are many stops along the way toward that final reductio ad absurdum. Symbolism, as we can see now, was actually the first stop, requiring the artist to express his innermost being in a private code. Once the public codes lose their potency and art becomes progressively more internalized, the controls fall away one by one until in the end no values are left at all. Even private codes are seen to be ephemeral, the whims of the moment, no more lasting than any others.

The transition of French art and letters from symbolism to absurdism was presaged before World War I in the comic theater of Alfred Jarry. First performed when the playwright was only twenty-three, his *King Ubu* (1896) turned a schoolboy's satire of a pompous schoolmaster into a powerfully derisive vision of *la bête humaine*, in the person of the bourgeois Ubu, who becomes king of Poland until at last his people can bear him no longer. The Irish symbolist poet Yeats, in the audience on the first night, correctly identified *Ubu* as a sign of things to come, the displacement of symbolist subtlety by "the Savage God" of comedy.

Jarry went on to invent "pataphysics," which he called "the science of imaginary solutions," in his Rabelaisian *Exploits and Opinions of Dr. Faustroll, Pataphysician* (1911). When this logic of the absurd reached the public, its creator was already dead, and his place as the comic tribune of the avant-garde had been taken by another young Bohemian, Guillaume Apollinaire. Poet, art critic, and playwright, Apollinaire delighted in iconoclasm, eccentricity, and innovation as ends in themselves. His last major work, *The Teats of Tiresias* (1917), was a triumph of inanity and, like *King Ubu*, a landmark in the history of absurdist theater.

Apollinaire also died early, a victim of wartime influenza in 1918, but by then the war had given birth to the first self-conscious movement of absurdists, christened "Dada," and founded at the Café Voltaire in Zurich in 1916 by a mixed group of French, German, and other fugitives from the war. *Dada*, in the nonsense manifesto of its spokesman Tristan Tzara, "signifies nothing." It is also the French for a child's hobbyhorse. Bringing together such deliberate eccentrics as the French artists Jean Arp and Marcel Duchamp, the German writer Hugo Ball, the German painter Max Ernst, the Rumanian Tzara, and the French poet André Breton, Dada was a multimedia phenomenon, embracing literature, painting, sculpture, theater, and everything in between. Its experiments were both unprecedentedly bold and funny, but its chief passion was nonsense, hurled like a weapon against the sacred canons of art, against the war and the self-important bourgeois social order that had unleashed it, and ultimately against the whole value system underlying Western civilization. After the war, Dada flourished for a few hectic years in Paris and Berlin.

We need not follow the history of absurdist art and literature in detail through the second and third generations of French irrationalism. It continued in the surrealism of Breton, Paul Eluard, Jean Cocteau, and René Magritte; the existentialist novels and plays of Sartre and Camus; the "new novel" of Alain Robbe-Grillet and Michel Butor; the "raw art" of Jean Dubuffet; and, above all, in the absurdist theater of Eugène Ionesco, Jean Genet, and the Gallicized Irishman Samuel Beckett. Some of this work has been romantic in its intensity: Eluard, for example, in his idolization of woman, or Camus in the heroic altruism of his last novels. The surrealists even expected a kind of psychotherapeutic healing from their exploration of the unconscious. But most French absurdism is distinguished by a toughness and a comedic insolence that denies dignity to the targets of its anger.

For in the end it must be said that the absurdists are also angry men. Not a few have turned to political radicalism, including communism, at some stage in their lives. If they laugh, it is the laughter of attack. Their denunciation of values has been too savage to conceal their longing for values. When Ionesco, for example, takes as the setting for his play *Unhired Killer* (1957) a "radiant city" uniting all the latest comforts and ingenuities of modern science where no one wants to live because it is stalked by an unknown crazed assassin, he does more than point to a fly in the ointment of modernity. The radiant city is a symbol of broken promises and shattered dreams. One is also reminded of the bitterness of Voltaire in *Candide*, itself a tale of the absurd, steeped in the author's accumulating disappointments with man and God. French irrationalism is full of the crisp and lethal humor of *Candide*, preserving intact this much of its inheritance from the Gallic national soul. It could not have been more appropriate that Dada was born (albeit in Zurich) at the Café Voltaire.

The Kingdom of God: Russia

"Russian thought," writes V. V. Zenkovsky, "has been condemned by history to a deep bifurcation."[12] One branch of the Russian intellectual road has led westward, toward rationalism, the other eastward, toward the mystical Christianity of the Russian Middle Ages. The two branches have sometimes threatened to reunite, as both Westernizers and Slavophiles have found inspiration in the Christian, idealistic, mystical, and romantic tendencies of Western thought, but in the second half of the nineteenth century they parted foreve. First the positivists and then the Marxists made a clean break with Russia Christianity. Following the Revolution of 1917, Marxism became the official world view of the new Soviet state. On the branch leading eastward, irrationalism joined forces with the Slavophile and Christian heritage to gain a clear ascendancy in the intellectual and artistic life of czarist Russia during its last quarter-century. After the collapse of czarism and the expulsion of its supporters and fellow travellers from Russian soil, irrationalism continued to flourish for a time among the White émigrés in various Western countries.

Russian irrationalism was nevertheless—during its heyday—a vigorous movement of thought and taste. With little Western influence, it followed its own distinctive course, generally marked by an impassioned commitment to traditional Christian values. It was also the most irrationalist of irrationalisms, the most extreme in its opposition to positivism in all its forms, and the most politically reactionary.

The cause of this national schizophrenia was the persistent and finally incurable failure of the czarist old order to bring Russia into the modern age. The process of industrialization that at last began to gather momentum in the 1890s came too late. The emancipated serfs remained alienated and depressed, except for a scattering of comfortable small farmers ("kulaks") who emerged to fatten on their flesh, especially after the encouragement they received from the Stolypin Law of 1906. The liberal bourgeoisie was small and ineffectual, the czarist regime unimaginative, the Russian army too poorly supplied, and the Russian economy too weak to fight the kind of total war that had to be fought in 1914–18. The Central Powers soon brought Russia to the verge of total national exhaustion and made revolution inescapable.

In Russia's desperate situation under its last two monarchs the response of its intellectuals and artists was, predictably, to turn to extreme remedies. A minority of irreconcilable revolutionists made preparations for the overthrow of czardom and its replacement by a socialist state. The majority clung all the more passionately to Holy Russia and the mystical genius of the Russian national soul, as if Russia could be saved only by becoming more and more single-mindedly Russian. German irrationalism adopted comparable strategies, but Germany already had the industrial and military might to translate its folkish fantasies into something like reality. For Russia it was all moonshine.

The father of Russian irrationalism in the nineteenth century was its greatest novelist, Fyodor Dostoyevsky. Despite his use of realistic techniques, Dostoyevsky had no spiritual affinities with the positivist generation to which he belonged. Like his exact French contemporary Baudelaire, he was a prototypical irrationalist, profoundly Russian in his espousal of the idea of Russia's mission of world redemption and his devotion to the Orthodox faith. The boldly drawn characters who inhabit his pages are monsters, like Stavrogin in *The Possessed* (1872), who have allowed modern ideas to destroy their faith in God, moral weaklings torn by sin and doubt, or men who have found the narrow path to peace through mystical illumination, such as Father Zosima in *The Brothers Karamazov* (1879–80). Dostoyevsky wielded an enormous influence for many years, but it was a conservative influence that strengthened the hand of the autocracy and widened the gulf between Left and Right in Russian thought. Although Lenin once dismissed Dostoyevsky's work as "trash," it unintendingly helped bring him to power.

The mystical pacifism to which Tolstoy turned in his last years was also a factor in the diffusion of irrationalism in late nineteenth-century Russia. Tolstoy avoided Dostoyevsky's political alliance with czardom, but he became no less fervently an enemy of positivism and the modern age. At about the same time, other contemporaries of Dostoyevsky and Tolstoy were preparing the ground for the triumph of irrationalism in philosophy and social thought. In a variant form of the Slavophile argument, Nikolai Danilevsky (who was later to influence Spengler) preached a vitalistic philosophy of history and evolution that hailed the Slavs as the next great world people, destined to establish a mighty Eastern federation with its capital at Constantinople. Boris Chicherin continued the attempts of the Russian romanticists to build a philosophy on Hegelian foundations, and Nikolai Fyodorov proposed the establishment of a brotherly kingdom of God on earth whose government would be neither autocratic nor democratic, but "psychocratic," the rule of consciousness redeemed by Christ. Outside the Russian mainstream, yet no less thoroughly irrationalist, was the worldwide Theosophical movement founded in Russia in 1858 by Helena Blavatsky.

All this activity during the positivist era provides ample evidence that Russia had by no means fully embraced the positivist creed even then. The initiatives of Dostoyevsky and his contemporaries led to a virtual explosion of irrationalist thought and art near the close of the nineteenth century. In philosophy and theology, art and music, poetry and fiction, two generations of irrationalists testify to the peculiar affinity of the Russian national spirit for the irrationalist world view.

The figure who stands as the cornerstone of the edifice of irrationalist thought in Russia during its first generation is Vladimir Soloviev. The son of the historian Sergei Soloviev, Vladimir was born in Moscow in 1853 and recapitulated during a stormy adolescence the whole recent history of Russian thought. At fourteen he lost his religious faith, becoming in the words of an old friend "a typical nihilist of the 'sixties," a follower of Pisarev and the German materialists. This phase ended with Soloviev's exposure to the thought of Spinoza at the age of sixteen. Spinoza led him back to theism and a sense of cosmic unity, as well as to the idealism of Hegel and Schelling. But his spiritual discoveries were not yet over. After submitting a brilliant master's thesis in 1874 on "The Crisis of Western Philosophy," subtitled "Against the Positivists," the precocious philosopher went abroad, first to London, then to Egypt in a search for occult wisdom reminiscent of the journeys of Mme. Blavatsky. Christian and mystical ideas blended with the teachings of his philosophical masters to produce, by 1880, a fully developed world view to which he adhered for the remaining twenty years of his life.

Soloviev argued that Western philosophies, such as empiricism and rationalism, mistakenly limited themselves to the knowledge that comes when the mind is detached from the being of what it seeks to know. In brief, the knowledge of reason and the knowledge of the senses were too subjective. Severely limited by the structure of the human mind and sensorium, they could not by themselves apprehend reality in its fullness. Only the direct mystical intuition of objective reality through faith could do this. Faith would make possible the organic integration of all the types of knowledge and bring us to what Soloviev termed "Godmanhood," divinity and humanness united in Christ. From his theory of integral knowledge Soloviev went on to contend that world history moved teleologically toward the realization of the Kingdom of God, to be achieved when the Orthodox and Western churches joined hands once more and the Russian nation, by the good example of its own holistic witness to being and truth, inspired the building of a universal theocratic society.

The fusion of religion, philosophy, historical thought, and apocalyptic utopianism in Soloviev's eloquent volumes won many converts among the younger thinkers who followed him. One of his most devoted friends and interpreters was Prince Yevgeny Trubetskoy, a substantial philosopher in his own right. Trubetskoy's major works included a two-volume analysis and criticism of Soloviev's thought, published in 1912, which he used as a springboard for presenting his own, more strictly Russian Orthodox views of God's action in the world. Trubetskoy's own action, when the Bolsheviks came to power in 1917, was to join a White army and participate in the counterrevolution. He died of typhus in 1920 just before the evacuation of his comrades from Russia. Still younger men who carried on Soloviev's spiritual and philosophical mission were the Orthodox priests Pavel Florensky and Sergei Bulgakov.

Better known in the West, however, were the lay philosophers Leo Shestov and Nikolai Berdyaev, both of whom wrote extensively during the years of their exile in Western Europe after the Revolution. Both were deeply religious thinkers, disciples of Dostoyevsky and Nietzsche who stressed the nonrationality of life and its moral struggle. As Shestov warned in his last book, *Athens and Jerusalem* (1938), the time had come for mankind to transcend the narrow limits of Hellenic rationalism and yield to the living truth of Revelation. Working along lines parallel to the existentialists and neo-orthodox theologians in Germany, Shestov and Berdyaev took the part of Jerusalem against a merely human Athens.

Russian aesthetic culture during the irrationalist ascendancy rivaled French and German, although unfamiliarity with the Russian language prevented the poets, in particular, from gaining the hearing in the West that they deserved. Symbolism reached Russia about the same time as it reached the German-speaking world. Dmitry Merezhkovsky and his wife Zinaida Hippius, both poets, led the symbolist movement in Russia in the 1890s and 1900s. Merezhkovsky was also something of a religious thinker, the founder of an important society of religious philosophers in St. Petersburg in 1901. He accused traditional Christianity of excessive otherworldliness and looked forward to the establishment of a millennial new order combining Christian and secular values in a consecrated unity, a Joachite reign of the Holy Ghost embodying both the divine and the human principle. The Revolution of 1905 found in Merezhkovsky and Hippius ardent supporters, but they opposed Bolshevism. Leaving Russia in 1919, they settled in Paris, developing fascist sympathies in their old age.

By the mid-1900s, Merezhkovsky had already been eclipsed as Russia's leading symbolist poet by a much younger man, Alexander Blok. He, too, invested symbolism at first with religious content, under the inspiration of Soloviev; later he turned to Slavophile themes, became involved in the defense of the Bolsheviks (who had little use for him), and died at the age of forty in 1921, steeped in melancholy and doubt. Also of the second irrationalist generation were the neoromantic poet and novelist Boris Pasternak, whose *Dr. Zhivago* (1956) outraged Soviet authorities because of its antirevolutionary sentiments, and the émigré novelist Vladimir Nabokov, now an American writer, although before he became an American citizen in 1945, he wrote his books in Russian for the Russian émigré communities of Western Europe. Nabokov's reputation has risen steadily among Western critics over the past twenty years. Working rich veins of allegory and sardonic humor, he takes as his themes the perennial problems of art and love. A comparison with Thomas Mann is not, perhaps, wide of the mark.

In painting, music, and dance, the Russian irrationalists have surpassed themselves. Their musical achievement was no doubt to be expected, after the triumphs of the romantic and national schools of Tchaikovsky and Rimsky-Korsakov in the nineteenth century. Alexander Scriabin and Sergei Rachmaninov followed the romantic impulse to its furthest limits, in Scriabin's case with the help of mystical ideas derived from Theosophy. The émigré composer Igor Stravinsky defies classification, like most universal geniuses. His early ballets were neoromantic. He then entered an austere neoclassical phase. In old age, after settling in California, he wrote in every style from jazz to church music to atonal works in the manner of Schönberg and von Webern. But despite the terseness and mathematical rigor of his musical language, Stravinsky's work grew organically out of late Russian romanticism. In its exoticism, demonic energy, religious feeling, and compulsive avant-gardism, it belongs more to the irrationalist world view than to any other.

Some of Stravinsky's best scores were originally written for the remarkable productions of the impresario Sergei Diaghilev. Founder of the Ballets Russes and a prodigy of taste and organization, Diaghilev integrated the talents not only of the leading dancers of the early twentieth century (most of them Russian), but also many of its greatest artists and composers. His seasons with the Ballets Russes from 1909 to 1929 were triumphs of artistic synthesis and innovation. Among the other Russians whose work he commissioned were the composer Sergei Prokofiev, the choreographers Mikhail Fokine and Leonid Massine, and the artists and designers Leo Bakst, Alexander Benois, Nikolai Roerich, and Pavel Chelishev. Diaghilev's aesthetic hedonism could have found no place in Soviet life, but in France and elsewhere in the Western world he filled a need for twenty surprising years.

Most surprising of all was the appearance of artists of international stature in Russia during the irrationalist period. Russian art had remained derivative and second-rate throughout the nineteenth century, but early in the twentieth it found itself. Some of this self-discovery was aided by the commissions of Diaghilev. Independently, the Russian painter Vasily Kandinsky became the first modern artist to execute purely abstract canvasses (about 1910), reflecting his mystical view of the artist's role. Somewhat later, Marc Chagall developed a highly personalized form of symbolic expressionism, a graphic "remembrance of things past" to which he has added in recent years the spiritual vision of his windows for the cathedrals of Metz and Reims and the synagogue of the Hadassah-Hebrew Medical Center in Jerusalem.

But of course irrationalism did not exhaust the fertility of the Russian mind or its artistic sensibilities in the twentieth century. Outside our purview here is the evolution of Marxist thought and socialist realism in the arts and letters in the U.S.S.R. The Marxism of Gyorgy Plekhanov and Vladimir Lenin, the cinema of Sergei Eisenstein, the poetry of Vladimir Mayakovsky and Yevgeny Yevtushenko, the novels of Maxim Gorky and Mikhail Sholokhov, and the music of Sergei Prokofiev (after his return to Russia in 1933) and Dmitry Shostakovitch take us into a world of quite different values from those of the Russian irrationalists. The irrationalists created their works chiefly for a privileged elite; they are hypersensitive, introverted, richly imaginative, and often otherworldly. Soviet culture is for the people and for this world. Even today in the Soviet Union an "underground" of irrationalist writers and artists thrives; examples of its protest against the ruling Marxist orthodoxy are the essays and tales of the imprisoned writer Andrei Sinyavsky, who used the pseudonym of Abram Terts. But on the whole Russia has become a Marxist country, embarked on a course that separates it in the most definitive way from the culture of the capitalist West. How Soviet thought and art relate to the world view of the foreseeable future is discussed in the Epilogue that directly follows this chapter.

Above the Fray: Great Britain and the United States

Of all the great powers in Western civilization, two alone have had cause to be reasonably well satisfied with the twentieth century. As from moated castles, Great Britain and the United States have watched the agony of the European continent, sent troops twice to rescue France from a Germany that had grown too big for the proper functioning of the international balance of power, and now imagine themselves standing guard against the danger that Soviet Russia will succeed where Germany failed. Behind their salty moats, Great Britain and the United States have remained relatively secure. *Au-dessus de la mêlée européenne,* never invaded, never occupied, never subjected to "totalitarian" rule, traumatized by no revolution, equipped with remarkably stable two-party bourgeois democracies, enjoying at least the illusion of universal affluence and class harmony, blessed with the pressure valves of easy migration to the open spaces of the Commonwealth and the Golden West, their native citizens could not (until recently) feel the sick dismay with modernity that has swept through continental Europe in our century.

Lacking even a well-entrenched national tradition of antiscientific and antimodernist thought, the Anglo-Saxon countries have participated only marginally in the irrationalist rebellion. Where irrationalism has shown itself at all, it has often arrived in the form of an imported delicacy, German or French or Russian in origin, freely adapted and blended to suit Anglo-Saxon tastes. Even as a home-grown product, it has tended to be significantly milder than its continental equivalent.

Whatever acceptance irrationalism has gained in Britain and America is due to a variety of situations more or less unrelated to one another. An obvious point, important also in explaining the origins of Anglo-American romanticism, is the relatively smaller weight in the Anglo-American intellectual tradition of the purely rationalist component of what we have called the rationalist world view. Enlightenment rationalism was an amalgam of two distinct metals: Baconian empiricism and Cartesian rationalism. In the main, British thinkers and their colonial followers took more account of the former than of the latter. They could tolerate insults to Descartes with more patience than insults to Bacon. A practical, commercial people with little dependence on the logical and organizing powers of centralized bureaucracies, they trusted their senses more implicitly than their reason. To the extent that irrationalism is just what the word means literally, the rejection of reason, the Anglo-American mind was already programmed to find it less offensive than the French mind. Perhaps man and his universe were, after all, less reasonable, less logical, less orderly than the philosophes had thought. It was not such a loss!

The very ease with which the Anglo-American could accommodate himself to some of the premises of irrationalism greatly diminished its shock value. Edmund Wilson's observation that the French symbolists had to fight their way to the freedoms of wild self-expression that English poets—untrammeled by the iron laws of prosody of the Académie Française—had always enjoyed, goes right to the heart of the matter.[13] The Anglo-Saxon thinker and writer felt less need than his French contemporary to enlist in the twentieth-century rebellion against reason, but he could do so with less embarrassment and self-consciousness, at the cost of making less difference.

Irrationalism also owes some of its appeal (such as it is) in the English-speaking countries to the irruption of the outside world into British and American society. The steady flow of immigrants from the European mainland at the end of the nineteenth and the beginning of the twentieth centuries, followed by the exodus of mainland Jewish intellectuals and other fugitives from fascism and communism, has overloaded the assimilative powers of Anglo-Saxon culture and pumped alien values into it, including some of the irrationalism of modern Europe. The vogue in Anglo-Saxondom of Freudian and Jungian psychoanalysis, neo-orthodox theology, and existentialism has been due as much to the presence of Continental émigrés in its midst as to the presence of Continental works of thought and art in its bookstalls, museums, and concert halls. From Einstein, Mann, and Tillich to Schönberg, Mannheim, and Stravinsky, many of Europe's best minds have lived a good part of their lives in the English-speaking world, affecting it more powerfully than they could otherwise have done.

Some of this irruption from the "outside" world has originated in enclaves of non–Anglo-Saxon culture within the English-speaking countries. Half of the leading protagonists of irrationalism in modern British literature, for example, have been Irish. In the United States, black and Appalachian Scotch-Irish influences have been extensive, especially in music. Since Cooper the Amerindian has also been a presence in American thought and art, and like Irish and black culture, the culture of the Amerindian is predominantly nonrational, reflecting the values of a pre-urban society.

Even the purest-blooded city-dwelling Angles and Saxons, no matter what their advantages, are not so high above the fray that they could fail to feel the impact of the disorientative events of twentieth-century history, including its intellectual history. The erosion of the old certainties in ethics and aesthetics, the confusions of modern physics, the discovery of the irrational in human behavior, and the threat to humanistic values of modern industrialism are well known to the Anglo-Saxon peoples. Even from the distance of their moated castles, they took full notice of the march of fascism across Europe, and they yield to no one in their hysterical fear of Soviet and Asian socialism.

In recent decades, I must add, the luck of the Anglo-Saxons has begun to dissipate. The British have lost their empire and fallen on hard times that find them, after many centuries of European leadership, lagging behind the major Continental powers in per capita wealth. Their American cousins remain prosperous. But much has gone wrong since 1945, beginning with the subhuman decision to obliterate two Japanese cities with atomic bombs that summer, and continuing with massive national resistance to the long overdue liberation of racial minorities at home, the consistent policy of military and economic support of reactionary regimes throughout the Third World, and the swift evolution of American capitalism to the status of a new monopolistic-imperialist world power. The metamorphosis of the old sylvan republic of the eighteenth century into the missile-rattling racist empire of the late twentieth is nothing mysterious. Every step of the change can be understood historically and was no doubt unavoidable. But as more and more Americans come to realize what has happened, both rational and irrational responses on the part of the freshly enlightened can be expected to follow. The "Beats" of the 1950s and the "Hippies" of the 1960s represented the first waves in the progressively deepening alienation of thinkers and artists in American society from its capitalist ancien régime. In their own day they were also prime examples of a native American irrationalism that had little to do with European influence.

Of the two major English-speaking cultures, the British and the American, the greater complexity and variety of America may give the impression that it has been more vulnerable to the seductions of irrationalism, but I would guess not. On the whole, the sufferings of Great Britain have been significantly greater in our century than those of the United States. It has lost more in war. Its power and wealth have dwindled all too visibly since the splendors of the nineteenth century, and a more openly and consciously fought class struggle has produced sharper contrasts in political thought. Beginning with the only half-serious weltschmerz of the Decadents of the 1890s, British culture has displayed a consistently greater receptivity to the irrationalist world view than its counterpart across the Atlantic.

As during the romanticist era, the chief glory of British irrationalist culture is not philosophy or the social sciences, where it has performed indifferently, but literature. C. P. Snow's thesis of the "two cultures" bears a special relevance to twentieth-century Britain. By and large, science, philosophy, and the social sciences have gone one way, nurtured by the national genius, whereas avant-garde literature, with the fine arts and music in tow, has moved in the opposite direction, toward irrationalism. In a sense, this is only another side of British national genius. The classical-rationalist-realist sequence in French literary history did not occur with the same brilliance and vigor in Great Britain; a disorganized free-booting lot, British writers evaded—as I remarked above—the academicization that overtook French letters in the late seventeenth century. Their hero was Shakespeare, not Corneille. After a weak classical revival in the eighteenth century, the neo-Shakespearian romanticism of the nineteenth proved such a success that it persisted all through the decades of the realist and naturalist secessions. Thackeray and Eliot notwithstanding, it inspired much of the best Victorian prose and poetry. In particular the late romantic aestheticism of John Ruskin, the pre-Raphaelites, Algernon Swinburne, and Walter Pater furnished an authentic native background for the earliest incursions of the irrationalist spirit in the 1880s.

The first generation of British literary irrationalists consisted almost exclusively of writers not of English birth. Fusing the aesthetics of the late Victorian romantics with French symbolism and Celtic mysticism, the Irish poets William Butler Yeats and George William Russell ("A. E.") initiated a renaissance in Irish letters whose influence reverberated throughout the English-speaking world. The Nietzschean vitalism of the Anglo-Irish playwright Bernard Shaw and the dandyism of his fellow Irishman Oscar Wilde also played their part in exposing the British public to irrationalist themes. An Anglicized Pole, Joseph Conrad (born Korzeniowski), wrote novels that carried psychological insight and metaphysical angst to depths unprecedented in English fiction. The roster of irrationalist writers of the first generation is rounded out by three distinctive, if minor, English poets who excelled in the treatment of decadent themes—Arthur Symons, Lionel Johnson, and Ernest Dowson. But this was also the generation of many notable exponents of literary realism, men such as H. G. Wells, John Galsworthy, and Arnold Bennett, who kept their distance from the avant-gardism of their more sophisticated contemporaries and found warmer receptions in the confident zeitgeist of pre-1914 Britain.

For Britain the second irrationalist generation, born between 1875 and 1900, was the most venturesome and the most successful by the canons of present-day criticism. It included the author of *Ulysses* (1922) and *Finnegans Wake* (1939), the inimitable Dubliner James Joyce. His novels are cornucopias of symbolism and linguistic wizardry, rich enough to furnish full-time employment to hundreds of professors of English on both sides of the Atlantic. Two scholarly periodicals are entirely devoted to Joyce studies, one of the greatest academic industries of all time.

Other masters of the second generation deserving notice are Virginia Woolf, who like Joyce made effective use of the "stream of consciousness" technique in her novels; the neoromanticists E. M. Forster and D. H.

Lawrence, trenchant critics of modern civilization; the American-born poet and dramatist T. S. Eliot, a convert in middle life to Anglicanism, which permeated all his best work after 1930; and the novelist, essayist, and (in his last years) literary impresario of mysticism, Aldous Huxley. The first and second generations were also prolific in writers of fantasy, such as Arthur Machen, Algernon Blackwood, Lord Dunsany, J. R. R. Tolkien, and C. S. Lewis.

Of authors born since 1900, hardly one equals the giants of the first and second generations, but the poets W. H. Auden and Dylan Thomas, the novelists William Golding, Lawrence Durrell, and Anthony Burgess, and the absurdist playwrights Harold Pinter and Tom Stoppard all have something to say. In science fiction, a recently invented genre of special importance to students of modern consciousness, British writers since about 1960 have proved more imaginative than their colleagues in the realms of official high literary art. The best work of Brian Aldiss, John Brunner, J. G. Ballard, and Michael Moorcock—perhaps more accurately described as anti-science fiction—is as innovative as anything coming from the pens of mainstream writers, although a few of them too (Huxley, Orwell, Burgess) have tried their hand at science fiction, with superb results.

In the fine arts and music, the irrationalist world view has inspired one or two major figures in each generation. Aubrey Beardsley ranks as the most gifted illustrator of the Decadence of the 1890s, although his career was cut short by tuberculosis at the tender age of twenty-five. The organic abstractions of the sculptor Henry Moore, the spiky surrealistic landscapes of Graham Sutherland, and the sadistic canvasses of Francis Bacon rank among the more powerful visions of modern art. After centuries of sterility, British music revived with the nostalgic pastoralism of Frederick Delius. The tone-poems, based on Celtic legend, of Sir Arnold Bax, and the many scores, often inspired by English folk song, of Ralph Vaughan Williams further helped to establish a national school of British music.

But the philosophers, as we suggested above, are a different breed. Limited chiefly to logical and linguistic analysis in the tradition of Hume and Mill, British philosophy in the irrationalist age is the counterpart of the movement launched in Austria by Mach. Indeed, the two movements intersected one another at various points and eventually flowed together in the 1930s and 1940s, as the rise of Hitlerism made Central Europe an impossible environment for the free unfolding of positivist thought.

In Britain the fountainheads of the new philosophy were two Cambridge men of the first irrationalist generation, G. E. Moore and Bertrand Russell. Beginning with a lucid refutation of the claims of idealism, Moore specialized in commonsense analysis of the traditional problems of philosophy, from which sprang the analytical movement associated with Gilbert Ryle, John Austin, and John Wisdom, philosophers of the second generation at Oxford whose influence reached its zenith in the 1950s. For the analysts, philosophy must limit itself to the elucidation of concepts and words. It is the science of thinking clearly and knowing what we mean—or, to quote Wittgenstein, "the battle against the bewitchment of our intelligence by means of language." The other principal school, which soon joined forces with Viennese logical positivism, took its cues from Russell and his project for the formal logical analysis of scientific discourse. Its best known advocate in the second generation has been A. J. Ayer.

For all their stringent rationalism and positivism, however, the British analytical schools do link up with irrationalism at one point, the same point that we noted in discussing the Vienna Circle. By turning from metaphysics and other traditional philosophical problems to the clarification of discourse, whether ordinary or scientific, the British philosophers have in effect abandoned those problems to other seekers—to poets, prophets, playwrights, whoever chooses to take them on, reasonably or (more likely) otherwise. In A. W. Levi's phrase, analytical philosophy has succumbed to "the lure of the part," the fascination with the microcosmic.[14]

Levi himself confesses to having succumbed to the lure of the whole, in the form of the "process" philosophy of another Englishman, Alfred North Whitehead, which reminds us that not all British philosophy since 1890 has been committed to the analytical movements. Whitehead's savory goulash of Platonism, vitalism, relativity theory, British empiricism, and several other ingredients has enjoyed a stubborn following in many corners of the Anglo-Saxon world since the 1920s. In some of its tenets it adheres closely to the irrationalist world view. There was a generous admixture of irrationalism in the neo-Hegelian idealist systems that ruled over British academic philosophy in the closing decades of the nineteenth century, most prominently in the thought of F. H. Bradley; and irrationalism also pervades the grand-scale evolutionary cosmology of the Manchester sage Samuel Alexander, whose concept of a "nisus in Space-Time" welled out of the same vitalistic, romantic, striving idealism as Bergson's doctrine of the vital thrust.

The twentieth century has not been a great era in political philosophy and the social sciences for Britain. Most of the best thought in any case has been utilitarian and positivist along already well established national lines. The conspicuous exceptions manifest a half-hearted, eclectic irrationalism with little influence outside the Anglo-American world, as in the political psychology of Graham Wallas, the commingled idealism and evolutionary naturalism of the sociology of L. T. Hobhouse, the historicism (based on the thought of the Italian idealist philosopher Benedetto Croce) of R. G. Collingwood, and the stupefying mélange of Spengler, St. Augustine, Jung, and British empiricism in Arnold J. Toynbee's *A Study of History* (1934–61). Although Toynbee's efforts to enunciate empirically verified laws of historical change evoke memories of Buckle and Spencer, his true calling, which he is too British to admit, is that of the prophet of world spiritual regeneration. The contradiction between his self-image as a commonsensical British social scientist and his real vocation as a messianic irrationalist philosopher has caused his work, in the eyes of all but a few (mostly American) devotees, to fall between two stools. Had he been born German, or Russian, he might have cut a much wider swath through the intellectual history of the twentieth century.

American irrationalism is simply a gentler version of British, with surprisingly few harkings-back to the powerful romanticist movements of the mid-nineteenth century. As in Britain, the writers and artists have represented it more faithfully than the thinkers. Lagging twenty or thirty years behind Europe, American literature missed the fin-de-siècle mood and joined the surge to irrationalism in the years just before World War I. The American first generation consisted of men and women born between 1875 and 1900: the cubist of prose Gertrude Stein (born 1874), who brought her eccentric art to full fruition as an émigré to Paris; the symbolist poet Ezra Pound, most seminal of modern American writers, who did his best work in England and Italy; the neoromanticist poet e.e. cummings; and the symbolist novelist William Faulkner.

Alongside these distinguished innovators appeared an assortment of more traditional writers. Realists and romantic realists of the type of Zola or Dreiser, they were among America's leading playwrights and novelists in the 1920s and 1930s, but not members in good standing of the irrationalist avant-garde. I refer now to Sinclair Lewis, Eugene O'Neill, F. Scott Fitzgerald, and Ernest Hemingway, all of the first American generation, and a few writers born soon after 1900, such as John Steinbeck and James T. Farrell. Even after World War II, realism continued to thrive, as in the plays of Tennessee Williams and Arthur Miller, or in the novels of Norman Mailer and John Updike. But the second American generation has included writers closer to the European mainstream. William Burroughs's *Naked Lunch* (1959), the surrealistic memoirs of a former heroin addict, opened a new era in American literature. His friend, the poet Allen Ginsberg, is another influential avant-gardist of the new wave. Also important are the novels of Kurt Vonnegut, Jr., and John Barth, and the absurdist theater of Edward Albee.

The irrationalist era has finally seen the appearance of serious American composers, struggling with modest success against the unmusicality of Anglo-Saxon culture. Charles Ives (born 1874) was the first substantial figure, followed by a variety of essentially neoromantic musicians, such as Aaron Copland and Samuel Barber. The second American generation has proved bolder, especially in the experimental scores of John Cage, whose work excels the Dadaists in its droll determination to *épater le bourgeois*. Cage's experiments with randomly produced and electronic sounds constitute an almost complete break with Western musical tradition. A typical Cage opus is his "Imaginary Landscape" for twelve radios. The performers twiddle the dials of their radios at will, duplicating the chaos of sonic "reality."

But the major American achievement has been jazz, country, and rock music. Despite merciless commercial exploitation, these are all powerful folk idioms drawn from the culture of blacks, rural poor whites, and other minorities on the outer fringes of the great American social consensus. The proof of their intrinsic vitality is their appeal far beyond America's frontiers. No product of American culture has traveled so well.

Americans have been similarly inventive in the realm of the fine arts. After a beginning even slower than in literature, a swarm of gifted artists born since about 1900 have filled galleries and museums with work of international reputation. The older realism hung on tenaciously through the 1930s, but since then Americans have achieved great success in abstract expressionism and the new schools of "pop" (popular) and "op" (optical) art. The luminaries include Alexander Calder, the inventor of "kinetic" sculpture; Jackson Pollock and Willem de Kooning, the founders of "action" painting; and the "pop" artists Roy Lichtenstein and Andy Warhol. Whereas the abstract expressionists probe the innermost self, pop art directly represents the objects of popular culture, sometimes in a sarcastic or mocking vein adapted from Dada, sometimes with a seemingly uncritical detachment that mocks only the elitist art of the past. For all its calculated banality, there is an ultimate irrationalism in pop art that surpasses even that of the symbolists and surrealists. Pop art is anti-art, a confession (which in some cases needs to be taken seriously) that the artist no longer has anything to express, that reason and emotion both are extinct, that (in Warhol's slogan) "everybody should be a machine."

In philosophy, after the plunge toward a uniquely American school of irrationalism taken by William James at the turn of the century, the leading minds have worked their way back toward positions closer to positivism than to irrationalism. The evolutionary naturalism of James's successor John Dewey retained much of the Jamesian concern for human subjectivity and attempted a synthesis of world views that would eliminate the traditional dichotomy between subject and object. But Dewey did so in a way that brought him into psychic harmony with the goals and methods of modern scientific civilization. He was the epitome of the liberal progressive who has no fear of science or technology because he sees them as mere instrumentalities, man-made and therefore at man's service. Of Dewey's best known contemporaries, George Santayana constructed an eclectic system from fundamentally naturalist premises, and Josiah Royce expounded an American version of Hegelian idealism. Again, the irrationalist world view exerted some influence, but both philosophers were too attached to what Santayana called "the life of reason" to take a radically irrationalist stance in the European manner.

American philosophy since Dewey, Santayana, and Royce has been rigorously academic and close to its roots in American and British thought. British logical positivism and analytical philosophy have won significant American followings. Ralph Barton Perry, C. I. Lewis, and others have offered revisions of pragmatism. Naturalism in the Dewey tradition dominated for many years the distinguished department of philosophy at Columbia, and the chief exponent of idealism since Royce has been Brand Blanshard of Yale. Blanshard's idealism, however, is of the most austerely rational sort, diametrically opposed to the irrationalist world view. Irrationalism operates only in selected portions of the thought of a few recent American philosophers: in the Whiteheadian philosophy of Charles Hartshorne, in the existentialism of John Wild, in the neo-orthodox Christianity of Reinhold Niebuhr. There is also a generous residue of the old Emersonian spirit in the romantic social philosophy of Lewis Mumford.

But this is to consider only the genteel and the academic. In the last two decades, beyond gentility, an irrationalist "counterculture" has arisen that few American academic philosophers are able to understand, much less join. With its rejection of technology and bureaucracy, its neo-Rousseauian cry for a return to nature, and its fascination with the consciousness-expanding potentialities of Eastern religions and psychedelic drugs, the counterculture displays an irrationalist passion alien to American culture, except perhaps for the more extreme forms of New England Transcendentalism. Too anti-intellectual to generate a philosophy of its own, the counterculture has expressed its values most convincingly in its rock and folk music, improvisatory theater, underground journalism, free verse, and experimental lifestyles. Only rarely, as in Charles Reich's *The Greening of America* (1970), has it tried to articulate its world view in a more or less conventional prose medium.

The American irrationalist counterculture has been painfully amorphous and youth-centered. It is perhaps not assimilable by the still younger generation now arriving on the scene. Nevertheless it has been a phenomenon of the highest importance. As in Europe many years earlier, the penetration of radical irrationalism into the national soul expresses profound dissent from the premises under which life is lived in a modern industrial urbanized society. American irrationalism was at first either too eclectic to have much impact, restricted to émigrés and a few avant-gardists, or drowned out by the voices of confident positivists. The counterculture of the 1960s, despite its failure to produce "great books," touched American life at deeper levels. America, too, has discovered the worms in the fruit of modernity. Whatever happens to the specific complex of values adopted by the irrationalists of the 1960s, it seems improbable that Anglo-American thought and art will ever be able to return to the relative insularity of the first half of the twentieth century. America, and Britain also, are "above the fray" no longer.

Summation

Although the twentieth century has been a time of rising affluence for most Western peoples, the dominant note of its intellectual and artistic life has been discontent. The events of the century have eroded Western man's faith in progress, in the nation-state as the guardian of peace and liberty, and in the systems of value that have helped to sustain our civilization for more than a thousand years. Both traditional values and their modern surrogates have not weathered well in our mental climate. The world view most fully expressive of our discontents is "irrationalism," which argues that man and his cosmos are fundamentally nonrational, moved by forces beyond the ken of empirical science, and comprehensible (if at all) only by direct intuitive perception or some other nonrational mode of knowing.

Irrationalism is thus a new form of romanticism, a new attempt to resist the march of modern scientific civilization. Like romanticism, it has often spurred the progress of modernity, by its internal contradictions, its radical experiments with traditional forms of thought and art, its tendency to rush impatiently from savior to savior, and its moral excesses. But more than romanticism, it has sought deliberately to reverse the course of mankind's historical development in defense of personal, tribal, or sectarian values. Even more than romanticism, it views reality in subjective terms, taking whatever meaning it has—and it may have none—from action, will, and striving, and not from any scientifically definable essence or nature. In its most extreme forms, irrationalism does not hesitate to declare reality wholly meaningless.

Even much of the positivist thought of the twentieth century, continuing its development from nineteenth-century origins, has reached conclusions that are congruent with the tenets of irrationalism. This is especially true of the neopositivist philosophies that envisage no role for their discipline apart from logical analysis of science and language. All the other traditional problems of philosophy are ruled invalid and entrusted for "solution" to the preferences and feelings of individuals.

Irrationalism seldom exists in its purest form, but it has inspired such characteristic recent systems of thought as vitalism, existentialism, and neo-orthodox theology, and such movements in the arts and letters as symbolism, expressionism, surrealism, and the theater of the absurd. Its greatest nineteenth-century heralds were Nietzsche, Baudelaire, and Dostoyevsky; among its major twentieth-century exponents are Bergson, Heidegger, and Berdyaev. In political thought, its disciples have ranged all the way from Mussolini to Sartre and radical segments of the new American counterculture.

The most obvious contrasts in national expressions of irrationalism are those between the countries of continental Europe and those of the English-speaking world. Europe has suffered more acutely from the political and social problems of the century and has felt more urgently drawn to the kinds of interpretations and remedies supplied by the irrationalist world view. The German-speaking countries, France, and pre-Bolshevik Russia were the natural homelands of irrationalism. Britain and the United States have shared in its later development, but it has tended to assume weaker forms in Anglo-Saxondom, above all in philosophy and social thought.

Of the three major continental countries, irrationalism was especially powerful in Germany (together with Austria) during its first two generations, consisting of men and women born between 1850 and 1900. The German academic elite set the pace, feeling its special position in German society threatened by the onrush of industrialism and social democracy. The most malevolent offspring of German irrationalism was the fascism of Hitler. France also came to irrationalism early, disappointed by the decline of her world power and torn by class struggle. The first French irrationalists were poets and artists; France led Europe in the versatility and radicalism of its avant-garde aesthetic culture. Russia, too, found irrationalism congenial to its national spirit. Most Russian irrationalists centered their hopes on a revival of Orthodox Christianity. But with the collapse of the autocracy in 1917, irrationalism was officially proscribed on Russian soil and its place taken by Marxism-Leninism. It survived for another generation among the many White émigrés living in the West.

In Britain and America, irrationalism has won most of its victories in literature. It enjoyed great success in British letters in the decades immediately following World War I, but in the United States, late as usual in following European trends, the best period for irrationalism arrived only in the late 1950s. America has become the center of a worldwide irrationalist culture, or counterculture, that exposes the senescence of monopolistic-bureaucratic national establishments and may help to prepare the way for important structural changes in the societies of the future.

But irrationalism itself is also senescent. Having exhausted most of its possibilities in three generations of intense intellectual and aesthetic activity, it will soon yield to a new world view. We cannot bring our study to a close without making an effort in good faith to foresee the form that such a world view may take.

Epilogue

The Next World View

Several conclusions that will make our task of exploring the future a little less arduous are in order.

First, it is clear that during the last three hundred years of Western intellectual history thought and taste have broadly conformed across national frontiers to the systems of fundamental values and meanings that we have called world views. At any one time, a single world view has tended to dominate the Western mind. During the period of its ascendancy, it has been ascendant nearly everywhere, although the peripheral cultures of Russia and America have typically lagged a few years or decades behind the cultures of the Western heartland. The most overwhelming fact of Western intellectual history is the internationalism of world views.

Second, the influence of the world view is seldom confined to intellectual culture. It reaches into aesthetic culture as well and may even find fuller expression of its values in works of art than in works of formal thought. Only in the case of the first world view examined above, the rationalism of the Enlightenment, did aesthetic culture receive its primary inspiration from a rival source.

Third, each successive world view has assumed a different form in each national culture that it penetrates, witnessing to the special refractive powers of national "spirits" in modern Western civilization. Such spirits are neither eternal nor mysterious, originating as they do in the concrete material circumstances of each society. But once crystallized, they acquire a life of their own that may outlast the material circumstances in which they formed. Of the five national spirits under close attention in this study, two formed in the age of rationalism (British and French) and three in the age of romanticism (German, Russian, and American). Especially in the realm of thought, Britain and France have shown throughout the modern period a greater affinity for rationalist and positivist values, Germany and Russia for romanticist and irrationalist values. The United States has occupied a position somewhere in between, growing closer to the Anglo-French model than to the German-Russian.

Fourth, there is a direct correlation between world views and the modernization process. The world views of the "naturalist" family (including rationalism and positivism) support and accelerate modernization, those of the "idealist" family (including romanticism and irrationalism) restrain or resist modernization. That Britain and France have long been the most economically and politically modernized of major Western countries, explains why these are also the countries whose national "spirits" have been most closely identified with rationalism and positivism. Germany and Russia, less modernized, have been more closely identified with romanticism and irrationalism. As the United States has advanced from the status of a relatively poor colonial society to the most fully modernized country in the world, it has predictably become more inclined to the values of the world views of the naturalist family. Achieving modernization in recent decades through a revolutionary change of political and economic systems, Russia has also effected a revolutionary shift of allegiances from its traditional idealist orientation to the naturalist orientation of Marxism. The same shift is now occurring in East Germany.

Fifth, world views of the naturalist and idealist families have alternated with one another dialectically, both in the West as a whole and in the separate national cultures. After an ascendancy of at least six generations, rationalism yielded near the end of the eighteenth century to romanticism, which in turn yielded after two generations to positivism. The ascendancy of positivism also lasted two generations, followed at the end of the nineteenth century by irrationalism, which was the dominant world view of the West for about three generations and has now become largely senescent except for its part in launching the anti-establishmentarian counterculture in America.

Simple extrapolation from this dialectical pattern would lead us to assume that the next world view will spring from the naturalist family of world views. It will be, if that pattern holds, a neorationalist, neopositivist weltanschauung. It will favor continued modernization and oppose efforts to restore premodern values and institutions.

As far as it goes, such extrapolation is, I think, sound. But we need to know more than the rhythm of Western intellectual history to be able to speculate intelligently about the next world view. Great forces are in motion in world history that may well act to modify or even supplant the cyclicalism of the last few hundred or few thousand years.

One possibility is, of course, that we shall have no world view at all, either because humankind will "outgrow" the need for collective belief systems and become intellectually atomized, or because humankind will become atomized in a more literal sense, by a round of thermonuclear wars. The former is conceivable, but would contradict all that we know about human nature and history. Such benevolent anarchy is, at best, many centuries away and may never arrive. The latter is also conceivable and, indeed, more plausible. But we need not pursue it further here, since it would either end Homo sapiens entirely or return him to his neolithic beginnings and compel world history to repeat itself from scratch, as in Walter M. Miller's brilliant apocalyptic fantasy *A Canticle for Leibowitz* (1959).

Assuming that modern civilization and the need for collective belief-systems both survive, what are the forces now at work in the world that bear on the question of the next world view? I should like to call special attention to just three: the integration of humankind, the growing need for science and reason, and the obsolescence of capitalism.

Despite all we have said about the crystallization of national cultures and national spirits in the Western world, it seems unlikely that these national differences will matter as much in future centuries as they have done in the past three. The differences are already less important than they were a few decades ago, and they continue to shrink, under the impact of irreversible tendencies toward ever greater political, economic, social, and cultural integration. As part of the same centrifugal process, the physical and psychic space between the West and the non-Western world is also shrinking. The West is assimilating vital fragments of the culture of the non-Western civilizations. The non-Western civilizations, in the throes of modernization, are becoming more and more like the West, which is the prototypical modernized society, the society that happened through various historical accidents to pass through modernization first.

The logical and world-historically predestined conclusion of this integrative process is the formation of a single planetary civilization, which nothing can prevent except the catastrophe of Armageddon. Indeed, successful attempts to frustrate its formation are likely to be the chief causes of new global wars if they should occur. But from the point of view of the intellectual history of the future, the relevance of world integration is clear: unless disaster intervenes, we must expect the progressive diminution of both national and civilizational differences and the appearance of a universal world view acceptable to both East and West in which the old national souls will play little or no part. Even at the zenith of the national system in Western civilization, as we have seen, the same world view prevailed at about the same time everywhere in the civilization. The various national refractions were significant, but not paramount. As the nations themselves bit by bit dissolve into the City of Man, so will their souls.

My second point helps to explain the apparent ruthlessness of the first. Why the growing uniformity? Apart from the perennial trends toward greater uniformity visible in the histories of all civilizations (trends that account for the growth of the nations themselves from feudal particularism at the end of the Middle Ages), the integrative process goes forward under special urgencies peculiar to our time. One of these is the brutal fact that modern science arms nations with weapons far too destructive to use, which nevertheless they ultimately will use as long as they remain sovereign entities preserved at the psychic level by national cultures and souls. Another is our accelerating need as a species for the rational scientific management of the total resources of the planet, which in turn is likely to create a more or less homogeneous world culture grounded in the methods, assumptions, and techniques of modern science.

The need for more, rather than less, science and reason in the affairs of humankind is not a matter of preference at this stage in world history but a matter of survival. We have all at once reached a point at which population and consumer demand threaten to outrun resources and consumer supply by a margin that is politically, if in no other way, insupportable. Public expectations have risen too fast and too high to make the predictable shortfalls in living standards acceptable to rich and poor zones of the world alike. The situation is particularly desperate in the latter, where many crowded nations are on the road to almost certain doom. To ward off economic and ecological disaster, to prevent a ruinous competition for diminishing resources between rich and poor countries, and to maintain the immense future population of the earth at a level of optimal well-being will require all the rational and scientific management and all the technical and industrial ingenuity of which humankind is capable. Even if the prophets of world economic collapse are unduly pessimistic, the task of keeping a planet of seven billion people (its minimum population by the year 2000) in tolerable health and wealth will still demand heavy investments of human rationality. The abandonment of reason, the abandonment of science and technology, the abandonment of industrialism are no longer options available to humankind. If they ever were, they are available no longer.

This is not to say that material standards of life must soar worldwide to the levels already enjoyed by certain favored elites like the Western haute bourgeoisie, or that humanity must permit the eternal maintenance of such levels even among such elites. But limits exist beyond which few men and women are likely to be movable. We must not expect humankind as a whole, in the West or in the East, to adopt vows of poverty.

Under the circumstances, I suggest again that we shall need all the help the scientific mind can provide in the next several generations. A neorationalist, neopositivist world view will create a world culture both supportive and reflective of the scientific search for survival on a planet of limited resources and rising expectations.

But the human predicament involves more than the pressure of population on resources. Technological solutions alone will not save us. The blissful wisdom of *idiots savants* such as Buckminster Fuller notwithstanding, the crisis of humankind in the last quarter of the twentieth century is also a political crisis. As always in human affairs, we must ask the question: how are the available resources and the power they represent being shared among the members of the human family? When certain countries enjoy one hundred times the per capita wealth of others, when certain individuals receive one thousand times the personal incomes of others, and when such wealth is translated into equally disproportionate political power and influence, it is absurd to congratulate ourselves on the arrival of the "democratic" age. In fact, although wealth is more broadly distributed than in past societies, the exploitation of man by man continues in our century, at a time when the worldwide dissemination of democratic values has unmasked its existence and rendered it unacceptable to the mass of the world's people.

In some respects, the dominant form of exploitation in the modern world, the capitalism of the Western bourgeoisie, has become even more oppressive than it was during its classical age in the nineteenth century. As foreseen by Marx, it has now entered its final period, a period characterized by rampant neo-colonialism on the international scene and by the almost complete disappearance of free enterprise. Only the competition between the capitalist powers and those in the so-called socialist camp prevents one side or the other from fully absorbing every poor nation in the world into a regime of political and economic domination far more effective than anything possible under the old imperialism. Meanwhile, as laissez-faire capitalism changes into state-protected monopoly capitalism, it wins a progressively firmer grip on the Western working classes. Duped by advertising, brainwashed by politicians and educators, bribed by welfare-statism, and regimented by corporate bureaucracies, workers in the capitalist world find themselves at the mercy of a small elite of rich men whose modest public profiles conceal vast power and privilege. The workers' plight is often as bad or worse in the would-be socialist countries, where the place of the capitalist is filled by party and government functionaries.

This latter-day capitalism and its counterpart in the "socialist" world are nonetheless dying systems of social relations. They suffer from bouts of paralyzing economic depression, and the stubborn disaffection of many of their victims. As the cheaply recoverable raw materials in the earth's crust vanish, the struggle for resources among rival elites will further undermine their capacity to govern. They will no longer be able to afford wholesale bribery of their populations. Rigid and unimaginative in their old age, the elites and the systems of private and state capital they represent will collapse.

Of course all attempts to foresee the future are hazardous. Like the dictatorship chronicled in Jack London's futurist novel *The Iron Heel* (1907), a regime that lasted three miserable centuries, political orders may arise out of odd circumstances and interrupt the evolution of social democracy. But I am convinced that in the end humanity will win through to a world commonwealth that is both just and free. I am also convinced that the foundation of the dominant world view of such a commonwealth already exists. Of all the philosophies available to the species in this hour of challenge and decision, the one that appears most likely to prevail is Marxism.

I do not say Marxism as interpreted by any one Marxist thinker, including Lenin, or Marxism as promulgated by the ruling party of any present-day Marxist state. Nor am I thinking of a petrified Marxism that consists only of the authentic texts of Karl Marx. I refer rather to a living Marxism, capable of much the same diversity and responsiveness to new situations as Christianity or Confucianism or Hinduism in their respective golden ages, or as the empirical natural sciences today.

In any event, no philosophy developed in the modern era has been able to weather so well the ideological storms of the twentieth century and to escape the boundaries of its own time and place of origin with so much of its essential doctrine intact as Marxism. Other philosophies have come and gone, from the positivism of Comte and Spencer to the fascism of Maurras and Gentile. But Marxism lives and grows. It nourishes thinking people throughout Eastern Europe and Russia, even when it is shamefully misused by the party apparatus. It is a major force in Western Europe. Marxism dominates much of the advanced contemporary thought of Asia, Africa, and Latin America. It has inspired the North American "New Left," and influenced segments of the otherwise irrationalist American counterculture. Marxism has shaped some of the most powerful independent minds of the century, and oriented many of its greatest artists and writers. Cutting across the irrationalist grain of recent thought and taste, Marxism looks forward to a postmodern democratic world society guided by reason.

The suitability of Marxism as the nucleus of the next world view is borne out by its richnness as well as by its radicalism. Although no philosophy in the world is more unambiguously committed to the goal of a rational, secular, and industrial society, Marxism also has organic links to older world views and a spectrum of national spirits. It uniquely combines German idealism and materialism, French scientific humanism and socialism, and British political economy. From the romanticist world view it draws its dialectical philosophy of history and its Rousseauian sense of community. Adapted since Marx's death to the needs of non-Western societies, Marxism in the Third World incorporates significant elements of the ancient thought of Asia and Africa. Yet at its roots Marxism is a cosmopolitan science, which strives toward the creation of a unified world order submerging the claims of rival national brotherhoods in the higher brotherhood of humankind. Brotherhood—and sisterhood as well, for Marxism is militantly feminist, opposing the exploitation of woman no less than the exploitation of man.

If world history is the world court, and truth (as American pragmatists would argue) is what works, then Marxism also passes the test of historical concreteness. Despite the indefensible atrocities of certain national regimes calling themselves Marxist, thinkers and political movements guided by Marxism have been in the vanguard of the struggles of the oppressed throughout the world since the middle of the nineteenth century. One-third of the world's peoples are already—with varying degrees of authenticity—professed Marxists. It is surely not excessive to forecast that by the end of the century, most of Asia, Africa, Latin America, and southern Europe will have converted to a Marxist public philosophy. Only in North America do the prospects look somewhat dim at this writing.

Indeed, the coming triumph of Marxism may seem an unreal prospect to affluent North Americans. The United States has become a little like old imperial China, a nation whose early unification and prosperity had the unfortunate effect of freezing her further development. From the world's greatest nation, China turned into one of its most backward. The early successes of the United States may have a comparable outcome, and the republic may eventually end her career as the bulwark of worldwide reaction, seeking to protect the privileges of a ruling class more obsolete than the mandarins and warlords of Manchu China.

As an American I hope this will not happen. The counterculture of the 1960s, now in retreat and disarray, serves as a reminder that it need not happen, that there are resources of mind and will in the republic not at the call of her governing elites. These human resources may come forward again in some future national crisis to do their part in restraining or removing established power.

Marxism, it is true, played only a minor role in the counterculture of the 1960s. Anti-establishmentarian Americans may have opted for the irrationalist world view precisely because the value-structure of the capitalist national establishment was predominantly rationalist and positivist. But a second wave of anti-establishmentarian activism may choose a different orientation. Americans may learn that irrationalism, however exotic in the American context, is already an old and exhausted game. Under current world conditions, it is a flight from social responsibility that plays into the hand of the elites, who do not hesitate to enlist its services as the contemporary opiate of the masses. From gurus and granola capitalism has nothing to fear. It can even turn a profit by commercializing them (and does).

But there is a value-system also out of step with official America that can transform the republic much more fundamentally. Marxism accepts industry and technology, but harnesses them in the people's struggle for a liberated world society. Although it embraces what we have called modernity, it also transcends modernity. From its humane science will grow the world view of the twenty-first century.

Notes

Chapter 1: World Views and National Souls

[1]See *The Journal of the History of Ideas: A Quarterly Devoted to Cultural and Intellectual History*, 1940–, and the German journal, *Deutsche Vierteljahrsschrift für Literaturwissenschaft und Geistesgeschichte*, 1923–. Leading texts are Willson H. Coates, Hayden V. White, and (first volume only) J. Salwyn Schapiro, *An Intellectual History of Western Europe*, 2 vols. (New York: McGraw-Hill, 1966–70), and Roland N. Stromberg, *An Intellectual History of Modern Europe*, 2d ed. (Englewood Cliffs, N.J.: Prentice-Hall, 1975). See also Franklin Le Van Baumer, ed., *Main Currents of Western Thought*, 3d ed. (New York: Knopf, 1970).

[2]Reprinted in Fritz Stern, ed., *The Varieties of History* (New York: Meridian, 1956), p. 175.

[3]For attempts to define the discipline, see Baumer, "Methodology and Interpretation," in Baumer, *Main Currents of Western Thought*, pp. 3–14; Baumer, "Intellectual History and Its Problems," *Journal of Modern History* 21 (September 1949):191–203; Carl L. Becker, "Climates of Opinion," in Becker, *The Heavenly City of the Eighteenth-Century Philosophers* (New Haven, Conn.: Yale University Press, 1932), pp. 1–31; George Boas, *The History of Ideas: An Introduction* (New York: Scribner's, 1969); Crane Brinton, *Ideas and Men: The Story of Western Thought* (Englewood Cliffs, N.J.: Prentice-Hall, 1950), pp. 3–28; Felix Gilbert, "Intellectual History: Its Aims and Methods," in Felix Gilbert and Stephen R. Graubard, eds., *Historical Studies Today* (New York: Norton, 1972), pp. 141–58; John C. Greene, "Objectives and Methods in Intellectual History," *Mississippi Valley Historical Review* 44 (June 1957):58–74; John Higham, "Intellectual History and Its Neighbors," *Journal of the History of Ideas* 15 (June 1954):339–47; Hajo Holborn, "The History of Ideas," *American Historical Review* 73 (February 1968):683–95; H. Stuart Hughes, *Consciousness and Society: The Reorientation of European Social Thought, 1890–1930* (New York: Knopf, 1958), pp. 3–32; Arthur O. Lovejoy, Jr., "The Study of the History of Ideas," in Lovejoy, *The Great Chain of Being* (Cambridge, Mass.: Harvard University Press, 1936), pp. 3–23; Quentin Skinner, "Meaning and Understanding in the History of Ideas," *History and Theory* 8 (1969):3–53; Roland N. Stromberg, "Some Models Used by Intellectual Historians," *American Historical Review* 80 (June 1975):563–73; and W. Warren Wagar, "Introduction," in Wagar, ed., *European Intellectual History since Darwin and Marx* (New York: Harper and Row, 1967), pp. 1–11.

[4]Gilbert, "Intellectual History: Its Aims and Methods," p. 155.

[5]See Dilthey, "Die Typen der Weltanschauung und ihre Ausbildung in den metaphysischen Systemen," 1911, in *Gesammelte Schriften*, 16 vols. (Stuttgart: B. G. Teubner, 1957–72), 8:75–118. See also H. A. Hodges, *The Philosophy of Wilhelm Dilthey* (London: Routledge, 1952), especially chap. 3.

[6]Dilthey, "Traum," in William Kluback, *Wilhelm Dilthey's Philosophy of History* (New York: Columbia University Press, 1956), p. 107. See Karl Jaspers, *Psychologie der Weltanschauungen* (Berlin: Springer, 1919).

[7]See Pitirim A. Sorokin, *Social and Cultural Dynamics*, rev. ed. (Boston: Extending Horizons, 1957).

[8]See W. T. Jones, *The Romantic Syndrome: Toward a New Method in Cultural Anthropology and History of Ideas* (The Hague: Nijhoff, 1961).

[9]See Arnold J. Toynbee, *A Study of History*, 12 vols. (New York: Oxford University Press, 1934–61); William H. McNeill, *The Rise of the West: A History of the Human Community* (Chicago: University of Chicago Press, 1963); Crane Brinton, *The Anatomy of Revolution*, rev. ed. (Englewood Cliffs, N.J.: Prentice-Hall, 1952); and Rushton Coulborn, ed., *Feudalism in History* (Princeton, N.J.: Princeton University Press, 1956).

[10]Johan Huizinga, in Stern, ed., *The Varieties of History*, p. 291.

[11]Gustave Le Bon, *The Psychology of Peoples* (New York: Macmillan, 1898), pp. 5–6, 11, and 13.

[12]Ernest Barker, *National Character and the Factors in Its Formation* (New York: Harper, 1927), pp. 18 and 125.

Chapter 2: Rationalism

[1]Quoted in Ernst Cassirer, *The Philosophy of the Enlightenment* (Princeton, N.J.: Princeton University Press, 1951), p. 163.

[2]Alexandre Koyré, *From the Closed World to the Infinite Universe* (Baltimore, Md.: Johns Hopkins Press, 1957), p. vi.

[3]Cassirer, *The Philosophy of the Enlightenment*, p. 43.

[4]See Kearney, *Science and Change, 1500–1700* (New York: McGraw-Hill, 1971).

[5]Cassirer, *The Philosophy of the Enlightenment*, p. 22.

[6]Gay, *The Enlightenment: An Interpretation*, 2 vols. (New York: Knopf, 1966–69), 1:14.

[7]Quoted in Paul Hazard, *European Thought: The Critical Years (1680–1715)* (New Haven, Conn.: Yale University Press, 1953), p. 213.

[8]Cassirer, *The Philosophy of the Enlightenment*, pp. 201–9.

[9]See Norman Hampson, *The Enlightenment* (Baltimore, Md.: Penguin, 1968), p. 128 and passim.

[10]F. Heer, *The Intellectual History of Europe* (London: Weidenfeld and Nicolson, 1966), p. 47.

[11]See Gay, *The Enlightenment*, 2:63–69.

[12]Ibid., 2:229.

[13]Ibid.

[14]Heer, *The Intellectual History of Europe*, p. 320.

[15]Kearney, *Science and Change*, p. 230.

[16]Quoted in W. H. Bruford, *Germany in the Eighteenth Century: The Social Background of the Literary Revival* (Cambridge: Cambridge University Press, 1935), p. 1.

[17]W. M. Simon, *Germany: A Brief History* (New York: Random House, 1966), p. 64.

[18]Heer, *The Intellectual History of Europe*, p. 183.

[19]See Hans Rogger, *National Consciousness in Eighteenth-Century Russia* (Cambridge, Mass.: Harvard University Press, 1960), pp. 78–79 and 82.

[20]See V. V. Zenkovsky, *A History of Russian Philosophy*, 2 vols. (New York: Columbia University Press, 1953), 1:19–22.

Chapter 3: Romanticism

[1]Irving Babbitt, *Rousseau and Romanticism* (New York: Meridian, 1955), pp. 37 and 269.

[2]Berlin in H. G. Schenk, *The Mind of the European Romantics* (London: Constable, 1966), pp. xv–xvi.

[3]F. Heer, *The Intellectual History of Europe* (London: Weidenfield and Nicolson, 1966), pp. 448–49.

[4]Jacques Barzun, *Classic, Romantic, and Modern* (Boston: Little, Brown, 1961), chap. 1.

[5]See Anderson, "German Romanticism as an Ideology of Cultural Crisis," *Journal of the History of Ideas* 2 (June 1941), 301–17.

[6]Heer, *Intellectual History of Europe*, p. 412.

[7]Ibid., p. 430.

[8]W. T. Jones, *The Romantic Syndrome: Toward a New Method in Cultural Anthropology and History of Ideas* (The Hague: Nijhoff, 1961), p. 173.

[9]Stephen F. Mason, *A History of the Sciences* (New York: Collier, 1962), pp. 350 and 356.

[10]George H. Sabine, *A History of Political Theory*, 3d ed. (London: Harrap, 1951), p. 558.

[11]Morse Peckham, *Beyond the Tragic Vision: The Quest for Identity in the Nineteenth Century* (New York: Braziller, 1962), p. 135.

[12]Basil Willey, *Nineteenth Century Studies: Coleridge to Matthew Arnold* (New York: Columbia University Press, 1949), p. 122.

[13]Edwin B. Burgum, "Romanticism," *The Kenyon Review* 3 (Autumn, 1941), 479–90.

[14]Barzun, *Classic, Romantic, and Modern*, p. 134.

[15]Quoted in John B. Halsted, ed., *Romanticism: Problems of Definition, Explanation, and Evaluation* (Boston: Heath, 1965), p. 5.

[16]Christopher Herold, *Mistress to an Age: A Life of Madame de Staël* (Indianapolis, Ind.: Bobbs-Merrill, 1958), p. 197.

[17]Sidney Harcave, *Russia: A History* (Philadelphia: Lippincott, 1952), p. 222.

Chapter 4: Positivism

[1]Franklin Le Van Baumer, *Main Currents of Western Thought*, 3d ed. (New York: Knopf, 1970) p. 456.

[2]W. M. Simon, *European Positivism in the Nineteenth Century* (Ithaca, N.Y.: Cornell University Press, 1963), pp. 3–4.

[3]Merz, *A History of European Thought in the Nineteenth Century*, 4 vols. (Edinburgh: Blackwood, 1912–28), 1:155–56.

[4]Frank E. Manuel, *The Prophets of Paris* (Cambridge, Mass.: Harvard University Press, 1962), p. 164.

[5]Simon, *European Positivism*, especially pp. 269–71.

[6]Elie Halévy, *The Growth of Philosophical Radicalism* (Boston: Beacon, 1955), p. 34.

[7]George H. Sabine, *A History of Political Theory*, 3d ed. (London: Harrap, 1951), p. 573.

[8]Lange, *The History of Materialism*, 3d ed., three volumes in one (London: Routledge, 1925), 2:245.

[9]V. V. Zenkovsky, *A History of Russian Philosophy*, 2 vols. (New York: Columbia University Press, 1953), 1:321.

Chapter 5: Irrationalism

[1]H. Stuart Hughes, *Consciousness and Society: The Reorientation of European Social Thought, 1890–1930* (New York: Knopf, 1958), pp. 33–37.

[2]Franklin Le Van Baumer, *Religion and the Rise of Scepticism* (New York: Harcourt, Brace, 1960), pp. 187–91.

[3]See Fritz Ringer, *The Decline of the German Mandarins: The German Academic Community, 1890–1933* (Cambridge, Mass.: Harvard University Press, 1969).

[4]Quoted in E. H. Carr, *What Is History?* (New York: Knopf, 1962), p. 149.

[5]I. M. Bocheński, *Contemporary European Philosophy* (Berkeley and Los Angeles: University of California Press, 1961), p. 140.

[6]See George L. Mosse, *The Crisis of German Ideology: Intellectual Origins of the Third Reich* (New York: Grosset and Dunlap, 1964).

[7]Gerhard Masur, *Prophets of Yesterday: Studies in European Culture, 1890–1914* (New York: Macmillan, 1961), pp. 263–64.

[8]Willson H. Coates and Hayden V. White, *An Intellectual History of Western Europe* (New York: McGraw-Hill, 1966–70), 2:325.

[9]See Ernst Nolte, *Three Faces of Fascism: Action Française, Italian Fascism, National Socialism* (New York: Holt, Rinehart and Winston, 1966).

[10]Arnold J. Toynbee, *A Study of History* (New York: Oxford University Press, 1934–61), 5:383–84 and 6:49–132.

[11]See Philippe Jullian, *Esthètes et magiciens* (Paris: Perrin, 1969), translated as *Dreamers of Decadence: Symbolist Painters of the 1890s* (New York: Praeger, 1971).

[12]V. V. Zenkovsky, *A History of Russian Philosophy*, 2 vols. (New York: Columbia University Press, 1953), 2:924.

[13]See Edmund Wilson, *Axel's Castle: A Study in the Imaginative Literature of 1870–1930* (New York: Scribner's, 1931), pp. 16–17.

[14]See Albert William Levi, *Philosophy and the Modern World* (Bloomington, Ind.: Indiana University Press, 1959), chap. 11.

Appendix I
The Generations

Note: Not all the thinkers, writers, and artists listed under a given world view are the best possible exemplars of that world view, but each contributed to its development in some significant way. "Great Britain" includes Ireland, "France" includes French-speaking Belgium and Switzerland, "Germany" includes German-speaking Austria and Switzerland. The date on the left of each name is the date of birth, the letter(s) on the right denotes field(s) of principal achievement.

Legend: N = Natural sciences
P = Philosophy, theology
S = Social, political or economic thought, historiography
L = Literature
A = Art, architecture
M = Music

1. Rationalism

Great Britain

1540 Gilbert (N)	1632 Locke (P)	1675 Clarke (P)
1561 Bacon (P)	1635 Hooke (N)	1676 Collins (P)
1578 Harvey (N)	1642 Newton (N)	1678 Bolingbroke (P,S)
1583 Herbert (P)	1657 Tindal (P)	1685 Berkeley (P)
1588 Hobbes (P)	1659 Defoe (L)	1688 Pope (L)
1614 More (P)	1667 Swift (L)	1694 Chesterfield (L)
1627 Boyle (N)	1670 Toland (P)	1697 Hogarth (A)
1628 Ray (N)	1671 Shaftesbury (P)	1705 Hartley (P)
1630 Barrow (N)	1672 Steele (L)	1707 Fielding (L)
1631 Dryden (L)	1672 Addison (L)	1709 Johnson (L)

1711 Hume (P)
1721 Smollett (L)
1723 Reynolds (A)
1723 Smith (S)

1723 Ferguson (P)
1727 Gainsborough (A)
1728 Adam (A)
1733 Priestley (N,P)

1737 Paine (S)
1737 Gibbon (S)
1743 Paley (P)
1748 Bentham (P,S)

France

1588 Mersenne (N,P)
1592 Gassendi (N,P)
1593 Le Nain (A)
1594 Poussin (A)
1596 Descartes (N,P)
1606 Corneille (L)
1622 Molière (L)
1623 Pascal (N,P)
1636 Boileau (L)
1638 Malebranche (P)
1639 Racine (L)
1645 La Bruyère (L)
1647 Bayle (P,S)
1657 Fontenelle (P)
1658 St. Pierre (S)

1683 Réaumur (N)
1689 Montesquieu (S)
1694 Voltaire (P,L)
1694 Quesnay (S)
1698 Maupertuis (N,P)
1699 Chardin (A)
1701 La Chalotais (S)
1707 Buffon (N)
1709 La Mettrie (P)
1712 Rousseau (S,L)
1713 Soufflot (A)
1713 Diderot (P,L)
1715 Condillac (P)
1715 Helvétius (P)
1717 D'Alembert (N,P)

1723 D'Holbach (P)
1727 Turgot (S)
1732 Beaumarchais (L)
1736 Ledoux (A)
1736 Lagrange (N)
1740 Sade (P,L)
1741 Houdon (A)
1743 Lavoisier (N)
1743 Condorcet (S)
1746 Monge (N)
1748 David (A)
1749 Laplace (N)
1754 Destutt de
     Tracy (P)
1757 Cabanis (P)

Germany

1571 Kepler (N)
1632 Pufendorf (S)
1635 Becher (N,S)
1646 Leibniz (N,P)
1655 Thomasius (P)
1679 Wolff (P)

1694 Reimarus (P)
1700 Gottsched (L)
1714 Gluck (M)
1714 Baumgarten (P)
1724 Kant (N,P)
1728 Mengs (A)

1729 Lessing (P,L)
1732 Haydn (M)
1733 Wieland (L)
1751 Tischbein (A)
1756 Mozart (M)

Russia

1711 Lomonosov (N)
1722 Skovoroda (P)

1744 Novikov (L)
1749 Radishchev (L)

1774 Fonvizin (L)

United States

1696 Johnson (P)
1703 Edwards (P)
1706 Franklin (N,L)
1723 Witherspoon (P)

1735 J. Adams (S)
1738 West (A)
1738 Allen (P,S)
1743 Jefferson (S)

1745 Rush (N)
1755 Hamilton (S)

2. Romanticism

Great Britain

1729 Percy (L)
1729 Burke (P,S)
1736 Macpherson (L)
1741 Fuseli (A)
1757 Blake (L,A)
1759 Burns (L)
1760 Beckford (L)
1763 Cobbett (S)
1764 Radcliffe (L)
1770 Wordsworth (L)

1771 Scott (L)
1772 Coleridge (S,L)
1774 Southey (L)
1775 Turner (A)
1775 Lamb (L)
1775 Lewis (L)
1776 Constable (A)
1778 Hazlitt (L)
1784 Hunt (L)
1785 De Quincey (L)

1788 Byron (L)
1792 P. Shelley (L)
1795 Carlyle (S,L)
1795 Keats (L)
1797 M. Shelley (L)
1801 Newman (P)
1812 Dickens (L)
1812 Pugin (A)

France

1712 J. Rousseau (S,L)
1743 St.-Martin (P)
1744 Lamarck (N)
1754 Bonald (S)
1754 Maistre (S)
1766 Maine de Biran (P)
1766 De Staël (L)
1767 Girodet-Trioson (A)
1768 Chateaubriand (L)
1770 Sénancour (L)
1772 Fourier (S)
1773 Sismondi (S)
1776 Ballanche (S)
1780 Nodier (L)

1782 Lamennais (P,S)
1782 Auber (M)
1790 Lamartine (L)
1791 Géricault (A)
1791 Meyerbeer (M)
1792 Cousin (P)
1795 Thierry (S)
1796 Corot (A)
1796 Enfantin (S)
1797 Vigny (L)
1798 Michelet (S)
1798 Delacroix (A)
1802 Dumas (L)
1802 Hugo (L)
1803 Mérimée (L)
1803 Berlioz (M)

1804 Sand (L)
1804 Sue (L)
1804 Sainte-Beuve (L)
1808 Barbey d'Aurevilly (L)
1808 Nerval (L)
1809 Proudhon (S)
1809 Borel (L)
1810 Musset (L)
1811 Gautier (L)
1812 T. Rousseau (A)
1814 Viollet-le-Duc (A)
1818 Gounod (M)
1822 Franck (M)

Germany

1724 Kant (N,P)
1730 Hamann (P)
1740 Jung-Stilling (P)
1743 Jacobi (P)
1744 Herder (P,S)
1749 Goethe (L)
1752 J. Müller (S)
1752 Klinger (L)

1759 Schiller (L)
1762 Fichte (P)
1763 Jean-Paul (L)
1764 Gentz (S)
1765 Baader (P)
1767 A. Schlegel (L)
1768 Schleiermacher (P)
1768 Werner (N)

1769 Arndt (S,L)
1770 Beethoven (M)
1770 Hegel (P)
1770 Hölderlin (L)
1772 Novalis (L)
1772 F. Schlegel (L)
1773 Fries (P)
1773 Tieck (L)

1773 Wackenroder (L) 1779 Savigny (S)   1789 Carus (A)
1774 Friedrich (A)   1781 Arnim (L)   1789 Overbeck (A)
1775 Schelling (P)   1781 Krause (P)   1794 W. Müller (L)
1776 Görres (P)   1782 Froebel (P)   1797 Heine (L)
1776 Hoffmann (L)   1785 J. Grimm (L)   1797 Schubert (M)
1777 Runge (A)   1786 W. Grimm (L)   1802 Lenau (L)
1777 Kleist (L)   1786 Weber (M)   1806 Stirner (P)
1778 Jahn (S)   1787 Uhland (L)   1809 Mendelssohn (M)
1778 Brentano (L)   1788 Schopenhauer (P) 1810 Schumann (M)
1779 A. Müller (S)   1788 Eichendorff (L)   1811 Liszt (M)
1779 Oken (N,P)   1788 Rückert (L)   1813 Wagner (M)

Russia

1766 Karamzin (S)   1799 Pushkin (L)   1811 Belinsky (P,S)
1774 Vellansky (L)   1803 Odoyevsky (P)   1812 Herzen (P,S)
1783 Zhukovsky (L)   1804 Khomyakov (P)   1813 Stankevich (P)
1794 Chaadayev (P)   1804 Glinka (M)   1814 Lermontov (L)
1799 Bryullov (A)   1806 Kireyevsky (P)   1814 Bakunin (S)

United States

1779 Allston (A)   1801 Cole (A)   1810 Parker (P)
1780 Channing (P)   1802 Ripley (P)   1811 Stowe (L)
1783 Irving (L)   1803 Brownson (P)   1814 Motley (S)
1789 Cooper (L)   1803 Emerson (P,L)   1817 Thoreau (P)
1789 Sparks (S)   1804 Hawthorne (L)   1819 Whitman (L)
1793 Doughty (A)   1807 Longfellow (L)   1819 Melville (L)
1794 Bryant (L)   1807 Whittier (L)   1823 Parkman (S)
1796 Prescott (S)   1809 Poe (L)
1800 Bancroft (S)   1810 Fuller (P)

3. Positivism

Great Britain

1748 Bentham (P,S)   1783 Thompson (S)   1812 Dickens (L)
1766 Malthus (S)   1790 Senior (S)   1815 Trollope (L)
1766 Dalton (N)   1791 Faraday (N)   1817 Lewes (P)
1771 Owen (S)   1797 Lyell (N)   1818 Congreve (P)
1772 Ricardo (S)   1806 J. S. Mill (P,S) 1818 Joule (N)
1773 J. Mill (P,S)   1809 Darwin (N)   1819 Kingsley (S,L)
1783 Hodgskin (S)   1811 Thackeray (L)   1819 Eliot (L)

1820 Spencer (P,S)
1821 Buckle (S)
1822 Galton (N)
1824 Kelvin (N)
1825 Stubbs (S)
1825 T. Huxley (N,P)
1826 Bagehot (S)
1829 Gardiner (S)

1831 Maxwell (N)
1831 Harrison (P)
1832 Stephen (S)
1832 Tylor (S)
1834 Acton (S)
1835 Jevons (S)
1838 Morley (L)
1840 Hardy (L)

1842 Hyndman (S)
1842 Marshall (S)
1849 Henley (L)
1852 Moore (L)
1854 Frazer (S)
1857 Gissing (L)
1857 Pearson (N,P)
1864 Schiller (P)

France

1760 St.-Simon (S)
1783 Stendhal (L)
1787 Guizot (S)
1788 Cabet (S)
1798 Comte (P,S)
1799 Balzac (L)
1801 Littré (P)
1805 Tocqueville (S)
1808 Daumier (A)
1809 Proudhon (S)
1811 Blanc (S)
1813 Bernard (N)
1814 Millet (A)
1816 Gobineau (S)
1819 Courbet (A)
1821 Flaubert (L)

1822 Pasteur (N)
1822 E. Goncourt (L)
1823 Laffitte (P)
1823 Renan (P,S)
1828 Verne (L)
1828 Taine (S)
1829 Prévost-Paradol
      (S)
1830 Fustel de
      Coulanges (S)
1830 J. Goncourt (L)
1830 Pissarro (A)
1832 Manet (A)
1832 Eiffel (A)
1834 Degas (A)
1839 Cézanne (A)

1840 Monet (A)
1840 Daudet (L)
1840 Zola (L)
1843 De Roberty (S)
1844 France (L)
1844 Monod (S)
1845 Guesde (S)
1848 Huysmans (L)
1849 Novicow (S)
1850 De Maupassant (L)
1852 Becquerel (N)
1858 Durkheim (S)
1859 Seurat (A)
1869 Worms (S)

Germany

1769 Humboldt (N)
1776 Niebuhr (S)
1777 Gauss (N)
1795 Ranke (S)
1800 Wöhler (N)
1801 J. Müller (N)
1803 Liebig
1803 Ruge (P,S)
1804 Feuerbach (P)
1804 Jacobi (N)
1808 Strauss (P)
1809 Bauer (P)
1813 Waitz (S)
1813 Ludwig (L)

1813 Hebbel (L)
1814 Giesebrecht (S)
1815 Menzel (A)
1815 Bachofen (S)
1817 Vogt (N,P)
1817 Sybel (S)
1817 Mommsen (S)
1818 Marx (P,S)
1818 Du Bois-
      Reymond (N)
1819 Fontane (L)
1820 Engels (P,S)
1821 Helmholtz (N)
1822 Mendel (N)

1822 Clausius (N)
1822 Ritschl (P)
1822 Moleschott (N,P)
1824 Büchner (P)
1826 Überweg (P)
1826 Bastian (S)
1826 Liebknecht (S)
1831 Schäffle (S)
1833 Dühring (P)
1833 Brahms (M)
1834 Haeckel (N,P)
1834 Treitschke (S)
1834 Weismann (N)
1838 Mach (N,P)

1838 Gumplowicz (S)   1844 Ratzel (S)   1856 Lamprecht (S)
1840 Bebel (S)   1847 Liebermann (A)   1857 Hertz (N)
1842 Ratzenhofer (S)   1849 Nordau (S,L)   1857 Sudermann (L)
1843 Koch (N)   1853 Ostwald (N,P)   1862 Hauptmann (L)
1843 Avenarius (P)   1854 Kautsky (S)

Russia

1793 Lobachevsky (N)   1828 Chernyshevsky (P) 1842 Vereshchagin (A)
1809 Gogol (L)   1829 Sechenov (N)   1843 Mikhailovsky (P,S)
1814 Bakunin (S)   1829 Lilienfeld (S)   1844 Repin (A)
1818 Turgenev (L)   1834 Mendeleyev (N)   1845 Metchinikov (N,P)
1820 S. Soloviev (S)   1837 Lesevich (P)   1849 Pavlov (N)
1821 Dostoyevsky (L)   1840 Pisarev (P)   1857 Plekhanov (P,S)
1823 Lavrov (P)   1840 Kovalevsky (N)   1860 Chekhov (L)
1828 Tolstoy (L)   1842 Kropotkin (S)

United States

1818 Morgan (S)   1841 Ward (S)   1855 Giddings (S)
1823 Le Conte (N,P)   1841 Holmes (S)   1856 Sargent (A)
1834 Whistler (A)   1842 Fiske (P)   1857 Veblen (S)
1835 Twain (L)   1842 W. James (P)   1859 Dewey (P)
1836 Homer (A)   1843 H. James (L)   1860 Garland (L)
1836 Harte (L)   1844 Eakins (A)   1861 Turner (S)
1837 Howells (L)   1845 Cassatt (A)   1870 Norris (L)
1838 H. Adams (S)   1848 B. Adams (S)   1871 Crane (L)
1839 Peirce (P)   1850 H. B. Adams (S)   1871 Dreiser (L)
1839 Gibbs (N)   1852 Michelson (N)   1876 London (L)
1840 Sumner (S)   1852 De Leon (S)
1841 Shaler (S)   1854 Small (S)

4. Irrationalism

Great Britain

1834 Morris (S,L)   1857 Conrad (L)   1865 Yeats (L)
1835 Butler (P,L)   1858 Wallas (S)   1865 Symons (L)
1837 Swinburne (L)   1859 Alexander (P)   1865 Kipling (L)
1839 Pater (L)   1861 Whitehead (P)   1867 Dowson (L)
1846 Bradley (P)   1863 Delius (M)   1867 Johnson (L)
1856 Wilde (L)   1863 Machen (L)   1867 A. E. (L)
1856 Shaw (L)   1864 Hobhouse (S)   1869 Blackwood (L)

1871 McDougall (S)
1872 Vaughan
  Williams (M)
1872 Beardsley (A)
1878 Dunsany (L)
1882 Joyce (L)
1882 V. Woolf (L)
1883 Bax (M)
1883 Hulme (P,L)
1884 W. Lewis (L)
1885 D. Lawrence (L)
1888 Eliot (L)

1888 T. Lawrence (L)
1889 Collingwood (P,S)
1889 Toynbee (S)
1892 Tolkien (L)
1894 A. Huxley (L)
1898 C. S. Lewis (L)
1898 H. Moore (A)
1903 Sutherland (A)
1904 Greene (L)
1906 Beckett (L)
1907 Auden (L)
1910 Bacon (A)

1911 Golding (L)
1912 Durrell (L)
1914 D. Thomas (L)
1917 Burgess (L)
1925 Aldiss (L)
1930 Ballard (L)
1930 Pinter (L)
1934 Brunner (L)
1937 Stoppard (L)
1939 Moorcock (L)

France

1815 Renouvier (P)
1821 Baudelaire (L)
1824 Puvis de
  Chavannes (A)
1826 Moreau (A)
1838 Fouillée (P,S)
1838 Villiers de
  L'Isle Adam (L)
1840 Redon (A)
1841 Le Bon (S)
1842 Mallarmé (L)
1843 Tarde (S)
1844 Verlaine (L)
1844 H. Rousseau (A)
1845 Boutroux (P)
1846 Bloy (P,L)
1847 Sorel (S)
1848 Huysmans (L)
1848 Gauguin (A)
1854 Rimbaud (L)
1854 Guyau (P)
1856 Moréas (L)
1857 Lévy-Bruhl (S)
1858 Durkheim (S)
1859 Bergson (P)
1859 Jaurès (S)
1861 Blondel (P)
1862 Debussy (M)

1862 Maeterlinck (L)
1862 Barrès (S,L)
1866 Satie (M)
1866 Rolland (L)
1868 Maurras (S)
1868 Claudel (L)
1869 Gide (L)
1869 Matisse (A)
1870 Denis (A)
1870 Le Roy (P)
1870 Louÿs (L)
1871 Valéry (L)
1871 Proust (L)
1871 Rouault (A)
1873 Jarry (L)
1873 Péguy (L)
1875 Ravel (M)
1876 Vlaminck (A)
1880 Apollinaire (L)
1881 Teilhard de
  Chardin (P)
1882 Maritain (P)
1882 Braque (A)
1883 Lecomte du Noüy
  (P)
1883 Varèse (M)
1884 Gilson (P)
1885 Mauriac (L)

1887 Arp (A)
1887 Duchamp (A)
1888 Bernanos (L)
1889 Marcel (P)
1892 Cocteau (L,A)
1895 Artaud (L)
1895 Eluard (L)
1896 Breton (L)
1898 Magritte (A)
1900 St.-Exupéry (L)
1900 Tanguy (A)
1901 Dubuffet (A)
1901 Malraux (L)
1905 Sartre (P,L)
1905 Mounier (P)
1908 Lévi-Strauss (S)
1908 Messiaen (M)
1908 De Beauvoir (P,L)
1908 Merleau-Ponty (P)
1910 Genet (L)
1910 Anouilh (L)
1912 Ionesco (L)
1913 Camus (L)
1922 Robbe-Grillet (L)
1926 Butor (L)
1930 Godard (A)
1932 Truffaut (A)

Germany

1827 Böcklin (A)	1870 Barlach (A)	1884 Beckmann (A)
1833 Dilthey (P,S)	1872 Klages (P)	1884 Rank (N)
1842 E. Hartmann (P)	1874 Scheler (P)	1884 Bultmann (P)
1842 Cohen (P)	1874 Cassirer (P)	1885 Berg (M)
1844 Nietzsche (P)	1874 Hofmannsthal (L)	1886 Barth (P)
1846 Eucken (P)	1874 Schönberg (M)	1886 Benn (L)
1848 Windelband (P)	1875 Rilke (L)	1886 Kokoschka (A)
1855 Tönnies (S)	1875 Mann (L)	1886 Ball (L)
1855 Chamberlain (S)	1875 Schweitzer (P)	1886 Koffka (N)
1856 Freud (N,S)	1875 Jung (N,S)	1887 Köhler (N)
1859 Husserl (P)	1876 Moeller van den	1887 Schwitters (A)
1860 Mahler (M)	Bruck (S)	1889 Hitler (S)
1862 Meinecke (S)	1876 Michels (S)	1889 Heidegger (P)
1862 Schnitzler (L)	1877 Hesse (L)	1889 Brunner (P)
1862 Klimt (A)	1878 Buber (P)	1891 Ernst (A)
1863 Rickert (P,S)	1879 Klee (A)	1893 Grosz (A)
1863 Sombart (S)	1880 Wertheimer (N)	1893 Mannheim (S)
1864 Weber (S)	1880 Keyserling (P)	1893 Rosenberg (S)
1864 Strauss (M)	1880 Spengler (S)	1895 Jünger (L)
1865 Troeltsch (S)	1882 N. Hartmann (P)	1902 Landgrebe (P)
1867 Driesch (N,P)	1883 Jaspers (P)	1906 Bonhoeffer (P)
1868 George (L)	1883 Kafka (L)	1917 Böll (L)
1870 Adler (N)	1883 Webern (M)	1927 Grass (L)

Russia

1821 Dostoyevsky (L)	1866 Kandinsky (A)	1887 Chagall (A)
1822 Danilevsky (S)	1869 Hippius (L)	1890 Pasternak (L)
1828 Chicherin (P)	1871 Bulgakov (P)	1891 Prokofiev (M)
1828 Fyodorov (P)	1872 Diaghilev (A)	1893 Mayakovsky (L)
1828 Tolstoy (L)	1872 Scriabin (M)	1898 Chelishev (A)
1831 Blavatsky (P)	1873 Rachmaninov (M)	1899 Nabokov (L)
1853 V. Soloviev (P)	1874 Berdyaev (P)	1918 Solzhenitsyn (L)
1862 S. Trubetskoy (P)	1874 Roerich (A)	1925 Sinyavsky
1863 Y. Trubetskoy (P)	1880 Blok (L)	("Abram Terts")
1865 Merezhkovsky (L)	1882 Stravinsky (M)	(L)
1866 Shestov (P)	1882 Florensky (P)	

United States

1873 Hocking (P)	1897 Faulkner (L)	1915 Motherwell (A)
1874 Ives (M)	1897 Hartshorne (P)	1920 Bradbury (L)
1874 Stein (L)	1898 Calder (A)	1922 Vonnegut (L)

1879 Lindsay (L)	1900 Copland (M)	1923 Lichtenstein (A)
1885 Pound (L)	1902 Wild (P)	1925 Rauschenberg (A)
1889 Sorokin (S)	1904 De Kooning (A)	1926 Ginsberg (L)
1889 Lippmann (S)	1910 Barber (M)	1928 Albee (L)
1892 Niebuhr (P)	1912 Cage (M)	1928 Reich (S)
1893 Krutch (P)	1912 Pollock (A)	1930 Warhol (A)
1894 e. e. cummings (L)	1913 N. Brown (P,S)	1930 J. Barth (L)
1895 Mumford (P,S)	1914 Burroughs (L)	

Appendix II

Comparative Chronologies

Note: The dates below indicate the approximate periods of greatest efflorescence for each world view in Western civilization as a whole and in the five national cultures studied in the text.

1. Rationalism

Western civilization:	1650–1790
Great Britain:	1620–1790
France:	1640–1810
Germany:	1690–1770
Russia:	1740–1800
United States:	1740–1810

2. Romanticism

Western civilization:	1790–1840
Great Britain:	1790–1840
France:	1820–1850
Germany:	1770–1830
Russia:	1820–1860
United States:	1830–1870

3. Positivism

Western civilization:	1840–1890
Great Britain:	1830–1890
France:	1850–1890

Germany: 1840–1890
Russia: 1860–1900
United States: 1870–1910

4. Irrationalism

Western civilization: 1890–1970
Great Britain: 1890–1970
France: 1880–1970
Germany: 1890–1945
Russia (and émigrés):   1890–1940
United States: 1920–1970

A Selected Bibliography of Scholarly Sources

A complete bibliography for a book of this kind would require the mention of almost every title published in the Western world since the invention of the printing press. Instead, I have listed a few choice volumes in only two categories: works dealing with the four world views and works dealing with the cultural and intellectual history of the five nations considered in the text. There is inevitably some overlap. Several of the books on world views discuss two or more and are listed under the world view that they treat at greatest length or with greatest insight. A few national studies contain material on other countries. For more general books, consult the bibliographical information in the notes for Chapter 1.

1. Rationalism

Becker, Carl L. *The Heavenly City of the Eighteenth-Century Philosophers* (1932).

Bronowski, J., and Mazlish, Bruce. *The Western Intellectual Tradition: Leonardo to Hegel* (1960).

Burtt, E. A. *Metaphysical Foundations of Modern Physical Science* (1927).

Butterfield, Herbert. *The Origins of Modern Science* (1949).

Cassirer, Ernst. *The Philosophy of the Enlightenment* (1951).

Gay, Peter. *The Enlightenment: An Interpretation* (1966–69).

Goldman, Lucien. *The Philosophy of the Enlightenment: The Christian Burgess and the Enlightenment* (1974).

Hall, A. R. *The Scientific Revolution, 1500–1800* (1954).

Hampson, Norman. *The Enlightenment* (1968).

Hazard, Paul. *The European Mind: The Critical Years (1680–1715)* (1952).

_____. *European Thought in the Eighteenth Century* (1954).

Koestler, Arthur. *The Sleepwalkers: A History of Man's Changing Vision of the Universe* (1959).

Koyré, Alexandre. *From the Closed World to the Infinite Universe* (1957).

Krieger, Leonard. *An Essay on the Theory of Enlightened Despotism* (1975).

Kuhn, Thomas. *The Copernican Revolution* (1956).
———. *The Structure of Scientific Revolutions* (1962).
Smith, Preserved. *A History of Modern Culture: The Enlightenment* (1934).
Webster, Charles, ed. *The Intellectual Revolution of the Seventeenth Century* (1974).

2. Romanticism

Aiken, Henry D., ed. *The Age of Ideology* (1956).
Barzun, Jacques. *Classic, Romantic and Modern* (1961).
Berlin, Isaiah. *Vico and Herder: Two Studies in the History of Ideas* (1976).
Brion, Marcel. *Art of the Romantic Era: Romanticism, Classicism, Realism* (1966).
Clark, Sir Kenneth. *The Romantic Rebellion: Romantic versus Classic Art* (1974).
Clive, Geoffrey. *The Romantic Enlightenment: Ambiguity and Paradox in the Western Mind (1750-1920)* (1960).
Frye, Northrop, ed. *Romanticism Reconsidered* (1963).
Furst, Lilian R. *Romanticism in Perspective: A Comparative Study of Aspects of the Romantic Movements in England, France, and Germany* (1969).
Halsted, John B., ed. *Romanticism: Problems of Definition, Explanation, and Evaluation* (1965).
Hayes, Carlton J. H. *The Historical Evolution of Modern Nationalism* (1931).
Hobsbawm, E. J. *The Age of Revolution, 1789-1848* (1962).
Löwith, Karl. *From Hegel to Nietzsche* (1964).
Mandelbaum, Maurice. *History, Man, and Reason: A Study in Nineteenth-Century Thought* (1971).
Marcuse, Herbert. *Reason and Revolution: Hegel and the Rise of Social Theory* (1941).
Meinecke, Friedrich. *Historism: The Rise of a New Historical Outlook* (1972).
Peckham, Morse. *Beyond the Tragic Vision: The Quest for Identity in the Nineteenth Century* (1962).
Praz, Mario. *The Romantic Agony* (1951).
Schenk, H. G. *The Mind of the European Romantics* (1966).
Talmon, J. L. *The Origins of Totalitarian Democracy* (1960).
———. *Political Messianism: The Romantic Phase* (1961).
White, Hayden V. *Metahistory: The Historical Imagination in Nineteenth-Century Europe* (1974).

3. Positivism

Barzun, Jacques. *Darwin, Marx, Wagner* (1941).
Butterfield, Herbert. *Man on His Past: The Study of the History of Historical Scholarship* (1955).
Chadwick, Owen. *The Secularization of the European Mind in the Nineteenth Century* (1976).
Eiseley, Loren. *Darwin's Century: Evolution and the Men Who Discovered It* (1958).

Heilbroner, Robert L. *The Worldly Philosophers: The Lives, Times, and Ideas of the Great Economic Thinkers* (1953).

Himmelfarb, Gertude. *Darwin and the Darwinian Revolution* (1959).

Laski, Harold J. *The Rise of European Liberalism* (1936).

Lichtheim, George. *Marxism: An Historical and Critical Study* (1961).

Lukács, György. *Studies in European Realism* (1950).

Morazé, Charles. *Triumph of the Middle Classes: A Study of European Values in the Nineteenth Century* (1966).

Nochlin, Linda. *Realism and Tradition in Art, 1848–1900* (1966).

Ruggiero, Guido de. *The History of European Liberalism* (1927).

Schapiro, J. Salwyn. *Liberalism and the Challenge of Fascism: Social Forces in England and France, 1815–1870* (1949).

Simon, W. M. *European Positivism in the Nineteenth Century* (1963).

4. Irrationalism

Arnason, H. H. *History of Modern Art: Painting, Sculpture, Architecture* (1968).

Barrett, William. *Irrational Man: A Study in Existential Philosophy* (1958).

Baumer, Franklin L. *Religion and the Rise of Scepticism* (1960).

Breisach, Ernst. *Introduction to Modern Existentialism* (1962).

Brown, J. A. C. *Freud and the Post-Freudians* (1961).

Esslin, Martin. *The Theatre of the Absurd* (1961).

Farber, Marvin. *The Aims of Phenomenology* (1966).

Fowlie, Wallace. *Age of Surrealism* (1950).

Hughes, H. Stuart. *Consciousness and Society: The Reorientation of European Social Thought, 1890–1930* (1958).

_____. *The Sea Change: The Migration of Social Thought, 1930–1965* (1975).

Jay, Martin. *The Dialectical Imagination: A History of the Frankfurt School and the Institute of Social Research, 1923–1950* (1973).

Jullian, Philippe. *Dreamers of Decadence: Symbolist Painters of the 1890s* (1971).

Levi, Albert William. *Philosophy and the Modern World* (1959).

Macquarrie, John. *Twentieth-Century Religious Thought* (1963).

Masur, Gerhard. *Prophets of Yesterday: Studies in European Culture, 1890–1914* (1961).

Nolte, Ernst. *Three Faces of Fascism: Action Française, Italian Fascism, National Socialism* (1966).

Shklar, Judith N. *After Utopia: The Decline of Political Faith* (1959).

Stromberg, Roland N. *After Everything: European Thought and Culture since 1945* (1975).

Wagar, W. Warren. *Good Tidings: The Belief in Progress from Darwin to Marcuse* (1972).

Whyte, Lancelot Law. *The Unconscious before Freud* (1960).

Wilson, Edmund. *Axel's Castle: A Study in the Imaginative Literature of 1870 to 1930* (1931).

5. Great Britain

Barker, Ernest, ed. *The Character of England* (1947).
Bowra, Maurice. *The Romantic Imagination* (1949).
Bennett, Jonathan. *Locke, Berkeley, Hume: Central Themes* (1971).
Brinton, Crane. *English Political Thought in the Nineteenth Century* (1933).
Buckley, Jerome Hamilton. *The Victorian Temper: A Study in Literary Culture* (1951).
Carré, Meyrick H. *Phases of Thought in England* (1949).
Fraser, George S. *The Modern Writer and His World: Continuity and Innovation in Twentieth-Century English Literature* (1964).
Frye, Northrop. *A Study of English Romanticism* (1968).
Halévy, Elie. *The Growth of Philosophical Radicalism* (1928).
Himmelfarb, Gertrude. *Victorian Minds* (1968).
Houghton, Walter E. *The Victorian Frame of Mind, 1830–1870* (1957).
Humphreys, A. R. *The Augustan World* (1954).
Hynes, Samuel. *The Edwardian Turn of Mind* (1968).
Robson, John M. *The Improvement of Mankind: The Social and Political Thought of John Stuart Mill* (1968).
Somervell, D. C. *English Thought in the Nineteenth Century* (1929).
Stephen, Sir Leslie. *History of English Thought in the Eighteenth Century* (1876).
Willey, Basil. *The Eighteenth Century Background* (1940).
_____. *More Nineteenth Century Studies: A Group of Honest Doubters* (1956).
_____. *Nineteenth Century Studies: Coleridge to Matthew Arnold* (1949).
_____. *The Seventeenth Century Background* (1934).

6. France

Barzun, Jacques. *Berlioz and the Romantic Century* (1950).
Brée, Germaine. *Women Writers in France* (1973).
Cazamian, Louis. *A History of French Literature* (1955).
Charlton, D. G. *Positivist Thought in France During the Second Empire* (1959).
Crocker, Lester G. *An Age of Crisis: Man and World in Eighteenth-Century French Thought* (1959).
_____. *Nature and Culture: Ethical Thought in the French Enlightenment* (1963).
Curtis, Michael. *Three Against the Third Republic: Sorel, Barrès, and Maurras* (1959).
Evans, D. O. *Social Romanticism in France, 1830–1848* (1951).
Gay, Peter. *Voltaire's Politics* (1959).
Green, F. C. *Jean-Jacques Rousseau: A Critical Study of His Life and Writings* (1955).
Guérard, Albert. *The Life and Death of an Ideal: France in the Classical Age* (1928).
Hughes, H. Stuart. *The Obstructed Path: French Social Thought in the Years of Desperation, 1930–1960* (1968).
Keeling, S. V. *Descartes* (1968).
Kors, Alan Charles. *D'Holbach's Coterie: An Enlightenment in Paris* (1976).

Manuel, Frank E. *The New World of Henri Saint-Simon* (1956).
_____. *The Prophets of Paris* (1962).
Mornet, Daniel. *French Thought in the Eighteenth Century* (1929).
Nadeau, Maurice. *From Baudelaire to Surrealism* (1957).
_____. *The History of Surrealism* (1965).
Peyre, Henri. *The Contemporary French Novel* (1955).
Shattuck, Roger. *The Banquet Years: The Arts in France, 1885–1918* (1958).
Soltau, Roger. *French Political Thought in the Nineteenth Century* (1931).
Spink, J. S. *French Free-Thought from Gassendi to Voltaire* (1960).
Wade, Ira. *The Intellectual Origins of the French Enlightenment* (1971).
Wright, Gordon. *France in Modern Times: 1760 to the Present* (1960).

7. Germany

Antoni, Carlo. *From History to Sociology: The Transition in German Historical Thinking* (1959).
Bossenbrook, William J. *The German Mind* (1961).
Bruford, W. H. *The German Tradition of Self-Cultivation: "Bildung" from Humboldt to Thomas Mann* (1975).
_____. *Germany in the Eighteenth Century: The Social Background of the Literary Revival* (1935).
Brunshwig, Henri. *Enlightenment and Romanticism in Eighteenth-Century Prussia* (1974).
Dahrendorf, Ralf. *Society and Democracy in Germany* (1967).
Gay, Peter. *Weimar Culture: The Outsider as Insider* (1968).
Heller, Erich. *The Disinherited Mind* (1959).
Hertz, Frederick. *The Development of the German Public Mind: The Age of Enlightenment* (1962).
Hook, Sidney. *From Hegel to Marx: Studies in the Intellectual Development of Karl Marx* (1950).
Iggers, Georg G. *The German Conception of History* (1968).
Kaufmann, Walter. *Nietzsche: Philosopher, Psychologist, Antichrist* (1956).
Kohn, Hans. *The Mind of Germany: The Education of a Nation* (1961).
Krieger, Leonard. *The German Idea of Freedom: History of a Political Tradition* (1957).
Mosse, George L. *The Crisis of German Ideology: Intellectual Origins of the Third Reich* (1964).
Pinson, Koppel S. *Modern Germany: Its History and Civilization* (1954).
Rieff, Philip. *Freud: The Mind of the Moralist* (1959).
Ringer, Fritz. *The Decline of the German Mandarins: The German Academic Community, 1890–1933* (1969).
Röpke, Wilhelm. *The German Question* (1946).
Stern, Fritz. *The Politics of Cultural Despair: A Study in the Rise of the Germanic Ideology* (1961).

8. Russia

Berdyaev, Nikolai. *The Russian Idea* (1948).

Billington, James H. *The Icon and the Axe: An Interpretive History of Russian Culture* (1966).

Haimson, L. A. *The Russian Marxists and the Origins of Bolshevism* (1955).

Harcave, Sidney. *Russia: A History* (1952).

Lampert, Eugene. *Studies in Rebellion* (1957).

Lavrin, Janko. *Pushkin and Russian Literature* (1947).

Lossky, N. O. *History of Russian Philosophy* (1951).

Malia, Martin. *Alexander Herzen and the Birth of Russian Socialism* (1961).

Masaryk, T. G. *The Spirit of Russia* (1919).

Rogger, Hans. *National Consciousness in Eighteenth-Century Russia* (1960).

Steiner, George. *Tolstoy or Dostoevsky: An Essay in the Old Criticism* (1959).

Struve, Gleb. *Russian Literature under Lenin and Stalin, 1917–1953* (1971).

Tompkins, Stuart Ramsay. *The Russian Intelligentsia: Makers of the Revolutionary State* (1957).

———. *The Russian Mind: From Peter the Great through the Enlightenment* (1953).

Ulam, Adam B. *The Bolsheviks: The Intellectual and Political History of the Triumph of Communism in Russia* (1965).

Venturi, Franco. *Roots of Revolution: A History of the Populist and Socialist Movements in Nineteenth Century Russia* (1960).

Wetter, Gustav A. *Dialectical Materialism: A Historical and Systematic Survey of Philosophy in the Soviet Union* (1959).

Zenkovsky, V. V. *A History of Russian Philosophy* (1953).

9. The United States

Barbour, Brian M., ed. *American Transcendentalism: An Anthology of Criticism* (1973).

Bercovitch, Sacvan. *The Puritan Origins of the American Self* (1975).

Commager, Henry Steele. *The American Mind: An Interpretation of American Thought and Character since the 1880's* (1950).

Gabriel, Ralph H. *The Course of American Democratic Thought: An Intellectual History since 1815* (1940).

Higham, John, et al. *History: The Development of Historical Studies in the United States* (1965).

Hofstadter, Richard. *Anti-Intellectualism in American Life* (1963).

———. *Social Darwinism in American Thought, 1860–1915* (1944).

Kazin, Alfred. *On Native Grounds: An Interpretation of Modern American Prose Literature* (1942).

Koch, Adrienne. *The Philosophy of Thomas Jefferson* (1943).

Marx, Leo. *The Machine in the Garden: Technology and the Pastoral Ideal in America* (1964).

Matthiessen, Francis O. *American Renaissance: Art and Expression in the Age of Emerson and Whitman* (1941).

Miller, Perry. *The New England Mind* (1939–53).

Parrington, V. L. *Main Currents in American Thought: An Interpretation of American Literature from the Beginnings to 1920* (1927–30).

Perry, Ralph Barton. *The Thought and Character of William James* (1935).

Persons, Stow. *American Minds: A History of Ideas* (1958).

Reck, Andrew J. *The New American Philosophers: An Exploration of Thought since World War II* (1968).

Riley, I. Woodbridge. *American Philosophy: The Early Schools* (1907).

Roszak, Theodore. *The Making of a Counter Culture: Reflections on the Technocratic Society and Its Youthful Opposition* (1969).

Schneider, Herbert W. *A History of American Philosophy* (1946).

Smith, John E. *The Spirit of American Philosophy* (1963).

Welter, Rush. *The Mind of America, 1820–1860* (1975).

White, Morton. *Social Thought in America: The Revolt against Formalism* (1949).

Wiener, Philip. *Evolution and the Founders of Pragmatism* (1949).

Index